DISCARD

# INDEX

—◆—

# UNCIVIL WARRIORS

# UNCIVIL WARRIORS

*The Lawyers' Civil War*

Peter Charles Hoffer

OXFORD
UNIVERSITY PRESS

# OXFORD
UNIVERSITY PRESS

Oxford University Press is a department of the University of Oxford. It furthers
the University's objective of excellence in research, scholarship, and education
by publishing worldwide. Oxford is a registered trade mark of Oxford University
Press in the UK and certain other countries.

Published in the United States of America by Oxford University Press
198 Madison Avenue, New York, NY 10016, United States of America.

CIP data is on file at the Library of Congress
ISBN 978–0–19–085176–7

3 5 7 9 8 6 4 2

Printed by Sheridan Books, Inc., United States of America

# CONTENTS

# PREFACE

———⊰◆⊱———

The second American Civil War from 1861 to 1865 (the first occurred during the War for Independence) is arguably the most important event in American history. It is also the saddest. The casualties in dead from wounds and disease numbered 720,000, over 9 percent of adult males according to the 1860 census. The total of those wounded in combat was nearly as high, and this does not count the psychological costs of these wounds to the soldiers and sailors. Over one million Confederates and over two million Union men served. Three out of four enlistees and draftees came home, but they were never the same. Those who waited for them to return were never the same. The war was not begun to end slavery, but in the end, emancipation became a justification for the sacrifices of the victors. For the defeated, secession and armed resistance were glorified as a lost cause.

Scholars supply civil war buffs with dozens of new books each year, and a recent count of books with Civil War in the title found over 1,100 in print. Wags joke that no Civil War diary will go unpublished, and it is true that print and online letters and journals comprise over twenty-six million hits on Google. No subject is better served by archivists, historians, and publishers than the Civil War, and yet it still calls on us to think and write about it.

This is a book about the Civil War lawyers, professional counsel who plotted the course of the war from seats of power. Both sides in the Civil War had their complement of lawyers and both sides' leading lawyers make their way through my account. This book, perforce, focuses primarily on the Union side, because, as we shall see, lawyers were a more important part of Union war planning and implementation than lawyers in the Confederacy. Because of this, there may appear to be a certain pro-Union bias in the following accounts. Additional bias may appear with regard to the treatment of the institution of slavery. I apologize if any of this partiality appears to influence the account unduly.

The war had a huge impact on the everyday activities of ordinary lawyers. There were lawyers stationed throughout the bureaucracies of the two combatants, and they performed important if sometimes little-known tasks. Other lawyers found themselves involved (sometimes as defendants) in wartime prosecutions. They dot the *Official Records of the Union and Confederate Armies and Navies*. In the following pages, we catch some glimpse of these men on both home fronts and follow some of them on to the battlefield, but my chief concern here is the lawyer/politicians of the Civil War. Thus, the work is a combination of the history of professions, political history, and legal history in the Civil War Era.

Last but hardly least, I know that I traverse ground muddied by the ankle boots of generations of Lincoln biographers and Civil War historians. Fortunately, I teach at one of the foremost training grounds of future Civil War scholars and am surrounded by colleagues and graduate students whose expertise in Civil War is extraordinary. I thank Stephen Berry, Matthew Hulbert, and John Inscoe for reading a preliminary draft of this manuscript. I have tried to avail myself of their immense knowledge and generous comments. The substantive legal aspects of the war have attracted attention recently as well. Legal historians Al Brophy, Williamjames Hull Hoffer, N. E. H. Hull, Earl Maltz, and William Nelson read the manuscript and offered immensely helpful comments, for which I am grateful. Although I am not a member of a political science faculty, the hardy fellows of the School of Public and International Affairs (SPIA)'s American Founding Group at the

University of Georgia, led by Keith Dougherty, were kind enough to read and comment on the manuscript in its later stages. To Keith, Mike Taylor, and the members of the group, I offer my thanks. The notes indicate further indebtedness to the abounding secondary sources. All errors are, of course, my own.

# UNCIVIL WARRIORS

# Introduction

## A Civil War of, by, and for Lawyers?

THE UNITED STATES AND the Confederate States of America engaged in combat to defend distinct legal regimes and the social order they embodied and protected. Considering the arguments on both sides, one could find in the Constitution grounds to assert the Union's perpetuity or reasons on which to base its dissolution. During the war, rival legal concepts of insurrection (a civil war within a nation) and belligerency (war between sovereign enemies) vied for adherents in federal and Confederate councils. In a "nation of laws," such martial legalism was not surprising, no more so than that the nation's lawyer/politicians—men who went from the practice of law into politics—found themselves at the center of the maelstrom. For these men, as for their countrymen in the years following the conflict, the sacrifices of the war gave legitimacy to new kinds of laws defining citizenship and civil rights.[1]

The war would affect almost all of the nation's lawyers, in 1860, according to the US census, some 101,000 men out of a free white male adult population of over 7 million. Many rushed to the colors. Others found jobs in the greatly expanded bureaucracies of the two governments. A few, the subjects of the pages that follow, played an even more important role. In positions of leadership they struggled to make sense of the conflict and, in the course of that struggle, began to glimpse a new world of law. It was a law that empowered as well as limited government, a law that conferred personal dignity and rights on those who, at the war's beginning, could claim neither in law. But not at first. For at first, adherence to an "old Constitution" in the words of Lincoln's first Inaugural Address, constrained the legal imagination.[2]

In the summer of 1862, former Supreme Court justice Benjamin R. Curtis was troubled for this very reason. A Whig in politics with a large and successful legal practice, he joined the US Supreme Court in 1851 and served for six years. After he resigned his post on the Court following a bitter dispute with Chief Justice Roger Taney in 1857 and returned to his thriving and prestigious private practice in Boston, he supported the candidacy of Abraham Lincoln and opposed secession. But in 1862, Curtis had become worried that Lincoln overstepped his constitutional role in proposing to emancipate slaves in Confederate territory. Rooted in the ground of the old Constitution, Curtis wrote what amounted to a legal brief against Lincoln's broad assumption of executive wartime powers. The short book became a bestseller among Northern Democrats and caused Lincoln genuine pain. Curtis's was a valedictory for an older jurisprudence of limited central government. Republicans like Lincoln had pledged themselves to it during the presidential campaign, but as New York Democrat Samuel Tilden—a lawyer/politician who supported Stephen Douglas's bid for the highest office—warned during the 1860 campaign, some Republicans seemed overly willing to "interfere with the affairs of other communities, and to seek to regulate and control them as they rightfully do their own." The danger of such interference was that it unbalanced the division of powers between federal and state governments embedded in the old Constitution. Curtis saw President Lincoln's actions coming dangerously close to this state of affairs. The exchange between Curtis and Lincoln in 1862 was virtual litigation, one of the many critical occasions when the lawyers in the Civil War employed their talents to vie for approval in the court of public opinion.[3]

In that endless summer of battle, with the fate of the Union hanging by a thread, Lincoln sought legal ways to justify his course of action and Curtis decried the seeming illegality of Lincoln's acts. Both men were lifelong practitioners of law, and both made sense of the crisis in legal terms. They were not alone in this. At the very center of the federal and Confederate governments, lawyers *as lawyers* played a vital role in the Civil War Era. Their ideas and acts were not confined to formal pleadings in courtrooms or the language of judicial opinions. Executive orders, treatises, election debates, even journal entries and letters were filled with legal ideas. These came from widely disparate sources reaching back to the first tracts on the laws of war and up to futuristic visions of civil rights. The lawyer/politicians were everywhere in the executive and legislative branches of government as well as the judiciary. From the framing of the first secession ordinance in Charleston and the drafting of the Confederate constitution in Montgomery through the last great act of wartime statesmanship—the passage of the Thirteenth Amendment in Washington, DC—government lawyers, performing as policymakers, litigators, and jurisprudents, shaped the Union and Confederate causes. Some of these legal practitioners, like Abraham Lincoln, James Buchanan, T. R. R. Cobb, Robert Toombs, Alexander Stephens, and Reverdy Johnson, are well known to history. Others, like the author of the South Carolina Ordinance of Secession, Francis H. Wardlaw, Buchanan's legal advisor Jeremiah Black, and Confederate lawyer/politician and soldier Patrick Cleburne, now rest in obscurity.

The extent to which two governments growing in size, expense, and powers waged a civil war based on older ideas of national governance would not have surprised lawyers on either side of the battle lines. Confederate lawyers believed that they were battling for the framers' "old Constitution." Lawyers in Lincoln's cabinet and the Republican majorities in Congress saw the cause of the Union rooted in the framers' constitution as well. As Abram D. Smith of the Wisconsin State Supreme Court put it in defense of his state's personal liberty laws, "The American people could no longer enjoy the blessings of a free government . . . whenever the state sovereignties shall be prostrated at the feet of the federal government." During the conflict, the justices of the United States Supreme Court struggled to find a way past the "old Constitution" to justify the prosecution of the war. With the wisdom of hindsight, one can see the gestation of federal supremacy, human rights, and governmental obligations emerging from the struggle, but that birth was a long and painful one.[4]

What did the presence of lawyers in the governments on both sides mean to the conduct of the war? Called the last war of gentlemen, it was, unlike civil wars before and after, remarkably rule-bound. Civil wars are customarily lawless events, by their very nature exhibiting extremes of brutality on both sides. While there were civilian casualties and the destruction of private property in the Civil War, the war was fought with a kind of genuine, if sporadic, lawmindedness, bordering on civility. After all, the leaders of the two sides had governed the nation together before secession. For example, Lincoln offered the rebels generous peace terms, hedged by legal requirements, on at least three occasions. On the eve of the first battle, he longed for a "civilized and humane jurisprudence" in which lawyer/politicians on both sides could find common ground. Confederate vice president Alexander Stephens labored almost incessantly to bring about an honorable peace. The war was horrific, but constrained. I propose to show that one important reason for this was the influence of the lawyers—making ours a Civil War by lawyers, of lawyers, and in the end, for lawyers.[5]

The lawyers transformed the war, but the war also transformed the lawyers' world. Not only did the war (and the reconstruction measures that immediately followed) provide new venues for legal work, but the war also changed the very nature of federalism. No longer would the national government be a junior partner in the federal system of states. The lawyers who managed the war might return to private practice when it ended, but the Union they left behind bore an entirely new constitutional face.[6]

Each of the chapters that follow, along with the prologue and epilogue, focuses on what may be called a legal "moment," a cross section or slice of time when a set of disputed questions about law was at issue. One may reply that such disputes, wars of words, had little impact on the course of politics or battle, but consider the null hypothesis: What if these legal questions had never been raised? If secession had not been defended as legal and contested as illegal, would there have been a Civil War at all? If Lincoln had not suspended the writ of habeas corpus and arrested Maryland pro-Confederate agitator John Merryman, then ignored Chief Justice Taney's opinion in the matter, would Maryland have joined its sister slave states in the Confederacy? If the Supreme Court had struck down the blockade as unconstitutional, would the Confederacy have won the war? If Lincoln had not found a legal ground to emancipate slaves in territories in rebellion, would the eventual end of slavery have come with the end of the war? If the lawyers in Congress had not found a way to end slavery after the war with the Thirteenth

Amendment, would slavery have survived the conflict? Each legal decision, as a legal decision, had a real-world impact. Legal words became
political and military deeds.[7]

One might, in contrary fashion, argue that by focusing on moments in
Civil War history that have inherent connection to law or that gave birth
to new laws, I am stacking the deck in favor of my thesis that lawyers had
a vital role to play during the war. In one sense, that charge is a fair one;
for of course I am making the best case I can for my contribution. But in
reply I ask whether the moments I have chosen were not crucial ones, not
just for law, but for the course of the war? I think they are.

The work here presented is a legal history, and it features a close reading of certain crucially important public texts. I have tried to empha-
size the way in which the Civil War lawyers' legal training, experience,
and approach to issues framed how they handled the great questions
of secession and the war. At the same time, those great questions were
never wholly legal ones. Political ambitions, military events, and personality played important roles as well. Hopefully, these essays navigate
a safe intellectual passage between the Scylla of too narrow a doctrinal
exegesis and the Charybdis of too broad a reliance on the externalities
of political biography.

In reading the texts I employ a method familiar to an older generation
of legal historians and intellectual historians that might be dismissed as
naïve realism. That is, I view the central documents as a product of
their times and the immediate purposes of those who conceived and
drafted them. I assay both public sources (the documents themselves,
speeches, official correspondence, contemporary publications) and private sources (memoirs, diaries, private letters) in this endeavor. There is
therefore a good deal here in the words of the lawyers, some of which
are "terms of art" (words whose legal usage is different from their common usage). I have tried to translate them into lay language when it
does not distort their meaning.

In the interests of keeping my focus and the reader's attention, I have
not spent much time on the course of ordinary litigation during the
war. Although the war dramatically affected the volume of that litigation and wartime legislation provided new forms of action (for example,
confiscation in the federal courts and sequestration in the Confederate
courts), these matters were quite distinct from the larger legal issues of

the war. I have devoted only one chapter to Civil War–era judges, and this to the justices of the US Supreme Court. While the judges and justices were lawyer/politicians before they ascended the bench, in the main they supplied what Judge Richard Posner has called "corrective justice" rather than applying law or lawyerly thinking to provide novel solutions to policy questions. In laymen's terms, this means that the judges and justice simply applied known law to particular cases. I did provide a fuller account of the Civil War–era federal judges in chapter 5 of *The Federal Courts: An Essential History* (2016).[8]

# Prologue

## The Inseparability of Politics and Law: The First Lincoln-Douglas Debate

THE WORLD OF LAW and lawyers was rapidly changing in the decades before the coming of the Civil War in ways that shaped the experience and the thinking of the wartime counselors. The rise of multistate insurance, transportation, and manufacturing operations provided new and lucrative opportunities for the legal profession. Single practice remained the norm, but more and more lawyers were forming partnerships. The partnership was a legal construct, a kind of contract among individuals. They owned and managed the business. Often contentious and rarely lasting for long, legal partnerships were hardly anything like the smooth-running corporate partnerships of today. Nevertheless, working with a law partner was an ongoing experience in cooperative endeavor. For example, Abraham Lincoln had three law partners, a mix and match of mentors and rivals, finally finding one, William Herndon, who understood and appreciated Lincoln's somewhat unique approach to lawyering. Lawyers had been drawn to public service from the founding of the Republic, but as sectional conflict loomed larger in the two decades before the war, lawyers seemed to play a more visible role in the nation's guidance. Sectional conflict was one of the reasons that men like Lincoln, Ohio's Salmon Chase, and New York's William Seward thought law and politics were so closely intertwined.[1]

Antebellum lawyer/politicians came in all shapes and sizes, from Alexander "Little Aleck" Stephens to "Fatty" [Howell] Cobb to the six-foot-four "Honest Abe." Some dressed like dandies. Others, like Lincoln, preferred "plain" clothing. However, all of these lawyers shared one trait or they would not have been successful. They were hard workers, putting in more hours than the farmer and the grocer whose suits they represented in court. The foremost manual of practice for the lawyers, David Hoffman's *A Course of Study* (1836), reminded all counselors that "to my clients, I will be faithful, and in their causes zealous and industrious." The lawyers read more than the average American. State case reporters, newspapers, and legal documents required lawyers' close attention. These men resembled a coterie of traveling salesmen, riding the judicial circuit from county seat to county seat, staying in the capital when the state supreme courts were in session. They kept their offices open from dawn to dusk, and whether, like Stephens and Lincoln, they were avid advice givers to all and sundry or preferred to listen, they were accustomed to dealing with all sorts of people. Lawyering was adversarial. That meant that lawyers argued with other lawyers in written briefs and in court. The adversarial system put a premium on winning rather than finding mutually acceptable solutions to disputes. Natural rivalries among these lawyers developed. That was law practice, and it left its marks on all of them.[2]

In Lincoln's day, even the most successful lawyers routinely faced a barrage of public scorn. In 1829, at his inauguration as Harvard law school's Dane Professor, US Supreme Court justice Joseph Story admitted that "the rebuke of public opinion follows close on every offense" lawyers committed in their private practices. Fiction writers found lawyers an inviting target. There was Southern wit George Washington Harris's account of a young Georgia lawyer "from town," who strutted and gobbled like a turkey, and a noble young practitioner like novelist Emma Southworth's fictional Ishmael, who sought to learn "jurisprudence, the science of human justice, the knowledge of the customs and laws and the rights of man" so that he could be a lawyer.[3]

Part of the transformation from private counsel to public official required some self-promotion, which lawyers seeking higher office provided. Two of Lincoln's law partners had important political careers in Illinois. Lincoln himself professed that lawyering could not be separated from the public good. As one scholar has summarized these attitudes, "For lawyers turned politicians/statesmen, the keys were twofold, constitution and the common law, both envisaged as foundations for institutions that would restrain or limit the power of the state and ensure liberty." Lawyer/politicians cast themselves as the guardians of public liberty just as in their practices they promoted private rights. "Or so they believed."[4]

Those lawyers who did succeed in gaining public positions proved that practicing law could be what law professor Henry St. George Tucker of Virginia called "the most successful path, not only to affluence and comfort, but to all the distinguished and elevated stations in a free government." The nation exhibited a "widely shared preoccupation with law and politics" according to one student of the first antebellum law schools, and success in politics required the same appearance of virtue as success in the other. True, there were winners and losers in most every case, but losing well might burnish a reputation when winning through guile might cost one the trust of future clients—and future voters. Lincoln urged lawyers to be honest, to discourage rather than stir up litigation, and to honor the law rather than abusing it. Joseph Story, perhaps the leading legal scholar of his day, as well as a greatly respected US Supreme Court justice, summed up the prevailing ideology of lawyering at the apex of practice: the lawyer was "the public sentinel" of virtue.[5]

Many of the lawyer/politicians in the following pages gained from legal practice a surer sense of themselves as advocates of political causes, for legal practice in the antebellum era was as much about advocacy of ideas as about "black letter" (formal lawbook) learning. The leaders of the profession, like Roger B. Taney, were distinguished for their skill at untangling issues, not particularly for their mastery of arcane knowledge, and for their representation of all kinds of clients. Such men were lucid and even passionate in oral argument. Future leaders of the bar like North Carolina's Thomas Ruffin developed their own styles of courtroom combat. Ruffin was "hardly ever courteous and not always respectful and frequently abusive." Not everyone fit this model, of course. By contrast, Georgia lawyer Alexander Stephens relied on his learning and eloquence to win cases. Virginia's Jubal Early admitted that "I had in a very limited degree the capacity for public speaking . . . and it was regarded that my forte at the law was not before a jury as an advocate, but on questions of law before the court." Early went on to political service when he was not volunteering for military service.

Both sets of qualities abetted lawyer/politicians' political advancement, for in many cases the very impulse that led them to practice law had fueled their ambition for public office. After which, their political energies could be devoted to legal subjects. Law practice and political office were like the coupling rods that propelled old-fashioned locomotive wheels: the action of one driving the motion of the other.[6]

On a dry, hot August 1858 afternoon in Ottawa, Illinois, two outstandingly successful Illinois lawyer/politicians met in electoral debate. This was the first of seven occasions when Democratic senator Stephen Douglas vied with his Republican rival for the Senate, Abraham Lincoln. In the days and weeks that followed, their words (transcribed at the time by newspaper reporters, and later corrected by both men) "were read and reread like a code that should have warned Americans of the whirlwind about to descend on them, if only they had known how to read them rightly." Both men infused the political issues they debated with legal concepts. In this, Lincoln and Douglas followed in the footsteps of Henry Clay, moving back and forth between both worlds, fusing the "energy and magnetism" of the politician with the mastery of detail and rhetorical skills of the lawyer.[7]

His former law partner recalled that "Lincoln's knowledge of law was very small when I took him in. There were no books out here in those days worth speaking of. I don't think he studied very much. I think he learned his law more in the study of cases. He would work hard and learn all there was in the case he had in hand. He got to be a pretty good lawyer though his general knowledge of law was never very formidable." Once in court Lincoln could "make as about as much of it as anybody." Lincoln had a diverse practice, a portion of which entailed pursuing deadbeat debtors on circuit, but he always had time to help younger lawyers and offered his advice freely. He even served as a "temporary judge" in more than three hundred cases. He shared his experience with a would-be younger partner in 1858: "If you wish to be a lawyer, attach no consequence to the place you are in, or the person you are with; but get books, sit down anywhere, and go to reading for yourself. That will make a lawyer of you quicker than any other way."[8]

Douglas was a fierce advocate in and out of some of the same courtrooms in which Lincoln practiced. One former colleague recalled that

Douglas's motto in court was "admit nothing and require my adversary to prove everything." For his own part, Douglas "was known to bluff, to turn facts, and distort evidence" to win cases. Douglas and Lincoln shared something else—both had railroads as clients. Lawyering for the Illinois Central Railroad that would cross Illinois into Kansas was one reason Douglas supported statehood for Kansas. For this and other reasons, Douglas's practice was more lucrative than Lincoln's, although by 1858 Douglas's practice had taken a back seat to his political career.[9]

Speaking first at Ottawa, Douglas's "melodious baritone" carried his words to a crowd estimated at ten thousand men and women. "I appear before you to-day for the purpose of discussing the leading political topics which now agitate the public mind." Those leading political topics were also legal topics—foremost among them the legality of the expansion of slavery into the western territories. One could separate the political from the legal, but Douglas wanted them joined. "[That] we are present here to-day for the purpose of having a joint discussion, as the representatives of the two great political parties of the State and Union, upon the principles in issue between those parties and this vast concourse of people, shows the deep feeling which pervades the public mind in regard to the questions dividing us." Those principles were legal ones too.[10]

America in 1858 was used to all manner of electoral campaigning on the stump, in Congress, in the newspapers, and with these debates—what amounted to a perpetual revival camp meeting. Not all of the candidates who took to the hustings were lawyer/politicians, but those who were, like Douglas, knew that just about every major political controversy in America had its legal side, and lawyers were the elite of the politicians. As French visitor Alexis de Tocqueville remarked, some years earlier, "In America there are no nobles or literary men, and the people are apt to mistrust the wealthy; lawyers consequently form the highest political class and the most cultivated portion of society. They have therefore nothing to gain by innovation, which adds a conservative interest to their natural taste for public order. If I were asked where I place the American aristocracy, I should reply without hesitation that it is not among the rich, who are united by no common tie, but that it occupies the judicial bench and the bar."[11]

Americans were thus accustomed to have the legal side of political arguments addressed directly. Douglas resumed: "Here I assert that
uniformity in the local laws and institutions of the different States is
neither possible or desirable." Instead, he offered the Democratic constitutional orthodoxy, what Lincoln's First Inaugural would call the
"old Constitution": domestic institutions rested on local law and must
continue to rest on local law for that law was the will of the people. To
his thinking, the framers of the Constitution had built that concept
into the nation's fundamental law. Their vision was a robust federalism
with strict limitations on the reach of the federal government into the
everyday lives of citizens of the states and everything not enumerated
in the Constitution was left to the states. Slavery, he recognized, was
a matter of such "domestic" law. Holding another in bondage without
the protection of the law would be a crime.

Roger Taney, chief justice of the highest court in the land, the US
Supreme Court, had said that slavery was national, not regional, in *Dred
Scott v. Sandford* (1857), and the debate in Ottawa was as much about
the Constitution according to Taney as it was about the cut and thrust
of two politicians on the speakers' platform. Douglas fumed: "We are
told by Lincoln that he is utterly opposed to the *Dred Scott* decision, and
will not submit to it, for the reason that he says it deprives the negro of
the rights and privileges of citizenship. That is the first and main reason
which he assigns for his warfare on the Supreme Court of the United
States and its decision." Of course, no politician in front of an audience
of voters was going to discourse on the technicalities of *Dred Scott* but
Douglas's version of Lincoln's views was singular and purposefully mis-
leading. Lincoln had never argued for citizenship rights for blacks. He
argued for their right to benefit from their labor. Douglas nevertheless
continued, "I ask you, are you in favor of conferring upon the negro the
rights and privileges of citizenship?"

Chief Justice Taney, in what amounted to an obiter dictum (a statement on the case that was actually not necessary to decide it) in his
*Dred Scott* opinion, had said that persons of African ancestry could
never be citizens. This aside could have decided the case if it turned on
Scott's citizenship, as opposed to the Court's deference to the Missouri
court finding, but one need not have been a citizen to bring a suit
in a federal court (foreigners did it all the time). Here it read not as

law but as a kind of sociology of racial incapacity. "In the opinion of the court, the legislation and histories of the times, and the language used in the Declaration of Independence, show, that neither the class of persons who had been imported as slaves, nor their descendants, whether they had become free or not, were then acknowledged as a part of the people, nor intended to be included in the general words used in that memorable instrument." This was not the opinion of the Court, because a majority of the justices did not sign on to Taney's opinion. It was, however, reflective of the thinking of a significant portion of the legal community, including Montgomery Blair, co-counsel who argued for Dred Scott's freedom. Taney's history was as subjective and dismissive as his reading of framers' texts. African Americans, he continued, "had for more than a century before been regarded as beings of an inferior order, and altogether unfit to associate with the white race, either in social or political relations; and so far inferior, that they had no rights which the white man was bound to respect; and that the negro might justly and lawfully be reduced to slavery for his benefit." Douglas seemed to agree.[12]

Douglas's stance did not rest on mere political expediency or the love of slavery; it rested on a conception of law. It was not a simple one of absolute states' rights—the unabridgeable sovereignty of the individual states in the federal Union in the old Constitution—for he denied the right of the state of Illinois to disobey the federal Supreme Court. Instead, it was a rule of law argument: the Constitution and the federal government had long accepted the notion that slavery was a domestic matter, a matter for the states. Lawyers always argued the law when it was in their favor. Douglas thought he had the law on his side. It was Lincoln, Douglas told the audience, who was acting outside the law.

Douglas argued as if the debate were an oral presentation before a court. He was accustomed to winning these oral contests and here he had Lincoln on the ropes. A little guilt by association might finish the job: "Mr. Lincoln, following the example and lead of all the little Abolition orators, who go around and lecture in the basements of schools and churches, reads from the Declaration of Independence, that all men were created equal, and then asks, how can you deprive a negro of that equality which God and the Declaration of Independence awards to him? He and they maintain that negro equality is guaranteed by the laws of God, and that it is asserted in the Declaration of Independence." But Douglas knew, and he told the gathering, that the Declaration was not law. It was at best aspiration, and though men of conscience might disagree about the godliness of keeping slaves, the law did not incorporate any particular religious injunction against slavery—no more than it incorporated religious defenses of slavery.

Douglas and his audience realized that law, in reality the absence of law, had become the most important public issue of the day. For four years after Douglas had led the fight in Congress to pass legislation (the Kansas-Nebraska Act) allowing voters in territories to determine whether they would seek admission to the federal Union as slavery or free states, pro- and antislavery forces in Kansas had rendered that land in blood. A proslavery constitution written in Lecompton, the territorial capital, had failed to win acceptance in Congress, with the consequence that Congress seemed unable to find a lawful solution to the violence. President Franklin Pierce and his successor, James Buchanan, had not been able to break the logjam in Congress. One reason for the dicta in Chief Justice Roger Taney's opinion in *Dred Scott* (portions of the opinion that were not necessary to decide the case) was his attempt to supply an answer to "Bleeding Kansas" from the bench. The problem of slave law was particularly important in Illinois. Its legislature had enacted provisions that favored slaveholders' rights, even though slavery per se was illegal. Law, lawmakers, and lawyers were at the heart of the issues in Illinois and the crisis in Kansas.[13]

Lincoln did his best to recover. His style was more attuned to addressing a jury of men like himself in a trial court than making fine points of law before an appeals court bench, and he began on a personal note. "When a man hears himself somewhat misrepresented, it provokes him—at least, I find it so with myself; but when misrepresentation becomes very gross and palpable, it is more apt to amuse him." He indicated as much when he referred to Douglas as "Judge Douglas," hinting that Douglas's view of the law came from above, from formal written sources like those a judge might deploy in an opinion, whereas Lincoln, the man of the people, would focus on the common sense and will of the people. Douglas's legislative stepchild was the Kansas-Nebraska Act of 1854, so it became Lincoln's target: "This is the *repeal* of the Missouri Compromise. The foregoing history may not be precisely accurate in every particular; but I am sure it is sufficiently so for all the uses I shall attempt to make of it." The disclaimer, really faux modesty (Lincoln was not a pedant, it implied), was preface, but the body of the comment said something entirely different, in a somewhat different tone. In it, Lincoln spoke with authority: "we have before us, the chief materials enabling us to correctly judge whether the repeal of the Missouri Compromise is right or wrong. I think, and shall try to show, that it is wrong; wrong in its direct effect, letting slavery into Kansas and Nebraska—and wrong in its prospective principle, allowing it to spread to every other part of the wide world, where men can be found inclined to take it." Lincoln ignored the self-determination argument that Douglas offered, and turned instead to slavery.[14]

Lincoln read from the Declaration of Independence as often as he could. It allowed him to shift the debate with Douglas from race, in which all concerned conceded differences, to slavery, which violated the basic premises of "all men are created equal" in the Declaration. He read its plain text and could not see how it could be understood to exclude any man. He thought it applied to people of color, and that was his chief disagreement with Taney's opinion in *Dred Scott*. Lincoln spoke as if the Constitution incorporated the Declaration. The Preamble to the Constitution, written by Gouverneur Morris in the last days of the convention, did include the phrase "the blessings of liberty," and not incidentally, for Morris was outspokenly opposed to slavery. In rewriting the document's Preamble to include the phrase, Morris was signaling a view that the convention had actually rejected, but by the time the Committee on Arrangement and Style reported its revisions to the convention, most everyone else had gone home. It might not have passed Lincoln's notice that the committee included Alexander Hamilton and Rufus King, also opponents of slavery.[15]

Lincoln's deft refocusing of the debate from race and racism to slavery required him to treat slavery in the Southern portions of the country as a regional custom rather than law. "When Southern people tell us they are no more responsible for the origin of slavery than we, I acknowledge the fact." Lincoln conceded the fact of slavery only, not its legality. "When it is said that the institution exists, and that it is very difficult to get rid of it, in any satisfactory way, I can understand

and appreciate the saying. I surely will not blame them for not doing what I should not know how to do myself." A very brief nod to the Constitution followed. A good brief in law will always acknowledge the opposing argument's most important points. "When they remind us of their constitutional rights, I acknowledge them, not grudgingly, but fully and fairly; and I would give them any legislation for the reclaiming of their fugitives, which should not, in its stringency, be more likely to carry a free man into slavery, than our ordinary criminal laws are to hang an innocent one." The dry (sometimes macabre) humor was characteristic of Lincoln, as one newspaper observed of his style of public address: "He abounds in good humor and pleasant satire, and often gives a witty thrust that cuts like a Damascus blade." The tail end of the concession, like the sting of a scorpion, poisoned the concession, for Lincoln, an accomplished criminal lawyer, knew how difficult it was for an innocent man, denied able counsel, to save himself from the rope.[16]

Lincoln's closing remarks in Ottawa anticipated a portion of his far more famous first Inaugural Address almost three years later. That too was a legal argument meant for a jury. The form of both addresses—conceding and then withdrawing concessions—was typical of his legal style and encapsulated his view of slavery over this critical period of his career. He seemed to concede the states' rights argument. "The great variety of the local institutions in the States, springing from differences in the soil, differences in the face of the country, and in the climate, are bonds of Union." Then he severed slavery from that general legal category. "But can this question of slavery be considered as among *these* varieties in the institutions of the country?" He answered his own rhetorical questions with what appeared to be an appeal to public opinion, but the public to whom he addressed the question already knew where he stood. "I leave it to you to say whether, in the history of our Government, this institution of slavery has not always failed to be a bond of union, and, on the contrary, been an apple of discord, and an element of division in the house." On June 16, in a speech accepting the Republican nomination for the Senate seat for which he vied with Douglas, Lincoln had issued his famous dictum that a house divided against itself could not stand. The speech opening with that invocation was widely publicized. He repeated its message in Ottawa. The laws of freedom and the laws of slavery were on a collision course. What would happen when they collided?[17]

Lincoln did not ask and did not want voters to violate the law. He was a believer in the rule of law. The *Dred Scott* decision put this faith in the law to the test. Could a house divided by law, a house with two sets of opposing laws, survive? One can sense in this first debate Lincoln's genuine anxiety about the potential for mob rule, widespread disregard of law, and lawlessness. He knew that mobs in the South had broken into federal post offices, a felony under federal law, and destroyed abolitionist literature. He had heard, in his brief stint in Congress, members of the House from slave states warn about a river of blood should Northerners stir slave rebellion. Yet his rejection of *Dred Scott* and the Kansas-Nebraska Act was within a lawyerly tradition; that is, he tried to narrow the application of Taney's comments and the threat to Free Soil in "Bleeding Kansas" by arguing that they were violations of law. As he had repeatedly said, "a reverence for the constitution and the law" was the only bulwark against violence.[18]

The remaining six debates introduced themes and variations on these positions, the two men becoming more comfortable, if that is the best word, with one another's styles. In these debates their differences hardened into vying constitutional doctrines. Looming above the two men, as they journeyed from town to town, and framing their views of the Constitution, was the growing national division over *Dred Scott*. In it, Chief Justice Roger Taney, joined by Associate Justice Peter Daniel, had opined that Congress did not have the constitutional authority to bar slavery from any territory, no matter what its inhabitants wanted. Portions of Taney's opinion posed a problem for Douglas. His defense of his Kansas-Nebraska Act's provision for popular sovereignty, that is, letting the people of a territory decide whether they would enter the Union as a free or slave state, did not fit Taney's insistence that the Fifth Amendment to the Constitution protected slave owners' property everywhere in the nation. Douglas's doctrine of popular sovereignty would be popular in the South if and only if it were conjoined with Taney's view of "slavery national."

At the next debate stop, in Freeport, Lincoln wanted to know where Douglas stood on Taney's views, and he responded, "The next question propounded to me by Mr. Lincoln is, can the people of a Territory in any lawful way, against the wishes of any citizen of the United States, exclude slavery from their limits prior to the formation of a State Constitution? I answer emphatically, as Mr. Lincoln has heard me answer a hundred times from every stump in Illinois, that in my opinion the people of a Territory can, by lawful means, exclude slavery from their limits prior to the formation of a State Constitution." The so-called Freeport Doctrine was popular with the audience there, because Freeport was located, like Ottawa, in the northern part of the state. Douglas's appeal to these voters would come back to haunt him when the debates moved to the Southern towns and, even more fatally, when he faced hostile Southern delegates at the Charleston Democratic presidential convention in 1860. There the die was cast—if there was no legal support for the expansion of slavery into the territories, Southern defenders of slavery would have no option but to seek a legal way out of the Union.[19]

Lincoln, by contrast, made clear that his aversion to slavery did not extend to its abolition where law established it. In this sense, he was a legalist like Douglas. A central part of this legalism was that slavery was sectional, not national. The same legalism found its way into the Republican platform of 1860, on which Lincoln ran for the presidency. "That the maintenance inviolate of the rights of the states, and especially the right of each state to order and control its own domestic institutions according to its own judgment exclusively, is essential to that balance of powers on which the perfection and endurance of our political fabric depends; and we denounce the lawless invasion by armed force of the soil of any state or territory, no matter under what pretext, as among the gravest of crimes." This law-and-order plank was a clear rebuff to the abolitionists, and hopefully, would reassure Southern politicians should Lincoln win. In the event, however, it did not.

The Lincoln-Douglas debates ended much as one would have expected: Douglas was reelected by the Democratic Party–dominated state legislature. The debates did have one unexpected consequence. Because of the telegraph and newspaper coverage, Lincoln was raised to national prominence. (It helped that he edited an edition of the debates from his own notes and had it published.) The debates also demonstrated that on the eve of the great schism of the Union, political issues and legal ideas were inseparable. It was thus entirely appropriate that the two contestants were lawyers, that Congress was dominated by men in the legal profession, and that the next great question national politics faced would be a legal one.

# I

## The Contested Legality of Secession

LINCOLN'S VICTORY OVER DOUGLAS and the other candidates in the presidential election of 1860 led to the dissolution of the Union. Secession swept over the Southern countryside like a tornado. Within a shorter time after the election of Lincoln than anyone in the North or South could have imagined, South Carolina lawyers crafted that state's Ordinance of Secession and Declaration of Causes for Leaving the Union. Lincoln and other Republicans hoped that conciliation was still possible, but agents had already departed Charleston to press other slave state legislatures to join in a new government. By February, six states' conventions had voted to join South Carolina in a separate government. The leaders of this movement met in Montgomery, Alabama, in that month and wrote a constitution, expecting that the bonds joining together the Confederate States of America would be as strong as those the framers of the federal Constitution had hoped to make for their new union. Authorities in Washington, DC, including the outgoing administration of James Buchanan and the incoming administration of Abraham Lincoln, faced a series of agonizing decisions. At their core, these were legal questions, and they taxed the skills of lawyer/politicians whose responses would determine the fate of the nation.[1]

In 1858 neither Lincoln nor Douglas fully anticipated the danger of secession. They should have. Southern federal district court judges sounded the tocsin during the debate over the Fugitive Slave Act of 1850. In an address at the laying of the cornerstone of the Virginia Military

Institute, Judge John White Brockenbrough warned that a "fanatical majority in Congress may effectively subvert the Constitution" and that such radicalism could undo the Union itself. In the same year, South Carolina delegates to a convention in Nashville in 1850 had raised this specter during the battle over the admission of California as a free state. Wiser men such as John C. Calhoun of South Carolina and Jefferson Davis of Mississippi had scotched it, but in his very last speech in the Senate, read to the members while Calhoun lay dying on a cot in their midst, he warned of secession if the Fugitive Slave Act were not passed. "Unless something decisive is done, I again ask, what is to stop this agitation before the great and final object at which it aims—the abolition of slavery in the States—is consummated? Is it, then, not certain that if something is not done to arrest it, the South will be forced to choose between abolition and secession? Indeed, as events are now moving, it will not require the South to secede in order to dissolve the Union. Agitation will of itself effect it, of which its past history furnishes abundant proof." So, too, in 1852, South Carolina's call for a gathering of Southern states to discuss secession was quieted by the caution of Southern members of Congress like Davis and the intervention of unionists like Alexander Stephens of Georgia. A movement to reopen the overseas slave trade, understood by its supporters as a spur to secession, also brought Stephens's condemnation. Stephens, a highly religious and moralistic lawyer and planter, in particular became the voice of legal reason in the Deep South when Lincoln won the presidential election in 1860.[2]

Stephens's career was eerily similar to Lincoln's though their personalities and physical appearance could not have been more different. Lincoln was outgoing; Stephens was introverted. Lincoln was tall and sinewy; Stephens was small and waiflike. But like Lincoln's, Stephens's family had moved a good deal, in his case from Pennsylvania to Georgia, where Stephens was born. Like Lincoln's parents, Stephens's were farmers. Like Lincoln, Stephens was a voracious reader and found a job teaching school. But unlike Lincoln's difficult relationship with his father, "little Aleck" worshipped his father and his death molded the son's melancholy and prickly nature. Like Lincoln, Stephens read law, passed the bar, and rode the circuit with the other lawyers and judges. His "eloquence and persuasiveness," despite his high-pitched voice (another trait he shared with Lincoln), won jury verdicts and friends. As his legal career prospered, the attraction of politics grew, and it took him to the Georgia Statehouse, and then to the US Congress from 1843 until 1859.[3]

Stephens had a gloom-and-doom view of the crisis of 1860. He wrote to a confidant in September 1860, when the question of secession was once again on the political agenda of his Georgia peers: "The truth is I have almost despaired of the Republic . . . . Men have no regard for past principles or professions. Consistency is wholly disregarded. Passion and prejudice rule the hour." The crisis was the antithesis of good lawyering and ignored "the real gravity and dignity of the questions before the country." Passing events only brought more concern for the fate of the Union and, equally important to Stephens, law and order. He had taken his stand with Douglas's popular sovereignty, and in speeches and newspaper pieces he tried to explain that the South's essential interests, in his words, were not abridged by letting the territories decide the question of slavery. Those who attributed bad motives to him were only appealing to "the game of the demagogue," to personal spite and "low, base, and mean" prejudice. A "wise, safe, and sound" policy lay in a steady course, not the radicalism or "revolution" of secession. This was the kind of reasoned argument that won Stephens case after case in the courts, for even as he pleaded for the Union in public prints he traveled the law circuit for his clients. For them he continued to win verdicts, but in the court of public opinion, he knew, he was losing.[4]

Stephens spoke to the Georgia legislature on November 14, 1860. In what was called his "Union speech" he laid out the grounds for staying in the federal system. In response to the secessionist jeremiad of his fellow lawyer T. R. R. Cobb, perhaps the foremost proslavery jurist in the land, Stephens counseled cool reason based on law. No overwrought posturing, no bravado, nothing but "good sense" was his offering. Lincoln had won legally and Georgia, a law-abiding state, had to accept the legality of his presidency. The state, he told its legislators, had always been a bedrock of the Constitution, and if the Union sank, "let us be found to the last moment standing on the deck with the Constitution of the United States waving over our heads." No one heckled the former congressman, his short, frail frame braced against the gusts of anti-Republican rhetoric, his shrill voice filling the chamber. It was the Constitution, not the party system, that mattered, for party was like a demon, and by abandoning the Constitution, Georgians would "at no distant day commence cutting one another's throats." He asked the legislature to call a convention and had, by the estimation of those present, prevented the legislature from simply declaring for secession; but he wrote to a friend a week later, "I fear we are past salvation. There is not enough patriotism in the country North or South to save it."[5]

After South Carolina announced its secession, but before Georgia had joined in the Confederacy, Stephens and Lincoln corresponded. It was a cordial but cautious exchange. The crucial point was whether the slave property owners of Georgia could trust the Republican Party to adhere to its campaign platform to leave slavery untouched. Lincoln told Stephens that the differences were not just legal but lay in the connection between the moral and the legal. "You think slavery is right, and ought to be extended, while we think it is wrong, and ought to be restricted." In fact, Stephens had no special brief to defend slavery (though he believed in the innate inferiority of the African race), but he feared that radical emotions, what he called fanaticism, would overbear legal protections for it. He told Lincoln that he loved the Union as much as anyone but that the states were independent sovereignties and in his mind secession was legal—bad policy that would have a bad end, but legal.[6]

Stephens was not the only leading Southern lawyer/politician to advise caution. In Virginia, the secession conference stuttered and wavered, in part because former US congressman and governor Henry A. Wise wanted to fight within the Union rather than against it. His legal practice soon gave way to political ambitions, and his energy in Democratic state and national politics was prodigious. Indeed, he hoped for a shot at the presidency in 1856, bowing with good grace when Buchanan became the nominee. Like Buchanan, Wise did not want the Union severed. Though he was a slaveholder himself, and feared the Republicans' motives, he was a staunch unionist until Lincoln called for volunteers to suppress the rebellion. Then, as always concerned about his popularity in Virginia, he issued bold though still equivocal calls for vigilance and preparedness. When Virginia did join the Confederacy, he donned the gray and served throughout the war in the Army of Virginia.[7]

John C. Breckinridge of Kentucky, vice president of the United States when South Carolina seceded, and during the first session of the Thirty-Seventh Congress a senator from Kentucky, was another unionist who, forced to choose, adhered to the Confederacy. Charming, with a "fine legal practice" in Lexington, Breckinridge was also a rising star in Democratic politics. He believed that slavery was a matter for the states, not the federal government, but that did not mean that a state had the right to leave the Union when it was affronted by federal policies. As he told an audience in Lexington, Kentucky, on September 5, 1860, during his campaign for the presidency, he would show voters "that the principles upon which I stand, are the principles of both the Constitution and Union of our country." Breckinridge had been chosen by the Southern wing of the Democratic Party to run against Douglas, and though he supported the right of slaveholders to take their slaves anywhere in the country, he denied being a disunionist. "All over the country the charge of Disunion is repeated against me and those who believe with me, by anonymous writers and wandering orators. Their whole stock in trade is Disunion! Disunion! Their continual cry is that this man and his party are attempting to break up the Union of these States. We say, how can principles be sectional or disunionist which are based strictly upon the Constitution." But events conspired against caution and delay, and men like Stephens, Wise, and Breckinridge could delay for only so long. [8]

Southern lawyer/politicians like Stephens, Wise, and Breckinridge were exceptions that proved the rule. Indeed, Southern lawyering—the practices of arguing before juries, reading texts in adversarial fashion, and taking political stances that marked antebellum lawyering—enabled Southern lawyers to lead a secessionist movement. Far more typical, then, was Charles Colcock Jones Jr. of Savannah, a lawyer and planter who represented more of elite Georgia professional opinion on the subject. At the outset of 1861, he wrote to his father, a leading Presbyterian minister, "I have long since believed that in this country have arisen two races which, although claiming a common parentage, have been so entirely separated by climate, by morals, by religion, by estimates so totally opposite of all that constitutes honor, truth, and manliness, that they can no longer exist under the same government." The young Jones might be forgiven this burst of secessionist passion—he had been practicing law for only three years—but T. R. R. Cobb of Athens, a much more established lawyer, three years earlier had warned that should Northern states not enforce federal laws on fugitive slaves, it would violate the Constitution. After Lincoln was elected, Cobb urged Georgia legislators to join a secessionist movement. Lawyering did not trump local allegiances. Nor did it dampen martial ardor. John Singleton Mosby, the most infamous of Southern "rangers" during the war, was a lawyer before it erupted.[9]

What Lincoln and Stephens feared but Cobb and Jones welcomed came to pass. The South Carolina Ordinance of Secession of December 10, 1860, followed by the Declaration of the Immediate Causes Which Induce and Justify the Secession of South Carolina from the Federal Union on December 24 of the same year, were legal documents that purported to prove that secession was not unlawful. That is, South Carolina could, within the framework of the Constitution, leave the Union. Removed from the First Baptist Church in Columbia because of an outbreak of smallpox in the city to the cavernous St. Andrews Hall in Charleston, the 106 delegates of the Secession Convention voted unanimously for secession. They then proceeded to Institute Hall to sign their names, witnessed by throngs of ladies and gentleman who filled the ground floor and balconies.[10]

Who had drafted the South Carolina declaration? Surely a lawyer, but which one? Later scholars suggested that William Ferguson Hutson, also a member of the committee, might have been the author. Hutson was a planter and a lawyer with a large practice in the southeastern corner of the state, but he was not particularly noted for his learning. If the draft was his, it would have to have been the final draft of a document he composed weeks before the convention met in anticipation of secession—hence weeks before he was selected to serve on the drafting committee at the convention. Contemporaries described that original document as far too long and too detailed for submission to the convention, a description that does not fit the elegant and forceful version finally reported out of the committee. John A. Inglis, the Maryland-born and bred member of the court of chancery and chairman of the drafting committee, has also been suggested as the author, but he chose Robert Barnwell Rhett to chair the committee, an unlikely step if Inglis had already prepared an ordinance. When, in the final days of the Civil War, Inglis was accused of being its author, he denied that he had any hand in drafting the ordinance. The ever-present fire-eater Rhett, who served on the committee, claimed that he had shaped it, but its steady and stately pace does not match his rhetoric before and during the secession convention. Consider his Address to the People of South Carolina: "All of the fraternity of feeling between the North and the South is lost, or has been converted into hate, and we, of the South, are at last driven together by the stern destiny which controls the existence of nations." This was hardly a work of reasoned legalism.[11]

The ordinance was not the work of hotheads and politicians but most likely a highly respected and able member of the South Carolina bar—Francis Henry Wardlaw. Wardlaw was a member of the court of chancery and then a justice in the state's highest court. Although not on the committee assigned the task, later recollections named him as its author. Certainly, he was the very model of the elite of the South Carolina bar. Men of highest caliber in the antebellum state's courts were expected to possess (in the words of one eulogy of former US senator A. P. Butler) "extraordinary faculties . . . popularity, quickness, sound judgment, integrity, and ability." Wardlaw possessed all of these qualities. Remarkably similar in appearance to Governor Francis Pickens, Wardlaw came from a family of lawyers, went to school at South Carolina College (later the University of South Carolina), and then read law and began a law practice in the Edgefield district. Election to the state legislature and the nullification convention of 1832, which created the South Carolina legislature and declared the tariffs of 1828 and 1832 unconstitutional, followed ten years of law practice. Like his better known fellow Carolinians James Henry Hammond and Rhett, Wardlaw edited a newspaper. In 1850, he was elected chancellor of the state and presided over its court of equity until, in 1859, he was elected to the state's court of appeals. On it, he sprinkled his opinions with his learning in English and continental law. He never lost his interest in politics and accepted election to the secession convention, where he avidly supported separation from the Union. Described in the press as "merry, cheerful and affectionate," he did not live long enough—he died on May 29, 1861—to see his eldest son die in the Civil War his draft helped bring on.[12]

Although there was no pressing need to go beyond the ordinance itself, the traditions of legalism that infused South Carolina's protests against the tariff in 1828 and 1832 persisted in the South Carolina secession convention. It would not be proper to depart the Union without showing that leaving was legal. That required a somewhat wordy and self-serving explanation: "And now the State of South Carolina having resumed her separate and equal place among nations, deems it due to herself, to the remaining United States of America, and to the nations of the world, that she should declare the immediate causes which have led to this act."[13]

Wardlaw had practiced common law and sat as a common law judge. He knew that in common law a legal brief stating the causes of the common law "action," the grounds for bringing the suit or the appeal, or here secession, would rest on sound doctrine, an offer of fact, citation of the applicable black letter (statute, constitutional) law, and a weighing of precedent (earlier cases on point).

Doctrine was jurisprudential reading of the law, that is, of its conceptual basis. Doctrine was the most important part of the South Carolina secession argument, although it included the other elements of a common-law argument. Ironically, the doctrinal model for the Declaration of Causes was the work of a man who although celebrated at the secession convention (his bust appeared at the top of an arch erected in Charleston during the convention) had worked hard throughout his career to prevent secession. John C. Calhoun had been a longtime member of Congress and former vice president. He died in 1850, his legacy a body of proslavery legal thought. He was not the first or even the foremost exponent of the states' rights theory, but his secretly drafted (at the time he was the vice president of the United States) Exposition of 1828 gave states' rights the constitutional foundation on which secession ultimately rested. Writing to defend South Carolina's opposition to the tariff of 1828, he argued, "Whereas the Congress of the United States . . . exceeding its just power to impose taxes and collect revenue for the purpose of effecting and accomplishing the specific objects and purposes which the constitution of the United States authorizes it to effect and accomplish . . . We, therefore, the people of the State of South Carolina, in convention assembled, do declare and ordain [that the tariff laws] are unauthorized by the constitution of the United States, and violate the true meaning and intent thereof and are null, void, and no law, nor binding upon this State, its officers or citizens."[14]

Calhoun had found precedent for such an avowal in Thomas Jefferson's Kentucky Resolutions and James Madison's Virginia Resolutions of 1798 against the Alien and Sedition Acts, but those resolutions did not fully embrace the doctrine of states' rights. Madison in particular opined that the Federalists of 1798 had violated the First Amendment, and hence the legislation was unconstitutional; Jefferson's call for interposition went further, but he did not call for nullification. Calhoun did. "Our system, then, consists of two distinct and independent Governments." While "the general powers, expressly delegated to the General Government, are subject to its sole and separate control . . . So, also, the peculiar and local powers reserved to the States are subject to their exclusive control; nor can the General Government interfere, in any manner, with them, without violating the Constitution." What was the remedy? "If the present usurpations and the professed doctrines of the existing system be persevered in—after due forebearance on the part of the State—that it will be her sacred duty to interpose—a duty to herself—to the Union—to the present, and to future generations—and to the cause of liberty over the world, to arrest the progress of a usurpation which, if not arrested, must, in its consequences, corrupt the public morals and destroy the liberty of the country." In Wardlaw's mind, and that of the committee responsible for the Declaration of Causes, South Carolina had exercised that "forebearance" for many years.[15]

Calhoun was not a democrat in the modern sense of the word. His ideal of popular sovereignty was the gathering of the propertied classes of men. The doctrinal lodestar was not the people themselves but a certain kind of gathering of certain kindred spirits in a convention whose members were chosen by qualified voters. The constitutional convention of 1787 was only one of these, assembled in a time of state constitutional conventions. These state conventions periodically reassembled to revise state government. While the revisions tended to open up the franchise to more and more white male voters, the democracy remained a body limited and defined by law. Thus, one could argue that the basis of the Union was not the federal Constitution's text, but the fact that the Constitution was written at and by members of a convention. Wardlaw invoked this principle in the very first passage of the South Carolina declaration—"The people of the State of South Carolina, in Convention assembled," referring to the convention of 1852.[16]

The declaration of 1860 also included a recital of facts. These grievances obviously and self-consciously resembled the list of grievances against King George III that comprised the body of the 1776 Declaration of Independence. At the center of this narration was South Carolina's continuous protest against the national government's violation of its own Constitution. "The people of the State of South Carolina, in Convention assembled, on the 26th day of April, A.D., 1852, declared that the frequent violations of the Constitution of the United States, by the Federal Government, and its encroachments upon the reserved rights of the States, fully justified this State in then withdrawing from the Federal Union; but in deference to the opinions and wishes of the other slaveholding States, she forbore at that time to exercise this right. Since that time, these encroachments have continued to increase, and further forbearance ceases to be a virtue." Those violations included various unconstitutional limitations on the rights of South Carolina slaveholders. "In the present case, that fact is established with certainty. We assert that fourteen of the States have deliberately refused, for years past, to fulfill their constitutional obligations, and we refer to their own Statutes for the proof." The gravamen—the complaint, was the free states' refusal to aid in the recapture and return of runaway slaves according to the rigorous procedure the Fugitive Slave Act of 1850 prescribed. As proof of this disregard of law in the free states' Personal Freedom Acts: "Those States have assumed the right of deciding upon the propriety of our domestic institutions; and have denied the rights of property established in fifteen of the States and recognized by the Constitution; they have denounced as sinful the institution of slavery; they have permitted open establishment among them of societies, whose avowed object is to disturb the peace and to eloign [remove at a distance] the property of the citizens of other States. They have encouraged and assisted thousands of our slaves to leave their homes; and those who remain, have been incited by emissaries, books and pictures to servile insurrection."

According to Wardlaw, who had taken part in the 1852 convention, the very language of the Constitution, read in the light of the common law of contract, added to the manner in which it was drafted and ratified, together supported the right of secession. This approach combined an early form of "textualism," taking the obvious public meaning of the document at face value, and "purposivism," looking at the supposed aims of the framers of the federal Constitution. "Thus was established, by compact between the States [a reference to Calhoun's compact theory of the Constitution], a Government with definite objects and powers, limited to the express words of the grant. This limitation left the whole remaining mass of power subject to the clause reserving it to the States or to the people, and rendered unnecessary any specification of reserved rights."[17]

If the contract or compact theory of the Constitution laid the basis for secession, the law of contract explained when secession could take place. Wardlaw: "We hold further, that the mode of its formation subjects it to a third fundamental principle, namely: the law of compact. We maintain that in every compact between two or more parties, the obligation is mutual; that the failure of one of the contracting parties to perform a material part of the agreement, entirely releases the obligation of the other; and that where no arbiter is provided, each party is remitted to his own judgment to determine the fact of failure, with all its consequences." These consequences included the rescission of the contract. "We affirm that these ends for which this Government was instituted have been defeated, and the Government itself has been made destructive of them by the action of the non-slaveholding States."

Finally, Wardlaw could cite precedent—the American Revolution: "In the year 1765, that portion of the British Empire embracing Great Britain, undertook to make laws for the government of that portion composed of the thirteen American Colonies. A struggle for the right of self-government ensued, which resulted, on the 4th of July, 1776, in a Declaration, by the Colonies, 'that they are, and of right ought to be, FREE AND INDEPENDENT STATES; and that, as free and independent States, they have full power to levy war, conclude peace, contract alliances, establish commerce, and to do all other acts and things which independent States may of right do.'" This second reference to Declaration of Independence tied together independence in 1776 and secession in 1860. South Carolina was one of those states, and became part of a confederation of the states with the understanding that "thus were established the two great principles asserted by the Colonies, namely: the right of a State to govern itself; and the right of a people to abolish a Government when it becomes destructive of the ends for which it was instituted." The founding of the nation rested on the right of the people to sever the bonds that tied it to such a confederation. South Carolina was once more an independent republic.

Wardlaw included all the elements one would find in a law pleading. One supposes that South Carolina could have promulgated a more forthright argument for secession, for as Wardlaw knew and the fire-eaters constantly repeated, secession was all about protection and expansion of slavery. As one Georgia Supreme Court justice put it, in 1855, the influence of the abolitionists who would be cited by Wardlaw at the outset of the 1860 declaration, left unconstrained, would lead to "insubordination, massacre of free citizens, and insurrection." But a jurist like Wardlaw respected the rule of law tradition just as he embraced the old Constitution of limited federal government and state sovereignty. For him the elements of common law pleading were not window dressing. They mattered. What is more, he may have even thought them persuasive in the present case, even if the details of the alleged violations of South Carolina's rights remained a little hazy. Whether the federal government in the person of the president of the United States or its Congress would accept secession as a fact or in law was another matter entirely.[18]

In the last month of his incumbency, President James Buchanan, a Pennsylvania Democrat, faced the dilemma of what to do about secession. Four years earlier he had selected a cabinet that showed clearly his obligations to the Southern wing of the Democratic Party. Those members included Howell Cobb of Georgia and John Floyd of Virginia. When Lincoln was elected, they expected South Carolina to secede. Cobb supported secession, Floyd opposed it, but they both urged Buchanan not to resist secession, and they resigned from the cabinet before their states seceded. Floyd was a lawyer/politician and former governor of Virginia whose steps were always dogged with accusations of self-dealing. He resigned from the cabinet at the eleventh hour, leaving without explaining why, again pursued by inquiries into his maladministration of the Department of War. Cobb explained his views on the eve of his resignation. He assumed that everyone knew that Lincoln and his party would not enforce the fugitive slave laws and would, given the opportunity, free the slaves. As a lawyer as well as a Southern man, he warned that the personal freedom laws of the North, aided and abetted by a Republican majority in Congress and a Republican chief executive, would "annul a plain provision of the Constitution of the United States." The Southern states would not, could not, remain in a union with such lawlessness, the "fruit of the principles and teaching of the Black Republican party." Both Cobb and Floyd would serve the Confederacy as general officers.[19]

Buchanan himself knew that the election of Lincoln was likely to renew South Carolina's drive to secession. Fiercely aggressive in his foreign policy, ever ready to commit federal troops and naval vessels to far-off military ventures, his view of his domestic powers was curiously subdued. Whether his reticence to react to secession was due to his hatred of the Republicans or to some atavistic desire to conciliate the Southern democracy, facing "the most wrenching crisis" of his presidency he blamed Congress for its inaction and refused to exercise any of his discretion as commander in chief of the United States' armed forces to coerce South Carolina to return to the Union or to punish the leading secessionists.[20]

In his Fourth Annual Message to Congress, on December 3, 1860, Buchanan explained where he stood as a matter of law, not politics. "Upon [the Southern states'] good sense and patriotic forbearance I confess I still greatly rely. Without their aid it is beyond the power of any President, no matter what may be his own political proclivities, to restore peace and harmony among the States. Wisely limited and restrained as is his power under our Constitution and laws, he alone can accomplish but little for good or for evil on such a momentous question . . . . They, and they alone, can do it." In other words, Buchanan accepted the strong states' rights position. "All that is necessary to accomplish the object, and all for which the slave States have ever contended, is to be let alone and permitted to manage their domestic institutions in their own way. As sovereign States, they, and they alone, are responsible before God and the world for the slavery existing among them. For this the people of the North are not more responsible and have no more right to interfere than with similar institutions in Russia or in Brazil."

On this view of a limited presidency and a robust states' rights rested a concept of executive restraint in a separation of powers system, suggesting that if any remedy in Washington, DC, was possible, it must come from the other branches of the federal government. "Apart from the execution of the laws, so far as this may be practicable, the Executive has no authority to decide what shall be the relations between the Federal Government and South Carolina. He has been invested with no such discretion. He possesses no power to change the relations heretofore existing between them, much less to acknowledge the independence of that State." The widespread disavowal of the *Dred Scott* decision in the North demonstrated that the federal courts could not provide that remedy. It remained to see if Congress could. He thought not. "Has the Constitution delegated to Congress the power to coerce a State into submission which is attempting to withdraw or has actually withdrawn from the Confederacy?" The use of the term "confederacy" suggested a pre-federal constitutional system. The ratification of the federal Constitution had ended the first confederacy and replaced the Articles of Confederation with a Union, but Buchanan declined to follow that logic. Instead, he told Congress that if it employed force against seceding states, "it must be on the principle that the power has been conferred upon Congress to declare and to make war against a State. After much serious reflection I have arrived at the conclusion that no such power has been delegated to Congress or to any other department of the Federal Government." His logic, in line with an extreme version of states' rights, assumed that secession would be the act of states, not citizens of the United States.[21]

Later that December, Buchanan read Wardlaw's defense of secession and explained once again to the "lame duck" Congress (according to the Constitution the newly elected Congress was not scheduled to sit until the end of the year) on January 8, 1861, why he could not suppress secession with force. "In my annual message I expressed the conviction, which I have long deliberately held, and which recent reflection has only tended to deepen and confirm, that no State has a right by its own act to secede from the Union or throw off its federal obligations at pleasure." That was not what he said, or believed, at the beginning of December. "I also declared my opinion to be that even if that right existed and should be exercised by any State of the Confederacy the executive department of this Government had no authority under the Constitution to recognize its validity by acknowledging the independence of such State." Bound by the law, the president could not overextend his authority. "This left me no alternative, as the chief executive officer under the Constitution of the United States, but to collect the public revenues and to protect the public property so far as this might be practicable under existing laws. This is still my purpose. My province is to execute and not to make the laws." This time, however, he passed the buck to Congress to deal with the crisis. Changing his stance on the authority of the legislative branch in the crisis, he added, "It belongs to Congress exclusively to repeal, to modify, or to enlarge their provisions to meet exigencies as they may occur." He had not found this power in Congress a month earlier. "The right and the duty to use military force defensively against those who resist the Federal officers in the execution of their legal functions and against those who assail the property of the Federal Government is clear and undeniable."[22]

Buchanan was a very successful lawyer before and during his stint in the Senate, and his messages on the secession crisis were legal briefs, albeit for inaction. Whether he was taking refuge in the legalism, genuinely felt bound by it, or was simply overwhelmed by the gravity and speed of secession and could not comprehend another answer to it than the ones he proposed, the fact remains that his answers were legal, not political or military. He had, according to one courtroom observer, "a combination of physical and intellectual qualities that contributed to make him a powerful advocate." With so much of lawyering depending on presence, Buchanan's six-feet-plus frame, his appearance of honesty and frankness, and his "indefatigable" preparation helped win him cases. But his career was interrupted by politics, so much so that he wrote to Andrew Jackson in 1835, "This change from law to politics and politics to law makes both pursuits very laborious. A man cannot do justice to both." Jackson, a lawyer himself and former judge who had chosen political office, undoubtedly knew what Buchanan meant. Once he had committed himself to political pursuits, he never looked back at the courtroom. From 1835 on, no mention of Buchanan as counsel appeared in the local court records. Yet even in Congress, as a diplomat, and in the presidency, "his was the oratory of a lawyer."[23]

In Buchanan's cabinet, there remained Jeremiah Black, a longtime friend from Pennsylvania; Edwin Stanton, a successful lawyer and politician from Ohio; and Joseph Holt of Kentucky, a third lawyer. The three men were different in their approach to the issues, however, in part because of their different personalities. Black was cautious and deeply religious, with a personal antagonism to slavery at odds with much of the Democratic Party's leadership. Stanton hid his antislavery views. Black made it a personal mission to forgive his enemies; Stanton relished revenge against his. Contemporary recollections of Black celebrated his "resonant wrath" when confronting what he saw as corruption and fraud. Stanton, self-taught, never fully confident, "could organize and control volumes of information in preparation for a complicated legal case. By dint of obfuscation, sarcasm, theatrics, and the browbeating of witnesses, he could sway judges and juries in the face of overwhelming contradictory evidence." Lincoln and Douglas had the same backgrounds and acquired the same skills but stopped short of Stanton's inclination to bully opponents. Black and Stanton were an odd couple, but Holt fit an older model of lawyer. A country lawyer and sometime newspaper editor from Kentucky, his stay in Mississippi in the cotton boom years of the 1830s bred in him a genuine hatred for slavery. Initially Buchanan's postmaster general, with the resignation of John Floyd, Holt became secretary of war. Fiercely loyal to both the Union and Kentucky, he later wrote to Governor James Speed (for publication), "In this struggle for the existence of our government, I can neither practice, nor profess, nor feel for neutrality . . . and find an abounding consolation in the conviction . . . that the popular heart of Kentucky in its devotion to the union is far in advance" of the neutral sentiments professed by its legislature. It was the "devotion to African Servitude" that had driven the Confederacy to its "treasonable enterprise." It was the sworn duty of the presidency to resist, with force if necessary, such an assault on the Union.[24]

In the troubled cabinet meetings of that winter, as Georgia's Cobb and others carried out their own version of secession by resigning and returning to their states, Black, Stanton, and Holt urged Buchanan to protect, with force if necessary, federal arsenals, post offices, and the District of Columbia itself. In these arguments, they were partially successful. But reinforcement or the calling up of troops to suppress a rebellion were beyond Buchanan's will, and perhaps his means as well. With the crisis growing and his former Southern allies gone, Buchanan was more and more dependent on his two counselors. Black in particular refused to let Buchanan back down on the evacuation of Fort Sumter, threatening to resign if Buchanan allowed Major Anderson and the garrison to pull out.[25]

Did Black also have a hand, perhaps the guiding hand, in drafting the January 8 Special Message? There is internal evidence that he did. Compared to the Fourth Annual Message on December 3, the Special Message has distinctly shorter sentences. It lacks the self-congratulatory tone of the Annual Message. Buchanan's interest in foreign affairs is absent, though the response of Britain and France to secession was of great importance to other leading politicians—for example, William H. Seward. The about-face on the role of Congress in the crisis was striking—for Buchanan was not a man who changed his mind easily. But the most imposing clue is the language itself, no longer the flowery stuff of Buchanan's courtroom oratory. Black's style of argument was more direct, almost fierce: "Even now the danger is upon us." "I have often warned my countrymen of the dangers which now surround us." These short, powerful sentences were not typical of Buchanan's style, nor was the firmness of his conclusion that "the seizing of this [federal] property, from all appearances, has been purely aggressive, and not in resistance to any attempt to coerce a state or states to remain in the Union."

On March 2, 1861, a movement in the Senate for a compromise based on longtime Kentucky senator John J. Crittenden's proposal failed, the Republicans voting as a bloc against it. Crittenden was a lawyer/politician who owned slaves and represented the substantial planter interest in the state. Some were proslavery unionists, if only marginally, and some would later serve the Confederacy. A few, like James Speed, a close friend of Lincoln's and a lawyer much respected in the state, not only chose the Union but would serve it. Speed became Lincoln's attorney general in the closing years of the war. While Kentucky and the other border states hung in the balance, Lincoln trying assiduously to keep them in the Union, the so-called Peace Conference met from February 4 to March 4, 1861. It did not have delegates from the seven states that had already seceded, but leading antebellum politicians from the border slave states did attend. The proposal that they compiled included amendments to the Constitution. But the amendments the conference agreed on pleased neither the incoming Republican majority nor the newly established Confederate States of America. Although the proposal seemed to protect slavery where it existed, it did not give the slave states what they wanted—the right to extend slavery into the territories—nor did it forbid slavery in the territories, the Free Soil platform. Predictably, it failed. Had it come before the election, it would have failed for the same reasons.[26]

At the same time the peace conference was assembling in the Willard Hotel, South Carolina attorney general Isaac W. Hayne, on behalf of South Carolina governor Francis Pickens, hand delivered to Buchanan a demand that South Carolina be given Fort Sumter in Charleston Harbor. Currently occupied by a small force of federal infantry, it had become a flash point in the crisis. Hayne and Pickens sought a legal transfer of the property, as though the transaction were one between private owners. Secretary of War Holt prepared an answer to which Buchanan subscribed. In a memorandum dated February 6, 1861, that reads much like the letter that a lawyer writes to a client explaining a property dispute, Holt wrote: "The title of the United States to Fort Sumter is complete and incontestable . . . . It has absolute jurisdiction over the fort and the soil on which it stands . . . . South Carolina can no more assert the right of eminent domain over Fort Sumter than Maryland can assert it over the District of Columbia. The President, however, is relieved from the necessity of further pursuing this inquiry by the fact that, whatever may be the claim of South Carolina to this fort, he has no constitutional power to cede or surrender it." Buchanan and Holt were responding to a political crisis with legalistic technicalities. Hayne, however, read the response as "highly insulting" and Buchanan noted that he had to pour oil on the troubled waters. "There was nothing insulting in the letter," he told former president John Tyler of Virginia, who brought word of Hayne's high dudgeon.[27]

Buchanan, with the wisdom of hindsight and some bitter reflection on the last days of his administration, in 1866 composed and published a defense of his actions. The fault, he found, lay in the failure of law. There was no federal judiciary in South Carolina after it seceded. The judicial branch of the government was thus powerless to indict and try the rebels in the vicinage of their destruction or taking of federal property. The federal judge, marshal, and attorney had resigned in order to serve the state. Congress had failed in its legal duties as well, refusing to give to the president the power to call up the state militias according to the 1795 act to suppress domestic insurrection. Buchanan was thus tied like Prometheus to the rock; no law-abiding president could authorize military action against South Carolina without violating the law. Quoting his January 8, 1861, message to Congress, he emphasized his official inability to deal with secession in legalistic terms: the danger "has already far transcended and cast in the shade the ordinary executive duties already provided for by law, and has assumed such vast and alarming proportions as to place the subject entirely above and beyond executive control."[28]

A failed negotiation would hardly have been news to an experienced lawyer. But Buchanan's client, the Union, had expected more of him, and his inability to work with any of the parties to the dispute demonstrated ineptitude. For negotiation to be successful, however, the parties have to want to come to a mutually acceptable agreement. The framing of the Constitution had been one such negotiation, and the question of slavery, so potentially divisive that South Carolina had threatened to absent itself from the Union in 1787, was on that occasion successfully handled. In part, Buchanan's failure lay in his inability to get the Republicans in Washington to assist him, an obstacle put in his path by another lawyer some 784 miles to the West who refused to break his silence.[29]

Far off in Springfield, Illinois, newly elected president Abraham Lincoln also read the South Carolina Ordinance and Buchanan's address to Congress. He responded to both documents with a legal brief imbedded in his first inaugural address. It was in form a summation of a case for the Union for a jury, a practice at which Lincoln excelled, intended for the unionists of the South. For Lincoln, then and later, saving the

Union was a "Constitutional duty." A few days before his scheduled departure from Springfield to Washington, DC, stealing time from the bustle of packing his family, in a "dingy, dusty, neglected backroom" of an in-law's office, Lincoln set about crafting his brief for the Union.[30]

Lincoln had laid out part of the ground for the Inaugural Address in his February 27, 1860, Cooper Institute Address in New York City. In form it was an answer to Chief Justice Roger Taney's obiter dictum in *Dred Scott v. Sandford* (1857) that the Missouri Compromise barring slavery from territories north of 36°30′ was unconstitutional. Lincoln had prepared the arguments after research at the Springfield Illinois State Library, in effect treating the proposed address as if he were arguing the case before the Supreme Court. His approach would today be called historical originalism, resting on his reading of the purposes and understandings of the framers of the Northwest Ordinance and the Constitution. "In 1784, three years before the Constitution—the United States then owning the Northwestern Territory, and no other, the Congress of the Confederation had before them the question of prohibiting slavery in that Territory." Among the members then were Roger Sherman, Thomas Mifflin, and Hugh Williamson, all three of whom "voted for the prohibition, thus showing that, in their understanding, no line dividing local from federal authority, nor anything else, properly forbade the Federal Government to control as to slavery in federal territory."[31]

That did not settle the issue, of course, for the final version of the ordinance was voted up in 1787, the same year the constitutional convention prepared its draft. "In 1787, still before the Constitution, but while the Convention was in session framing it, and while the Northwestern Territory still was the only territory owned by the United States, the same question of prohibiting slavery in the territory again came before the Congress of the Confederation." The prohibition passed and was included in the Constitution in Article IV, Section 3, Clause 2: "The Congress shall have Power to dispose of and make all needful Rules and Regulations respecting the Territory or other Property belonging to the United States; and nothing in this Constitution shall be so construed as to Prejudice any Claims of the United States, or of any particular State" and Article VI, Clause 1: "All Debts contracted and Engagements entered into, before the Adoption of this Constitution, shall be as valid against the United States under this Constitution, as under the Confederation." The upshot of this essay in originalist interpretation of the Constitution was clear: "The sum of the whole is, that of our thirty-nine fathers who framed the original Constitution, twenty-one—a clear majority of the whole—certainly understood that no proper division of local from federal authority, nor any part of the Constitution, forbade the Federal Government to control slavery in the federal territories; while all the rest probably had the same understanding. Such, unquestionably, was the understanding of our fathers who framed the original Constitution; and the text affirms that they understood the question 'better than we.'"[32]

Lincoln's view of the superintending authority of Congress to make rules for the territories, he thought, was understood by the members of the new Congress. "In 1789, by the first Congress which sat under the Constitution, an act was passed to enforce the Ordinance of '87, including the prohibition of slavery in the Northwestern Territory." Lincoln, addressing an overflow crowd of Republican supporters as though they were a collective bench, hammered home the point: "This shows that, in their understanding, no line dividing local from federal authority, nor anything in the Constitution, properly forbade Congress to prohibit slavery in the federal territory; else both their fidelity to correct principle, and their oath to support the Constitution, would have constrained them to oppose the prohibition."[33]

Lincoln feared that that secessionist opinion was rampant in the South, and he closed his address by connecting it to a wrongheaded view of the *Dred Scott* case and the role of the Supreme Court in constitutional adjudication. "Perhaps you will say the Supreme Court has decided the disputed constitutional question in your favor. Not quite so." Taney's dictum had only one subscriber among the majority, Justice Peter Daniel. It was not the decision of the Court; that required a majority of the members to sign on to an opinion. "But waiving the lawyer's distinction between dictum and decision, the Court have decided the question for you in a sort of way. The Court have substantially said, it is your constitutional right to take slaves into the federal territories, and to hold them there as property. When I say the decision was made in a sort of way, I mean it was made in a divided Court, by a bare majority of the Judges, and they not quite agreeing with one another in the reasons for making it; that it is so made as that its avowed supporters disagree with one another about its meaning, and that it was mainly based upon a mistaken statement of fact—the statement in the opinion that 'the right of property in a slave is distinctly and expressly affirmed in the Constitution.'" Nowhere in the Constitution's text was the right to hold slaves explicitly affirmed.[34]

An inauguration of a president is an explicitly legal moment. The president-elect takes an oath to preserve and defend the Constitution and is sworn into office. The address that customarily follows is not, however, required by law. It is usually a collection of bromides about the past and future of a great nation. On no occasion previously had the Union been in such peril as on March 4, 1861, however. At the center of that peril were two legal issues—the status of slavery and the purported secession of seven states from the Union. Lincoln went straight to the legal questions.

A little over one year after Lincoln's Cooper Union speech, he faced the unthinkable—a portion of the slave South had seceded. He thus amended his Cooper Union argument to make it more palatable to the South, though he did not change its conclusions. At the outset, Lincoln promised that the Republican administration would be bound by the law. During the deliberations of the various compromise committees over the period that Lincoln remained in Springfield, he had been asked what he would concede. He refused to step back from the Free Soil platform, but he wrote to Illinois senator Lyman Trumbull that he would enforce the Fugitive Slave Act, providing enforcement included protections for free blacks wrongly taken into custody. He began the Inaugural Address with the concession that "apprehension seems to exist among the people of the Southern States that by the accession of a Republican Administration their property and their peace and personal security are to be endangered. There has never been any reasonable cause for such apprehension." As the leader of the party as well as the nation, he offered that "the most ample evidence to the contrary has all the while existed and been open to their inspection. It is found in nearly all the published speeches of him who now addresses you." In particular, he repeated that "I have no purpose, directly or indirectly, to interfere with the institution of slavery in the States where it exists. I believe I have no lawful right to do so, and I have no inclination to do so." Proof lay in the platform on which he ran, and won, the presidency: "That the maintenance inviolate of the rights of the States, and especially the right of each State to order and control its own domestic institutions according to its own judgment exclusively, is essential to that balance of power on which the perfection and endurance of our political fabric depend; and we denounce the lawless invasion by armed force of the soil of any State or Territory, no matter what pretext, as among the gravest of crimes."[35]

Lincoln knew that the central grievance in the South Carolina Declaration of 1860 was the refusal of the free states to obey the Fugitive Slave Act of 1850. Lincoln had an answer to this fear, again grounded in law. "There is much controversy about the delivering up of fugitives from service or labor. The [Rendition Clause] is as plainly written in the Constitution as any other of its provisions . . . . It is scarcely questioned that this provision was intended by those who made it for the reclaiming of what we call fugitive slaves; and the intention of the lawgiver is the law. All members of Congress swear their support to the whole Constitution—to this provision as much as to any other." When he took the oath to preserve and defend the Constitution at the outset of his address, he committed himself to enforce the Fugitive Slave Act.

But that law was subject to the larger meanings of the Constitution, a theory of legal interpretation that Lincoln's generation understood. John Marshall as lawyer and then chief justice, for example, opened up the terse language of the Constitution by deploying the methods of a common-law lawyer. One looked at the intent of the lawmaker, the broad purpose of the law, and adapted plain text to novel situations. This kind of interpretive tool encompassed sources of law outside the text of the Constitution, including natural law concepts. Natural law applied to the "intercourse of nations" and their peoples was "the law of nations." Whether it was called the higher law or represented in references to the Declaration of Independence (a favorite of Lincoln's as it had been of John Quincy Adams's condemnations of slavery), it applied to acts of Congress and those bound to enforce federal law. Lincoln continued, "Again: In any law upon this subject ought not all the safeguards of liberty known in civilized and humane jurisprudence to be introduced, so that a free man be not in any case surrendered as a slave? And might it not be well at the same time to provide by law for the enforcement of that clause in the Constitution which guarantees that 'the citizens of each State shall be entitled to all privileges and immunities of citizens in the several States'?"[36]

Lincoln thus juxtaposed the legal status of slavery under the Constitution and his own view of the moral status of slavery, drawn from natural law. Slavery was established in state and federal statute law, and he was bound to obey it. But slavery was a moral wrong, and nothing in his oath or the duties of his office required him to say anything favorable about it. This was the central tension of Republican constitutional jurisprudence—slavery was a wrong with no legal remedy, a contradiction that the Anglo-American common law was not supposed to tolerate.

Handling the legal question of secession was far easier, for to Lincoln's mind it involved no inherent contradiction. That is, as matters of law, the issues of slavery and secession were separate in his mind, although the secession ordinances always joined the two. Within the law he could do nothing about slavery where law established it, but he could do something about secession. To it he applied the same succession of interpretive tactics as he had to slavery. "I hold that in contemplation of universal law and of the Constitution the Union of these States is perpetual. Perpetuity is implied, if not expressed, in the fundamental law of all national governments. It is safe to assert that no government proper ever had a provision in its organic law for its own termination. Continue to execute all the express provisions of our National Constitution, and the Union will endure forever, it being impossible to destroy it except by some action not provided for in the instrument itself." The purpose of the Union was implied in the text of the Constitution, though not explicitly stated. Had there been a provision for secession, it would have been provided.[37]

Lincoln next had to deal directly with the compact theory of the Union. "If the United States be not a government proper, but an association of States in the nature of contract merely, can it, as a contract, be peaceably unmade by less than all the parties who made it? One party to a contract may violate it—break it, so to speak—but does it not require all to lawfully rescind it?" Lincoln analogized the Union to a contract in only one passage, asking whether one party to a multi-party contract could rescind the entire contract without the consent of all the other parties, but this was a private law analogy, and he did not pursue it. In any case, posing questions did not answer them, Lincoln knew, and he turned, as had Wardlaw in the South Carolina declaration, to legal history. "Descending from these general principles, we find the proposition that in legal contemplation the Union is perpetual confirmed by the history of the Union itself. The Union is much older than the Constitution. It was formed, in fact, by the Articles of Association in 1774. It was matured and continued by the Declaration of Independence in 1776. It was further matured, and the faith of all the then thirteen States expressly plighted and engaged that it should be perpetual, by the Articles of Confederation in 1778. And finally, in 1787, one of the declared objects for ordaining and establishing the Constitution was 'to form a more perfect union.'" Finally, he assayed a reading of the plain text. "If destruction of the Union by one or by a part only of the States be lawfully possible, the Union is less perfect than before the Constitution, having lost the vital element of perpetuity."[38]

Having explained the principles of constitutional law as he understood them, Lincoln told the United States citizens in the seceding section of the country how he intended to enforce the law. "I therefore consider that in view of the Constitution and the laws the Union is unbroken, and to the extent of my ability, I shall take care, as the Constitution itself expressly enjoins upon me, that the laws of the Union be faithfully executed in all the States." Faithful execution of the laws was an executive mandate, part of the oath of office. It was also the command of the ultimate sovereign in a democratic republican system: "Doing this I deem to be only a simple duty on my part, and I shall perform it so far as practicable unless my rightful masters, the American people, shall withhold the requisite means or in some authoritative manner direct the contrary."[39]

Nothing could be more simply stated—Lincoln intended to enforce the laws. "I trust this will not be regarded as a menace, but only as the declared purpose of the Union that it will constitutionally defend and maintain itself." There was a carrot, "In doing this there needs to be no bloodshed or violence," and a stick, "and there shall be none unless it be forced upon the national authority." In case anyone did not understand what he meant, "The power confided to me will be used to hold, occupy, and possess the property and places belonging to the Government and to collect the duties and imposts." But Lincoln stopped short of calling secession itself an act of insurrection. Again he offered the carrot, "Beyond what may be necessary for these objects, there will be no invasion, no using of force against or among the people anywhere. Where hostility to the United States in any interior locality shall be so great and universal as to prevent competent resident citizens from holding the Federal offices, there will be no attempt to force obnoxious strangers [presumably Northern abolitionists] among the people for that object." But he held the stick in hand where it might be seen: "While the strict legal right may exist in the Government to enforce the exercise of these offices, the attempt to do so would be so irritating and so nearly impracticable withal that I deem it better to forego for the time the uses of such offices."[40]

In what may have seemed an unnecessary aside, Lincoln addressed the question of the federal post. "The mails, unless repelled, will continue to be furnished in all parts of the Union. So far as possible the people everywhere shall have that sense of perfect security which is most favorable to calm thought and reflection." This subtle reference to the fact that in the past, Southern mobs had entered federal postal facilities to find and destroy abolitionist literature was especially important to the abolitionists in the audience. Some radical abolitionists had had little objection to the departure of the hated slave South. Lincoln wanted them to know that he recognized their past travails and although he was not of their number, he wanted their allegiance.[41]

In the final portion of the Inaugural Address, Lincoln appealed to the sentiment and good sense of those who had raised the standard of rebellion. He did not (and never would) consider the states in the new Confederacy as independent, nor the Confederacy itself as a sovereign nation. They were merely the delusions of those who could be called back to their better natures. In form, the closing passage was an appeal to the jury of the sort which Lincoln had mastered over three decades of practice in trial courts. He wanted the jury to deliberate. "My countrymen, one and all, think calmly and well upon this whole subject. Nothing valuable can be lost by taking time. If there be an object to hurry any of you in hot haste to a step which you would never take deliberately, that object will be frustrated by taking time; but no good object can be frustrated by it." Nothing had changed with his election—"you still have the old Constitution unimpaired, and, on the sensitive point, the laws of your own framing under it." His final words were those a lawyer leaves a jury with—perhaps a jury that is leaning to an unfavorable verdict. "In your hands, my dissatisfied fellow-countrymen, and not in mine, is the momentous issue of civil war. The Government will not assail you." But Lincoln was a winner in a courtroom, and perhaps, just perhaps, his words would sway enough of Southern opinion, "the better angels of our nature."[42]

For one observer, newspaperman William Henry Hulbert, the Inaugural Address was a disappointment because it was too legalistic. "There was too much argumentative discussion of the question at issue, as was to have been expected from a man whose whole career has been that of an advocate." Abolitionists complained that Lincoln did not attack slavery directly. Somewhat less explicitly, others, notably Seward, criticized Lincoln for not doing with the Inaugural Address what he had not done in the weeks preceding it—give support to some kind of political compromise. Other contemporaries recognized that the tone was intended to conciliate. Later historians supplied another motive: that more compromises would undo the Republican victory. More severe modern critics regard the address as "a miserable failure." While Lincoln did make a political miscalculation of immense significance, believing wrongly that unionist sentiment in the South would ultimately swing the seceding states back into the federal union, his unwillingness to compromise rested on his view of the legalities of the situation. Law courts in his experience were not political bodies like electorates and legislatures. Courts had the authority to settle disputes by reference to established law. Lincoln believed that he had the law on his side. The court—here his countrymen—would surely come around to the proper decision.[43]

Knowing as we do that four years of carnage would follow them, the legalese of the South Carolina Declaration of Causes of Secession and Lincoln's First Inaugural Address may seem something belonging to a dream of peace before the nation awoke to war. Historians have labeled the former an attempt to maintain calm and reason and the latter an expression of faith and a rhetorical masterpiece of nonpartisanship and moderation. Surely it shows Wardlaw's and Lincoln's faith in the power of law to settle the most contentious issues. Throughout, the appeal of the two documents was to law-abiding men. That both the South Carolina Declaration and the First Inaugural Address failed to avert the Civil War was a proof that in the heat of secession politics, adherence to established law bowed to passion and fear.[44]

# 2

# A Tale of Two Cabinets and Two Congresses

IN THE SECESSION WINTER, Abraham Lincoln and Jefferson Davis assembled their cabinets. One sat in Washington, DC, the other first in Montgomery, Alabama, and then Richmond, Virginia. The first was guided by a lawyer, the second by a planter/soldier. Both were filled with ambitious and sometimes self-important counselors, but only one made effective use of their talents. Lincoln understood and valued the sometimes combative and always lawyerly talents of his team. Davis, though no lawyer, was a lawmaker (in the United States Senate) long enough to internalize the language of the law. For example, he knew what every important slave owner in the South knew, and in his first message to the Confederate Congress reported that "the right of property in slaves was protected by law" and was "recognized by the Constitution" and that the federal government had become "the theater of agitation and aggression against the clearly expressed constitutional rights of the Southern States." But he did not fully understand the thinking of the very able lawyers in his cabinet and did not make full use of it.[1]

The Thirty-Sixth Congress of the United States that witnessed the alleged creation of the Confederate States of America was a "lame duck," as the new Congress was not due to begin its work until December 1861. With the Civil War already under way, Lincoln called a special session of the Thirty-Seventh Congress's Senate to meet in Washington, DC, on March 4, and the first regular session of both houses commenced on July 4, 1861. The Congress was in session during most of the

48

Civil War years. The Confederate States Congress met first on February 18, 1862, and adjourned two months later. It met again that August and adjourned in the middle of October. Two more sessions were held, for four months in 1863 and three months over the winter of 1863–1864. Lawyers predominated in both Congresses, but the legislative output of the US Congress and its impact on the war and the peace far exceeded the role and importance of the Confederate States congress—in part because of states' rights provisions in the Confederate constitution, in part because Davis did not make much use of the Congress, and in part because the majority party in both houses of the Confederate States congress was not the party of the Confederate president.

In the first days of the great rebellion or the war against Northern tyranny (depending on one's perspective), one would have found lawyer/politicians everywhere in the councils of federal and Confederate government. Both sides turned to the lawyers to offer answers, reassure, and restore order. But they, like their fellow citizens, felt the terrifying prospect of a world at war. Looking back. Democratic lawyer/politician and Lincoln's secretary of the navy, Gideon Welles, remembered, "Few comparatively know or can appreciate the actual condition of things and state of feeling of the members of the [incoming Lincoln] administration in those days. Nearly sixty years of peace had unfitted us for any war, but the most terrible of all wars—a civil one was upon us, and it had to be met . . . promptly and decisively."[2]

When Lincoln won the presidency over Douglas, John Bell, and John C. Breckinridge, he turned to lawyers to populate his cabinet: Secretary of State Seward of New York, Secretary of the Treasury Salmon Chase of Ohio, Attorney General Edward Bates of Missouri, and Secretary of the Navy Welles of Connecticut. Postmaster General Montgomery Blair was a lawyer from a family of lawyers. Caleb Smith briefly served, but after a year of illness in Washington, returned to his law practice and later a federal judgeship in Indiana. Simon Cameron, the first secretary of war, was not a lawyer, but a year later he was replaced by Stanton. James Speed, a Kentucky lawyer and close friend of Lincoln, replaced Bates in 1864. Speed was from his early political career an opponent of slavery, calling it "legalized robbery," not an easy position to hold in a slave state like Kentucky. A fierce unionist, he wanted to confiscate the property of Confederate sympathizers, a measure of his passion early in the war rather than his adherence to more traditional ideas of property rights. Overall, one could not find a more able or imposing team of lawyers than this, though like many law partnerships, there was rivalry and contention among themselves and with senior partner Lincoln.[3]

What did it matter that Lincoln had virtual law partners in the cabinet? Shortly after Lincoln's cabinet was complete, he was asked by a friendly journalist why he had selected "enemies and opponents." Lincoln replied, "We needed the strongest men of the party in the Cabinet. We needed to hold our own people together. I looked the party over and concluded that these were the very strongest men." He did not add, or at least was not reported to add, that he had done the same with the opposition party's strongest men. Whatever did he mean by strongest, then? Seward was a leading politician, but to call Chase and Bates "strong" just because they had supporters at the Chicago Republican convention makes little sense. Certainly, they were not strong politically in the secession winter of 1860–1861. Other members of the cabinet, including Welles, Blair, Stanton, and Speed, were not Lincoln's political rivals in the sense that Bates and Chase were, nor were they particularly strong in any partisan sense, though they may have been rivals for his ear with the other members of the cabinet. Instead, like the "prairie lawyer from Springfield," they were all lawyers. This was their strength, and that strength they lent to his cabinet. Lincoln knew that the crisis was one of law, that secession was illegal in a profound way. As he told secessionists in his first inaugural address, "No State upon its own mere motion can lawfully get out of the Union; that resolves and ordinances to that effect are legally void, and that acts of violence within any State or States against the authority of the United States are insurrectionary or revolutionary, according to circumstances." The ship of state must be steered by lawyers because the crucial issues were not political, or even military (at this time at least), but legal. The only exception to his choice of lawyers for cabinet posts was Cameron, an early Lincoln supporter, and Lincoln soon showed Cameron, an avid corruptionist (he took bribes and did favors), the exit. As Lincoln was reported to say to his law partner William Herndon, "Law is nothing else but the best reason of wise men applied for ages to the transactions and business of mankind." The Civil War would test that faith.[4]

The sheer weight of legal talent would have made the cabinet meetings something extraordinary. Chase was called the "attorney general" of the antislavery movement, so often had he stepped forward to represent antislavery clients. Though self-taught with a "slender" knowledge of black letter law, and sometimes criticized as more a politician than a practitioner in the courtroom, Chase was more than competent in those subjects that interested him. Ambitious for advancement without sacrificing his radical views of slavery, he was a force to be reckoned with on that subject in any gathering. When not serving as the governor of New York State, Seward had a lucrative patent law practice, to which he added celebrated criminal defense cases. If sometimes deceitful and overly ambitious, he was a true law reformer, seeing in progressive legislation in New York a model for law reform nationally. He pressed for the end of imprisonment for debt, reducing the expense and complexity of litigation in state courts. Although "he may not have enjoyed his legal work, he was good at it." Lincoln often deferred to him, in part because of his status in the Republican Party, but also because of his legal acumen. Stanton may have been the most "brilliant"—certainly the most "successful"—of all of them at the bar. Bates was no slouch, however. A leader of the conservative, pro-Union Democrats in Missouri and a sometime candidate for the presidency, his legal practice paid for a large family and his political forays. He came to appreciate the idea of emancipation slowly, but when he did, he supported Lincoln's emancipation program. Of Lincoln, he wrote to a close friend, "Personally unexceptionable, his integrity unimpeached, his talents known and acknowledged, and his industry and moral courage fully proven."[5]

Once one sees that Lincoln had chosen a cabinet of top legal talent, the question of how he managed the cabinet becomes easier. The rivalries among them were the stuff of legend. Welles did not trust Stanton, and the feeling was mutual. No one fully trusted Chase, and he and Seward were rivals for domination of the meetings. Welles and Blair respected one another but feared cabals among the other members. Everyone else thought Seward had too much influence with Lincoln. Lincoln knew all this, and sought ways to promote the more admirable lawyerly traits in the cabinet. For example, Lincoln was wont to pose to his cabinet all the objections to a course of action, soliciting from them opinions on that course of action. Lawyers would recognize these as hypotheticals—not as evidence that Lincoln was unsure or wavering, but as ways of examining alternatives. What if we . . . but . . . in the case that . . . suppose—these are all introductions to the hypothetical. This method of reasoning was hardly new in law at the time, and Lincoln simply applied it to his interactions with the cabinet. It was not that he wanted them to air their differing political views or that among themselves they were haggling over politics, but he wanted them to compete in their answers, as though they were partners in his law firm.[6]

The first test of President Lincoln's mettle as a manager of a law firm came soon after the cabinet assembled. The commander of the federal forces, General Winfield Scott, passed to Lincoln Major Robert Anderson's report on the status of Fort Sumter, on March 11, 1861. Anderson did not think he could hold the fort without reinforcements. Should the fort be evacuated? Resupplied? Lincoln met every day with his cabinet to discuss the matter, pacing the room as the members spoke. Then they drafted their views in letters to him. The first of these exchanges hints at the way in which the law firm of A. Lincoln and partners operated.[7]

Seward replied to Lincoln's request on March 15, 1861. Lincoln had asked for a response in writing, though Seward was sitting in the old state department building a stone's throw away from the White House. It was not distance then, but something else that prompted Seward to reply in the manner he chose. In fact, asked about a legal matter (in effect, the legality of secession), he reverted to his lawyerly ways. His letter had the structure of a lawyer's response to a client's request. He urged Lincoln not to provoke the South, but to go slowly. "If it were possible to peacefully provision Fort Sumter, of course I should answer, that it would be both unwise and inhuman not to attempt it. But the facts of the case are known to be, that the attempt must be made with the employment of military and marine force, which would provoke combat, and probably initiate a civil war . . . . I would not provoke war in any way *now*."[8] Good counsel.

Shortly after the March 15 memo, Seward wrote a fuller and somewhat sterner memo to Lincoln. Nothing had been done to settle the Sumter question in the two weeks since the first letter. It seemed to Seward that Lincoln's caution had become a paralysis similar to Buchanan's. Dated April 1, 1861, it has been called the "April Fool's letter" and denounced as an attempt by Seward to strong-arm the president. Seward had been a very energetic governor of New York, and he thought that Lincoln, who had no executive experience, could benefit from a dose of his. Labeled "Some thoughts for the President's consideration," it was again a form of memo from a lawyer, this time to a recalcitrant party in a case that was not going well. "We are at the end of a month's administration and yet without a policy either domestic or foreign." The delay in formulating a plan was "not culpable" as "the need to meet applications for patronage have prevented attention to other and more grave matters . . . . But further delay to adopt and prosecute our policies for both domestic and foreign affairs would not only bring scandal on the Administration, but danger upon the country."

Seward served at Lincoln's pleasure, but the secretary of state post was the foremost in the cabinet, Lincoln had already shown great deference to Seward's opinions and experience, and this led Seward to be frank. "I am aware that my views are singular and perhaps not sufficiently explained. My system is built on this *idea* as a ruling one, namely that we must *Change the question before the Public from one upon Slavery, or about slavery* for a question upon *Union or Disunion* [italics in the original]." Slavery entailed legal questions, but its legality was well established, and Lincoln had already promised that he would not touch it where state law established it. The Republican Party was opposed to the expansion of slavery, but that was a party stance, not a legal one. Secession was an act whose legality was at issue; and this was Seward's point. "In other words," he told Lincoln, shift the subject from "what would be regarded as a Party question" to one of the crime of insurrection. In effect, Seward pressed Lincoln to take a legal rather than a political view of the crisis. Sumter had become a focus of partisan debate because of the "last [Democratic] administration." Instead, drop the Sumter issue and return to the question of the defense of federal property. "I would simultaneously defend and reinforce all the Forts in

the Gulf, and have the Navy recalled from foreign stations to be prepared for a blockade. Put the Island of Key West under Martial Law.
This will raise distinctly the question of *Union* or *Disunion*. I would
maintain every fort and possession in the South." Seward concluded
with broad hints that he, as legal counsel, should take the lead in this
shift of policy. "But whatever policy we adopt, there must be an energetic prosecution of it. For this purpose, it must be somebody's business
to pursue and direct it incessantly. Either the President must do it himself and be all the while active in it, or Devolve it on some member of
his Cabinet. Once adopted, debates on it must end, and all agree and
abide. It is not in my especial province. But I neither seek to evade nor
assume responsibility."[9]

The imposition of martial law was within the legal capacity of a president in time of domestic rebellion, so long as the regular courts of law
were not or could not operate. It applied as well to "the very ground"
over which an enemy had control or contested with the legal government. It could also be imposed by military commanders on the scene,
by the commissioners of military courts, or when a government's courts
were held in jeopardy. Traditionally, however, martial law was a last
resort in the United States. In addition, state courts were very wary of
federal martial law. Seward, a former governor, knew that martial law
could only be "temporary and local," and its application to localities
nominally at peace in the Union was an extreme extension of the presidential wartime power.[10]

Lincoln's memorandum response, written the same day (though the
original cannot be found in the Seward papers and Lincoln may have
delivered its contents orally, for that would be his custom in later days),
was similar to a reply one might give to a junior member of one's law
firm. It was not a rebuke to an inferior, for by experience and reputation Seward was Lincoln's equal, but a memo to oneself much as a
lawyer writes for oral argument. It repeated and then answered each
of Seward's points. "My dear Sir: Since parting with you I have been
considering your paper dated this day, and entitled 'Some thoughts for
the President's consideration.' The first proposition in it is, "1st. We are
at the end of a month's administration, and yet without a policy, either
domestic or foreign." Rather than consider Seward's point as an insult,
Lincoln answered as if it were a "count" in common-law pleading.

"At the *beginning* of that month, in the inaugural, I said 'The power confided to me will be used to hold, occupy and possess the property and places belonging to the government, and to collect the duties, and imposts.'" Lincoln could have defended himself by simply thanking Seward for his concern, or by replying briefly that a policy of patience would pay dividends, or by not replying at all. Instead, Lincoln filed a something like a demurrer, a statement at common law that the facts may be true but they do not amount to sufficient legal grounds: "This had your distinct approval at the time; and, taken in connection with the order I immediately gave General Scott, directing him to employ every means in his power to strengthen and hold the forts, comprises the exact domestic policy you now urge, with the single exception, that it does not propose to abandon Fort Sumpter [*sic*]." It was the insufficiency of Seward's argument that Lincoln asserted. Lincoln obviously found the formulary if not a comforting, at least a type, of response with which he was thoroughly familiar. Lincoln also objected to the relief or remedy that Seward proposed. "Upon your closing propositions, that 'whatever policy we adopt, there must be an energetic prosecution of it . . .' I remark that if this must be done, I must do it." What could have been an estrangement or worse, Lincoln's response turned into a legal exchange, polite but firm, and wholly in keeping with both men's professional experience. It did not revolve around politics but around a common understanding of what was permissible when lawyers disagreed. "When a general line of policy is adopted, I apprehend there is no danger of its being changed without good reason, or continuing to be a subject of unnecessary debate; still, upon points arising in its progress, I wish, and suppose I am entitled to have the advice of all the cabinet."[11]

Seward's caution, skill as a negotiator, and sense of legal context served him, and Lincoln, better in coming days. For example, during the crisis over the US Navy's stopping of the British ship *Trent* and the temporary arrest and internment of Confederate agents James Mason and John Slidell, a violation of the rights of a neutral (Britain), Seward's abilities as a government lawyer fully showed themselves. It was vital that Britain not side with the Confederacy (equally vital for Confederate hopes that it would). The British were furious at the violation (somewhat ironic in light of similar British violations of American neutrality during the Napoleonic Wars), and the ship and diplomats were soon allowed to go on their way. Seward's note to the British, read to the cabinet on December 25 and delivered to their ambassador in Washington, DC, on December 27, 1861, promised that the Confederate diplomats would be released and allowed to travel abroad. The message itself was long and detailed, a masterful miniature legal brief, including the history of British impressment of Americans and a treatise on international law regarding diplomats conveyed politely but without a hint of fawning. Lincoln conceded that the navy had acted without instructions. Then he added that the principles under which the ship should not have been stopped were "American principles" avowed by a long line of presidents and precedents when the United States had been a neutral power. Throughout all of this he reassured the British of the federal government's strong feelings of attachment to the English people. The result, according to ambassador to Britain Charles Francis Adams, another lawyer (he studied with Daniel Webster and practiced in Boston), was a triumph.[12]

The so-called *Trent* Affair was a diplomatic crisis rather than a legal one per se, though the law of war and the law of the seas (neutral rights under law of nations) entered into the British protest and the American response. Seward's response was a legalistic one, however, and historians have correctly noticed how legalistic American diplomacy has been. In part, surely, this is because the nation's great secretaries of state—Jefferson, John Quincy Adams, Daniel Webster, and Seward, to name but a few—were all very able lawyers.[13]

It is the form rather than the substance of these missives and those that followed that is important in the context of this book. When called upon to give opinions, Seward and Lincoln produced memoranda that a lawyer would provide to a client. Here form had great influence on substance; that is; instead of the informality of conversation among coworkers written down for convenience and clarity, Lincoln got legal advice and responded in similar form. The stiff formality of the correspondence was characteristic of this virtual law firm, never really a cabinet of cronies that other presidents before or after Lincoln selected. The closest comparison would be George Washington's first cabinet, itself filled with lawyers (Jefferson, Hamilton, and John Randolph were all lawyers) who were rivals, and incidentally functioned brilliantly. In both cases, the lawyers did not leave behind their favored way of communicating when they joined his administration.[14]

Confederate president Jefferson Davis's cabinet also featured a cadre of lawyers. The Confederate constitution, written by a lawyer, T. R. R. Cobb, provided that members of the cabinet also sit with the Confederate Congress, giving the lawyers in the cabinet a chance to advise its legislative branch that the lawyers in Lincoln's cabinet did not have, at least formally (although nothing stopped Seward in particular from acting as an unofficial and sometimes unwanted go-between for Lincoln and Republican members of Congress). Davis's lawyers included the versatile Judah P. Benjamin of Louisiana (who at different times was secretary of both state and treasury), Robert Toombs and Alexander Stephens of Georgia, Robert M. T. Hunter of Virginia, John C. Breckinridge of Kentucky (Buchanan's vice president), and Christopher Memminger of South Carolina.

Benjamin's accomplishments as a former US senator were largely financial, and as secretary of the treasury, he oversaw the Confederacy's seizure of Northern-owned properties and debts (so-called sequestration). Before the war he was described as New Orleans' most respected commercial lawyer, and during the war he was regarded by Lincoln and Davis as a brilliant lawyer; his abilities in that realm were helpful to the Confederate cause. A less successful stay as secretary of state (he could not gain recognition of the Confederacy in Europe) and an even more disastrous stint as secretary of war (he resigned in disgrace shortly after accepting the post), however, meant that in nonfiscal areas he was not so useful. After the war, Benjamin departed the United States and began a successful legal practice in his parents' hometown of London, England.[15]

Davis could have availed himself of the legal services of Robert Toombs, a very successful prewar lawyer who made even more money in law practice after the war. Though not at first very successful at the bar, Toombs soon gained a reputation as a superb courtroom orator. It was said that Stephens would begin his summations to the jury calmly, and only gradually build to an emotional climax, but his friend Toombs started and finished in high dudgeon. "A quick study" much respected for finding the key points in an argument, "always prepared" on the details of cases, he also had a "quick wit" that friends and adversaries both appreciated. Toombs was also a planter, US congressman (and sometime speaker of the House) and senator; genial, popular, he was a Whig in politics until the Whig Party folded its tent in Georgia, after which he joined the Democratic Party and then drifted into the secessionist faction in Georgia. Toombs was a rival of Davis for the presidency, and the two men did not get along during Toombs's short stay as secretary of state. It is not likely that Davis consulted Toombs on legal matters or that Toombs felt easy offering legal advice to Davis. Toombs soon departed to serve in the Confederate army, as did his rival, T. R. R. Cobb.[16]

Compare, then, how Seward and Lincoln resolved the Trent Affair and how Toombs bungled it. Slidell and Mason were both former US senators, Mason famous for reading John C. Calhoun's last speech to the Senate in February 1850. Slidell was highly regarded by some in the English government and praised for his depth and subtlety. When they were interned in Boston, while diplomatic negotiations for their release proceeded, Toombs had the opportunity to shift official views and public opinion in Britain to the Confederate side. Unlike Seward, his opposite number in the Lincoln cabinet, Toombs did not prepare special instructions for Mason and Slidell to seek recognition of the Confederacy, relying instead on the assumption that British need for raw cotton would inevitably lead to recognition. Nor did he participate actively in diplomatic correspondence with the British government. In any case, he sought and obtained his commission as a Confederate officer and left for war before Slidell and Mason sailed on the *Trent*. Toombs's replacement was Robert M. T. Hunter of Virginia, also a lawyer, and also in office for only a short time before he too left the State Department—in his case, for a seat in the Confederate Senate. Like Toombs, he thought that Davis disregarded criticism, and this soured their relationship. Moreover, Hunter did not see himself as a lawyer engaged in adversarial proceedings with the likes of Seward. He was outmaneuvered diplomatically by Seward but did not regard this disappointment as a setback, for his political ambitions lay in a different arena than diplomacy. As a result, he did not perform with the due diligence expected of a lawyer for the Confederacy and let the opportunity to gain recognition for the Confederacy slip away.[17]

T. R. R. Cobb, arguably the brightest, most tenacious, and most highly regarded lawyer in the first days of the Confederacy, did not serve in Davis's cabinet at all. Had he, its functioning might have been more effective. But he was not a politician and did not relish partisanship, except as it touched his brother, Senator Howell Cobb. Thomas Cobb had risen in Georgia legal circles not only through his brother's importance but also by marrying the daughter of Georgia's first chief justice, Joseph Henry Lumpkin. By his middle thirties, Cobb could boast of a very successful legal practice in Athens, Georgia, that included the buying and selling of slaves. With the help of his father-in-law, Cobb helped found the Lumpkin Law School at the University of Georgia. He did not have his father-in-law's zeal for reformism, but he did have his love of legal scholarship and education. This he poured into his immensely learned and thoroughly racialist *An Inquiry into the Law of Negro Slavery in the United States of America* (1858). Intended to be a scientific exploration of the reasons for slavery as well as its legal aspects, it was read at the time as a defense of slavery. It still bears that character. Cobb found that slavery was a natural, benign, and well-ordered system necessary for the two races to live in close proximity. He argued as well against the personal freedom laws of the North, for the nature of the slave, as property, did not change according to the incidents of the master and slave's travels in the free states. One can also read the treatise as a defense of private property as the highest good the law can preserve.[18]

Cobb's service to the Confederate cause had a more immediate aspect. He was a strong proponent of secession, and his public addresses in the early stages of Georgia's secession debate showed his legal talents and hint at the reason he did not offer them to Davis. For example, on November 13, 1860, at the Georgia state legislature sitting in Milledgeville, the political novice ("having never, in seventeen years, made a political speech") explained why secession was legal. He told the legislators that he belonged to no party and spoke not from the excess of enthusiasm that motivated other proponents of secession. He was a reasonable man offering reasons for secession in a reasonable fashion. No lawyer could have summarized the legal approach to an issue with any greater clarity. "Then, let all party animus be put aside" (anticipating rightly the personal animosities that would plague Davis's cabinet) and "come and take counsel together, how we shall avenge [Georgia's] wrongs, promote her prosperity, and preserve her honor."

Were there legal grounds for secession after Lincoln's election? Cobb thought so. Lincoln had only won the electoral votes of a section (the North) whose state legislators' personal liberty laws nullified the Fugitive Slave Laws of 1793 and 1850. "As a lawyer, I am prepared to say that parties to such a contract [as brought Lincoln the White House] who have thus violated its provisions when onerous to them, are not entitled to its privileges." Cobb's audience knew that he was a lawyer; why then restate the obvious unless to underline that this was a legal argument? But legal arguments were not the reason he urged on the Georgia legislature. As in his decision not to serve in a political capacity but to don the uniform and die for his country, Cobb insisted that honor, not some legalistic quibble, was the reason to depart the Union. "Let us determine to act, act like men, men who are determined to do or die." One is struck by the posture of Cobb's speech, promising a reasoned discourse, then offering a rousing call to virtual, if not actual, battle. Motivated by this kind of thinking, Cobb would naturally have disdained service in some musty Confederate government office. And the concept of Southern honor, so perfectly represented in Cobb, would similarly have preferred the real battlefield to the courtroom version. While he did linger at Montgomery long enough to help write the new Confederate constitution—he told fellow Georgians that it was merely their "old constitution" with states' rights assured—he was soon back in Athens recruiting for a regiment of volunteers to "Cobb's Legion" that he would lead.[19]

A more likely source of such advice was Cobb's Georgia nemesis and Toombs's great friend and ally Alexander Stephens, for Stephens never hesitated to offer his advice on matters of law and politics, but most vexing for the fate of the Confederacy was the detachment of this foremost lawyer from its day-to-day operations. Stephens, with great regret and foreboding, had followed his native Georgia into the new government. He signed the secession ordinance and traveled to the new capital of Montgomery, Alabama, to take part in the constitutional convention. Although he did not seek office, his pride led him to accept the vice presidency under Jefferson Davis, whom Stephens cordially came to hate. He did not write the Confederate constitution—that was largely the work of another lawyer, T. R. R. Cobb. Cobb did not have a post in the new government, however, as Stephens did. In fact, when Cobb could not get his brother Howell named president, his primary role in the Montgomery government was adding to the dysfunctionality of Davis's cabinet by trying to undermine Stephens and Toombs.[20]

Georgia had to ratify the new constitution, and Stephens accepted an invitation to speak about it at the Georgia ratification convention in Savannah. On March 21, he delivered the address. It was the moment when peaceful separation still seemed possible. It was a lull, as Charles Sumner described it, more like a desperate indrawn breath that could not be held for long. Stephens was ready to exhale. "I was remarking that we are passing through one of the greatest revolutions in the annals of the world. Seven States have within the last three months thrown off an old government and formed a new. This revolution has been signally marked, up to this time, by the fact of its having been accomplished without the loss of a single drop of blood." But it was a revolution in law, not in arms, that Stephens celebrated. And to his mind it must remain so to be successful. He told the gathering that a resort to arms would lead to the failure of the experiment in nation-building. "In reference to it [i.e., the new Confederate constitution], I make this first general remark: it amply secures all our ancient rights, franchises, and liberties. All the great principles of Magna Charta are retained in it. No citizen is deprived of life, liberty, or property, but by the judgment of his peers under the laws of the land. The great principle of religious liberty, which was the honor and pride of the old constitution, is still maintained and secured. All the essentials of the old constitution, which have endeared it to the hearts of the American people, have been preserved and perpetuated." The new constitution was rid of the old problems of tariffs, internal improvements, reelection of the president, and restrictions on slavery. Unlike the federal Constitution, that equivocated with slavery, "Our new government is founded upon exactly the opposite idea; its foundations are laid, its corner-stone rests, upon the great truth that the negro is not equal to the white man; that slavery subordination to the superior race is his natural and normal condition. This, our new government, is the first, in the history of the world, based upon this great physical, philosophical, and moral truth . . . . With us, all of the white race, however high or low, rich or poor, are equal in the eye of the law. Not so with the negro. Subordination is his place. He, by nature, or by the curse against Canaan, is fitted for that condition which he occupies in our system."[21]

But Stephens would not have been Stephens if he had not found something to worry about the new government. "Our destiny, under Providence, is in our own hands. With wisdom, prudence, and statesmanship on the part of our public men, and intelligence, virtue and patriotism on the part of the people, success, to the full measures of our most sanguine hopes, may be looked for." Thus far, familiar Southern patriotic boilerplate; now, the warning: "But if unwise counsels prevail[,] if we become divided[,] if schisms arise[,] if dissentions spring up[,] if factions are engendered[,] if party spirit, nourished by unholy personal ambition shall rear its hydra head, I have no good to prophesy for you. Without intelligence, virtue, integrity, and patriotism on the part of the people, no republic or representative government can be durable or stable." Stephens knew all about Thomas Cobb's machinations and the fever of party alignments.

The most immediate legal problem was whether the peace would continue. The framing of the Confederate constitution, seen from across the Mason-Dixon line, was an example of lawlessness, not of law. Stephens thought the prospects for peace looked better than they had when Lincoln delivered the inaugural address, for nothing had yet been done to reinforce Fort Sumter or to coerce Southern sympathizers in the border states. Lincoln was waiting, a kind of patience that Stephens conflated with unwillingness to begin hostilities, or so he told his audience.

In all, it was fine rhetoric, but not much in the way of lawyering. Good lawyering was based on dispute resolution, not hope. Good lawyering dealt with realities and contingencies. Stephens recognized as much. "But at first we must necessarily meet with the inconveniences and difficulties and embarrassments incident to all changes of government." The extent of these difficulties went far beyond "our postal affairs and changes in the channel of trade." Good lawyering looks to possible outcomes and prepares for all of them. Stephens seemed to be prepared in his November 1860 Union speech in the Georgia assembly. Now, events had moved so swiftly that he did not seem ready to counsel caution. A call to patriotism instead fueled those very impulses that he had condemned five months earlier. Good lawyering would have urged his new countrymen not to fire the first shot. No such caution appeared in his speech then or after, even though Stephens wanted a peaceful separation. When the war began, he kept this opinion to himself. Again, if he were a good counselor he would—he should—have said something.[22]

To be sure, although Davis had said that he wanted to avoid war and had sent a peace delegation to Washington, he also prepared for war. He called for volunteers before Lincoln did and pushed Toombs, his secretary of state, toward war. Davis viewed the mission to resupply Sumter as an affront to the honor of the South, something that no gentleman and former soldier could ignore. Stephens, at his home in Crawfordville, Georgia, had no part in these preparations and sought no part in them, although Davis made every effort to keep Stephens apprised of events, even telegraphing him that Seward wanted to avoid open hostilities. The telegraph lines ran along the railroad lines that connected to Montgomery, and Stephens could have weighed in at any time before the bombardment began. He did nothing.[23]

Compare Seward's and Stephens's roles as lawyers for their respective presidents: Seward was Lincoln's rival, and Lincoln thought long and hard before he offered Seward the first place—secretary of state—in the cabinet. Seward was well aware of the difference between the two men, in particular his own desire for a peaceful settlement based on compromise and Lincoln's refusal to compromise. Seward had perhaps overstepped his place, but Lincoln forgave him for his impatience and impertinence. Stephens was one of Davis's rivals for the Confederate presidency but was not present in Montgomery with the other members of the cabinet when Davis supported the decision to attack Fort Sumter. He had kept his own counsel when a more aggressive lawyering for the Confederacy might have saved many lives and changed the course of American history. Stephens's desire for peace was evident throughout the war, as he tried on numerous occasions to broker a peaceful end to the fighting, but he never truly pressed Davis in that direction. Or it may be that Davis did not understand the role of lawyers and thus did not appreciate good legal advice when he got it. One lawyer who entered the cabinet late in 1862, James Seddon, reported that Davis was the most difficult man with whom he had ever worked.[24]

Indeed, the relative success and failure of Civil War lawyers' advice in the two cabinets stemmed at least in part from Lincoln's and Davis's receptivity to such guidance. Lawyers had to listen to their opponents' arguments, at the very least because an opponent in court one day might be co-counsel the next. Lincoln knew how to listen. He made up his own mind, but that mind was open to a variety of options in legal moments. Lincoln had the capacity to develop his own opinion through interaction with others the way a good lawyer knows how to see the development of a case. Davis was far less tolerant of dissent. Once he had made up his mind, usually early in the process of decision making, he was close-minded. Indeed, he resented advice that did not jibe with his thinking. His wife, Varina, admitted that Davis, when crossed, came near to dueling, even with friends. Davis himself conceded, "When I am aroused in a matter, I lose control of my feeling and become personal." Although some of these differences, and the relative impact they had on the functioning of the two cabinets, depended on individual personality, that personality was shaped by life. Lincoln's kindness and good humor with his sometimes irascible and often feuding cabinet members reflected the experience of a successful law practice. Davis's personality, framed in years of military service and as a planter, then in the Senate debating society, would not have brought him much legal business even had he changed careers in mid-life. Lincoln's experience in the law helped make the law firm of A. Lincoln and partners perform well. Not so with Davis and his cabinet.[25]

At the outset and throughout the war, the US Congress took a major part, sometimes a leading part, in setting policy. Within Congress, the leaders were lawyers and their names are associated with legislative enactments that every teacher of American history knows. The Ohio Senate delegation was in some ways typical. "Bluff" Ben Wade demanded stiff penalties for Southern rebels; denounced Lincoln when he refused to comply; gained a permanent place for black troops in the US Army; almost succeeded in convicting Lincoln's successor, Andrew Johnson, on impeachment charges; and then returned to a private law practice. John Sherman, like Wade an antislavery lawyer and early convert to the Republican Party, not only supported the Thirteenth Amendment, the Fourteenth Amendment, the Fifteenth Amendment, and much of Reconstruction policy, but he also authored the first federal antitrust act. In between terms in Congress he served as secretary of the treasury. The Massachusetts senatorial team of Charles Sumner and Henry Wilson was just as distinguished. Both men were lawyers, both had impeccable educational credentials, and though they never really developed a substantial practice, both were passionate opponents of slavery and what Wilson later called the "slave power." Both would go on to sponsor civil rights bills in Congress. For example, the Civil Rights Act of 1875, Sumner's final effort, would become the basis for the Civil Rights Act of 1964. Wilson was responsible for the first federal educational act for the freedmen, a policy that would eventually become a broad commitment of federal aid to education. William Pitt Fessenden of Maine, a lawyer and one of the chief financial planners in the war-era Congress, was responsible for the borrowing policies of the Lincoln administration.

All of these lawyers, and their peers in the wartime congresses, assumed the paramount importance of lawmaking by elected officials. Sumner, for example, believed that legislation was the most republican form of lawmaking, and that through proper legislation the world could be reformed. On this basis he defended the civil rights acts and the Reconstruction amendments. The idea that legislation could change the world, a notion "exuberant and overflowing," was shared by other Republican lawmakers. For example, one saw it in the orations of Senator Lyman Trumbull of Illinois and Senator Wilson during the debates over the passage of the Thirteenth Amendment. Radical and conservative, Republicans demonstrated their faith in the power of legislation at one time or another in the wartime US Congress. Even when members professed unwillingness to use "ordinary legislation" to alter the status quo, they proceeded to do just that.[26]

Lawyers also played important organizational roles in the first Confederate States Congress, but its legislative efforts paled beside those of its rival to the North. In the senate, Clement Clay of Alabama was a veteran lawyer and state politician, then a US senator, before taking his seat in the senate in Richmond. After the war he returned to the practice of law in Alabama. Robert Ward Johnson of Arkansas had a similar career in law and politics, but after the war he practiced in Washington, DC. Benjamin Hill, of Georgia, another lawyer, not only survived the war but reentered the US Congress after peace was resumed. Thomas Semmes of New Orleans was a prominent lawyer before and after the war. James M. Baker of Jacksonville, Florida, similarly made a living at the bar before and after the hostilities. Augustus Maxwell, of Tallahassee, vaulted from law practice to the state attorney general's office, then to the Confederate Senate, then back to postwar Florida's supreme court. George Davis, of North Carolina, served in the Senate and then as Confederate attorney general. After the war, he returned to private practice in Wilmington, North Carolina. His fellow North Carolina senator, William Dortch, was also a lawyer. Robert Barnwell, of South Carolina, served in both the US Senate and the Confederate Senate. After the war, he gave up his law practice in favor of a career in higher education at what would become the University of South Carolina in Columbia. His colleague, James Orr, like many of the members, was a strong proponent of states' rights and the old constitution ideal. After the war, he served as South Carolina's governor.

The Confederate lawmakers were men of property and standing who believed in a rule of law. Some had opposed secession but remained loyal to their states when they voted to leave the Union. A few stayed in Richmond, but most went home after the shortened sessions of the Congress. With a few exceptions, like their constituents, they came to dislike Davis and resent the impositions of wartime on the people and property of the South. However, riven with personal and party differences, their work product—the legislation they authored and promoted—was slight and had little impact on the war, the Congress hardly making "a good reputation for itself." Although defenders of the Confederacy might celebrate the "outstanding leaders" of the body, who today, save the most knowledgeable of Civil War buffs, knows the authors of their few enactments?[27]

Of course, had the Confederacy survived, its Congress's legislation would have survived as well and made more of an impression on American history. But what would that impression have been? In its final days, the Confederate States Congress passed a bill that would have freed those slaves who took up arms for the Confederacy. That act, along with earlier attempts to increase fighting forces of the Confederacy, was perhaps the most striking step the Congress took. Even this was assaulted by critics as usurping the rights of the states and the people of the states. They would have done far less to ensure the abolition of slavery than the Thirteenth Amendment. The states' rights philosophy that undergirded Confederate constitutional thinking undermined Confederate congressional initiatives and sapped Davis's ability to defend the Confederacy.[28]

The differential impact on the conduct of government by the lawyer/politicians in the Union and the Confederacy was immense. Union lawyers' activity contributed to the Union's victory; Confederate lawyers' comparative inactivity worked toward the Confederacy's defeat. True, some Northern intellectuals had feared that secession and disunion would spread a contagion of disorder. Unitarian minister Henry W. Bellows was one of these, writing to his sister in December 1860 that "the possible insecurity of life and property, if secession and revolution should occur, [would drive] our populace into panic for bread and violence toward capital and order." Despite the political divisions among the Republicans and between the Republicans and the Northern Democrats, despite the personality differences, rivalries, and suspicions, the Lincoln cabinet and the Union Congress was an effective organization because of the ability of the Union's lawyer/politicians in Lincoln's administration to function throughout the crisis. Indeed, the functionality of this virtual law firm was the strongest possible disproof of one esteemed historian's "melancholy reflection that the political machinery of a great people broke down completely in the crisis and gave passion and crime the mastery over sober counsel, equity and justice." Even Stephen Douglas, who opposed all of the Republican policy initiatives, visited Lincoln when Sumter fell and wearing his lawyerly mantle promised "to sustain the president in the exercise of all his constitutional functions to preserve the Union, and maintain the government, and defend the Federal Capital." He publicly avowed, "A firm policy and prompt action was necessary," for "the country was in danger, and must be defended at all hazards, and at any expense of men and money." Indeed, in part because of the lawyers at Lincoln's command, sober counsel, equity, and justice triumphed over passion and crime.[29]

By contrast, according to Laura Edwards's fascinating and original legal history of the Civil War, "Richmond, the Confederacy's capital, developed a political culture of gossip, backbiting, and intrigue, as members of Congress, military commanders, and appointed officials charged each other with either failing or abandoning the Confederacy's true principles." Periodic motions of no-confidence in Davis failed to pass in the Confederate Congress, even though the only party represented was the Democrats, but "discord at the top" was notorious. Better lawyering might not have saved the Confederacy from these debilities (Washington, DC, was also a hotbed of gossip and backbiting), but the goals of good lawyering—to resolve disputes in a matter acceptable or at least accepted by all parties—would have made the Confederate central government far more efficient.[30]

Thus far I have suggested that the reason for the relative contributions of the lawyers in the two cabinets lay in a matrix of individual decisions and relationships. There may also be a more general phenomenon at work in the contrasting cultures of the two regions. While lawyers occupied roughly the same professional niche in North and South, and lawyer politicians like Seward and Howell Cobb came from both sections, the preference of Thomas and Howell Cobb for a military command over service in the Confederate government offers a tantalizing though highly speculative hypothesis. Neither man had military experience, but in their minds the election of Lincoln and the Black Republicans was an affront to the honor of the South that could only be defended on the field of battle. The Cobbs' decision is eerily similar to the decision that two other Southern lawyer/politicians made five years earlier. On May 22, 1856, South Carolina congressmen Preston Brooks and Laurence Keitt entered the Senate chamber where Massachusetts' Charles Sumner sat working at his desk. While Keitt held off onlookers with a pistol, Brooks beat Sumner senseless with a cane. Sumner's offense was a speech skewering another senator, South Carolina's Andrew Butler, with language that infuriated Brooks. After the assault, Northern papers decried Brooks's actions, while Southern papers lauded him and Southerners sent him dozens of canes to replace the one he broke over Sumner's supine body. Sumner, a lawyer himself, had used words (his speeches in the Senate sometimes ran on for days) to make the case against slavery. Brooks and Keitt adopted violence as the appropriate response. If service in Lincoln's cabinet was an analog for public litigation, perhaps one might, with the Cobbs, view the war as a duel. Certainly the rhetoric of secessionists swelled with personal affront at the abolitionists' depictions of slavery and slave societies. The speeches of both Cobbs echoed this outrage. Like Brooks, who declined to challenge Sumner to a duel because in his mind Sumner was no gentleman, the Cobbs may have decided that public insults were best repaid in blood. Brooks died before the war began, but Keitt joined the Cobbs in Confederate gray, and like Thomas Cobb, died in battle.[31]

# 3

## *In Re Merryman* and Its Progeny

AFTER THE FALL OF Fort Sumter, on April 16, 1861, Lincoln called for volunteers to put down the rebellion. Federal troops were already arriving in states that teetered on secession, like Maryland. In Baltimore, successful planter and businessman James Merryman was working hard to convince his fellow Marylanders to join the Confederacy. As an officer in the state militia, he had the means to cause serious problems for Union forces. When a mob attacked federal troops in the city, Lincoln ordered the arrest and detention of Merryman in a military facility and refused to honor a writ of habeas corpus to bring him before a civil court.[1]

To Lincoln and his advisors, the allegiance of the border slave states was vital to the war effort. Had Missouri, Maryland, Kentucky, and Delaware seceded, the Confederacy would have been far stronger. The border slave states contained over 35 percent of the South's whites, roughly one-third of the horses and mules, and 50 percent of the South's urbanization and industrial capacity; the federal capital would have been almost indefensible; and the Union Army would have had far more difficult access to the middle reaches of the Tennessee and Cumberland Rivers that would be so important to the Union's successes in the western theater in 1862. In the first days of the war the success of the Union war effort in the border states thus seemed to rest on a legal confrontation, this time between the US Supreme Court and the presidency—Chief Justice Roger Taney of Maryland and President Lincoln. Lincoln did not go into great detail in his order to General

Winfield Scott, commander of the federal forces, regarding the treatment of secessionist agitators in Maryland. But military necessity counseled that Lincoln give Scott the discretion to arrest and hold anyone raising rebellion. The question was whether promoting rebellion by speech, without accompanying acts in furtherance of that goal, was sufficient grounds for the imposition of martial law.[2]

The imposition of martial law was a back door to the suspension of habeas corpus. But Lincoln did not contemplate the "temporary and limited" replacement of civil law and its courts with courts composed of military officers operating under the laws of war at this time in Maryland. Nor did he seek a wholesale replacement of regular federal courts with military courts. The front door to the suspension of habeas corpus was congressional action, and that was not possible at the moment. Lincoln thus improvised a hybrid solution—the suspension of habeas corpus while the regular courts operated by treating a single individual—Merryman—under martial law. Note that martial law actually limits what military officers and courts can do, prescribing rules for evidence, trial, and punishment. At the outset of the Civil War, President Lincoln and Attorney General Bates could point to scattered precedent for the imposition of martial law, but it had always been a last resort—until April 1861.[3]

On April 25, 1861, Lincoln wrote to Scott, "I therefore conclude that it is only left to the commanding General to watch, and await their action, which, if it shall be to arm their people against the United States, he is to adopt the most prompt, and efficient means to counteract, even, if necessary, to the bombardment of their cities—and in the extremest necessity, the suspension of the writ of habeas corpus." Armed insurrection was an offense defined by congressional act in 1790 (Federal Crimes Act) and 1792 (the Militia Act), and Lincoln had the power to execute these laws (Article II, Section 3 of the Constitution)—but Lincoln hinted that should Scott's officers see or hear anything that might amount to future rebellious actions, they were to use preventive detention. Two days later, as evidence poured in about the seriousness of the secessionist activity, Lincoln again wrote to Scott: "You are engaged in repressing an insurrection against the laws of the United States. If at any point on or in the vicinity of the military line, which is now used between the City of Philadelphia and the City of Washington, via Perryville, Annapolis City, and Annapolis Junction, you find resistance which renders it necessary to suspend the writ of Habeas Corpus for the public safety, you, personally or through the officer in command at the point where the resistance occurs, are authorized to suspend the writ." Lincoln was now prepared to define the offense more precisely. He was the commander in chief, so his orders to Scott were entirely constitutional if the nation was at war, but he was not the prosecutor in chief if Merryman's crime were treason. Instead, it was the US attorney for the district, William Addison, who should have brought a criminal indictment if the charge were treason.[4]

Taney's ruling on the writ was delivered in the Baltimore special session of the Circuit Court for the District of Maryland (Supreme Court justices, Taney in this case, sat with district court judges when the federal circuit courts met) on May 28, 1861, but referred to the events of the previous two days. He had issued the writ on the request of George H. Williams, Merryman's attorney, the previous day, ordering General George Cadwalader to come to court and explain why he held Merryman in custody at Fort McHenry. Cadwalader, who had served as a volunteer officer in the Mexican American War and offered his services to the Union after the fall of Fort Sumter, refused, citing as his reason the president's order. Taney sent the federal marshal, Washington Bonifant, to Fort McHenry to deliver the writ and escort Merryman to court, but a sentry refused the marshal entrance.[5]

Although the legal issue was one of national importance, the entire affair had a local cast of characters. Cadwalader had a substantial legal practice in his Philadelphia home. His brother was a federal judge there. Taney, born and bred in eastern Maryland, had friends and family in attendance in the courtroom. Addison (a Franklin Pierce appointee and a Democrat) and Bonifant (a Lincoln appointee), apparently on opposite sides of the matter, were both well known in Baltimore's legal community. Merryman was a familiar figure in the city as well. Everyone knew everyone else—except for Lincoln. Lincoln was an outsider, literally and figuratively. But now, the confrontation between the absent president and the very much present chief justice was unavoidable.[6]

Taney left a written opinion with the clerk of the court (another government official, this one named by district court judge William Fell Giles, a Franklin Pierce appointee who made himself scarce on the final day of the hearing). It never mentioned Lincoln by name, but reading it one can see how much Taney resented Lincoln's pounding on the *Dred Scott* decision. "As the case comes before me, therefore, I understand that the President not only claims the right to suspend the writ of Habeas Corpus himself, at his discretion, but to delegate that discretionary power to a military officer, and to leave it to him to determine whether he will or will not obey Judicial process that may be served upon him." Lincoln was certainly allowed to give such orders to an officer in wartime at the front, but it was not clear to Taney that the nation was at war and Baltimore was not a front line of battle. Moreover, as his presence demonstrated, the civil courts were open for business in Maryland. Why would martial law apply? "No official notice has been given to the courts of justice, or to the public, by proclamation or otherwise, that the President claimed this power, and had exercised it in the manner stated in the return."[7]

Taney feigned astonishment at the entire proceeding, something of a pose because he knew very well what was happening in his native state. It was inching toward anarchy if not secession. Taney pouted: "I certainly listened to it with some surprise. For I had supposed it to be one of those points of constitutional law upon which there was no difference of opinion, and that it was admitted on all hands that the privilege of the writ could not be suspended, except by act of Congress." Taney also knew that Congress was no longer in session, so it could not suspend the writ. "The only power therefore which the President possesses, where the 'life, liberty, or property' of a private citizen is concerned, is the power and duty prescribed in the 3rd section of the 2nd Article, which requires 'That he Shall take care that the laws be faithfully executed.' He is not authorized to execute them himself or through agents or officers civil or military appointed by himself." Taney's view rested on a strong version of separation of powers in the federal government. According to it, the president was to execute the law as the courts found it, "as they are expounded and adjudged of by the Coordinate Branch of the Government to which that duty is assigned by the Constitution. It is thus made his duty to come in aid of the judicial authority, if it shall be resisted by a force too strong to be overcome without the assistance of the Executive arm." This construing of the Constitution would have made the executive subordinate in power to the judiciary: "He acts in subordination to judicial authority, assisting it to Execute its process & enforce its judgments."[8]

Taney's description of the proper relationship between the chief executive and the federal courts was disingenuous if not outright duplicitous. Taney had served as President Andrew Jackson's attorney general. He knew that Jackson never regarded himself or the office of the president as if he were merely the agent of the federal courts. What was more, Taney was Jackson's attorney general during the Cherokee cases, and in no fashion did he advise the president that he had to give effect to the Supreme Court's rulings in favor of the Cherokee against the state of Georgia (a stance repeated in his opinion for the Court in *US. v. Rogers* [1846]). Taney was no more or less culpable of duplicity than any of the leading politicians of the era; the important fact here is that he was a politician before he took a seat on the Court and he never lost his political view of judicial power. In other words, on the bench he remained a lawyer/politician, just as Lincoln remained a lawyer/politician in the White House.[9]

Taney was a Jacksonian Democrat sharing that party's attachment to states' rights, but an outright statement of that attachment would cross the line from judge to partisan. He had felt the bitter accusations of partisanship from Free Soil Northerners over his opinion in *Dred Scott*. Better, then, to rest his opinion on the separation of powers doctrine. "The documents before me show that the military authority, in this case has gone far beyond the mere suspension of the privilege of the writ of Habeas Corpus. It has, by force of arms, thrust aside the judicial authorities and officers to whom the Constitution has confided the power and duty of interpreting and administering the laws, and substituted a military government in its place, to be administered and executed by military officers." For Taney, government by military fiat was the portent of Merryman's detention. If the courts in the regular course of law could not constrain the military, the Republic was doomed. "For at the time these proceedings were had against John Merryman, the District Judge of Maryland, the Commissioner appointed under the act of Congress; the District Attorney, and the Marshal, all resided in the city of Baltimore, a few miles only from the home of the prisoner. Up to that time there had never been the slightest resistance or obstruction to the process of any court, or judicial officer of the United States in Maryland, except by the military authority."[10]

Had the military authorities suspected Merryman of committing a criminal offense under federal law, "it was [their] duty to give informa tion of the fact, and the evidence to support it, to the District Attorney; and it would then have become the duty of that officer to bring the matter before the District Judge or Commissioner, and if there was suf- ficient legal evidence to justify his arrest, the Judge or Commissioner would have issued his warrant to the Marshal, to arrest him; and upon the hearing of the case, would have held him to bail, or committed him for trial, according to the character of the offense." This was standard criminal procedure: in cases of suspected serious crimes, the accused would have been held, indicted, brought before a federal grand jury, and if it found a true bill on the indictment, tried in the circuit court over which Taney and Judge Giles presided. A jury of Merryman's peers in the vicinage would have heard evidence and rendered a verdict of fact. All this would suppose that a grand jury could have been impan- eled that did not know or at least sympathize with Merryman.

Taney must have been aware that ordinary criminal process would not have prevented Merryman from going free on bail and continuing to aid and abet the secessionist element in the state. Nevertheless, Taney reiterated that "there was no danger of any obstruction, or resistance to the action of the civil authorities, and therefore no reason whatever for the interposition of the military." He could have simply stopped there, but he did not, and one can only suppose that the passage that followed was dictated as much by anger as by a reasoned defense of the inde- pendence of the judiciary. Read aloud it reveals the emotional tone that Taney's critics, principally former justice Benjamin Curtis, found so objectionable in the chief justice's opinions. "And yet under these cir- cumstances a military officer, stationed in Pennsylvania, without giving any information to the District Attorney, and without any application to the judicial authorities, assumes to himself the judicial power, in the District of Maryland." High dudgeon.[11]

In an unfair and somewhat untruthful enlargement of the facts of the matter, Taney accused Cadwalader of undertaking "to decide what constitutes the crime of Treason, or rebellion, what evidence (if, indeed, he required any) is sufficient to support the accusation, and justify the commitment, and commits the party." Cadwalader was only following orders. The real miscreant, if there was one, was General Scott, but even he was under orders. It was Lincoln who was the problem, but could Taney accuse the president of breaking the law without fomenting a full-blown constitutional crisis within the already existing crisis of secession? Taney never named the president, but he did note, in an acerbic aside, that Lincoln was "elected for the brief term . . . of four years," hinting that conduct like this would surely limit Lincoln's stay in office to one term.[12]

Taney had been ill for years, and the crowd around his court saw a man bent with pain and age enter and depart. But his powers of intellect were not crippled and his capacity for indignation was, if anything, enhanced by his long years of service on the bench (at the time exceeded only by the tenure of John Marshall). Filled with references to Blackstone, Marshall, and Hamilton, the opinion can almost be read as a valedictory of his long service. Who better to explain to that country lawyer the meaning of the Constitution? "The Constitution provides, as I have before said, that 'no person shall be deprived of life, liberty, or property, without due process of law.'" These were the very words, from the Fifth Amendment, he had used in his *Dred Scott* dictum to declare that the right of the slave owner to his property could not be disturbed by an act of Congress. He then cited the Fourth Amendment, that "the right of the people to be secure in their persons, houses, papers, and effects against unreasonable searches and seizures, shall not be violated, and no warrant shall issue, but upon probable cause, supported by oath or affirmation, and particularly describing the place to be searched, and the persons or things to be seized.'" How this was relevant to the writ Merryman sought was not clear, but Taney was on point when he added, "It provides that the party accused shall be entitled to a speedy trial in a court of justice. And these great and fundamental laws, which Congress itself could not suspend, have been disregarded and suspended, like the writ of habeas corpus, by a military order, supported by force of arms."[13]

Taney closed not with an apology, but with a last slap at the president (albeit again without naming Lincoln). "I have exercised all the power which the Constitution and laws confer upon me, but that power has been resisted by a force too strong for me to overcome. It is possible, that the officer, who has incurred this grave responsibility, may have misunderstood his instructions, and exceeded the authority intended to be given him," in direct contradiction to the earlier accusation that Cadwalader had decided for himself what constituted treason. Taney had probably written the better part of his opinion even before his marshal was turned away at the gates of Fort McHenry, but he withheld the written version for the time being. "I shall, therefore, order all the proceedings in this case, with my opinion, to be filed, and recorded in the Circuit Court of the United States for the District of Maryland, and direct the clerk to transmit a copy, under seal, to the President of the United States. It will then remain for that high officer, in fulfilment of his constitutional obligation to 'take care that the laws be faithfully executed,' to determine what measures he will take to cause the civil process of the United States to be respected, and enforced."[14]

Just as he had with Seward's suggestions, Lincoln had no intention of allowing Taney to have the last word in this matter, as the suspension of the writ of habeas corpus was not likely to be confined to Maryland in the coming days. Although Taney did not actually order Lincoln to do anything (had he issued such an order, it would have been directed to Merryman's captors in any case), on July 4, 1861, in a message to the special session of Congress, Lincoln explained why he had to suspend the writ before Congress met, and why it might be necessary to suspend it in other areas of the country prone to secessionism. It is clear from the text itself that Lincoln was replying to Taney's opinion—note, for example, the not-so-subtle references to Taney's own words: "Soon after the first call for militia, it was considered a duty to authorize the Commanding General, in proper cases, according to his discretion, to suspend the privilege of the writ of habeas corpus; or, in other words, to arrest, and detain, without resort to the ordinary processes and forms of law, such individuals as he might deem dangerous to the public safety. This authority has purposely been exercised but very sparingly."[15]

On top of all this, Lincoln knew that days counted. The Constitution clearly stated that Congress could suspend the writ of habeas corpus in time of domestic insurrection, but Congress was not in session.

Lincoln relied on his "residual powers" as president to order the detention of Merryman. These powers ordinarily applied to foreign affairs,
wherein the president's discretion to act was based on the exigencies
of a particular situation. Read strictly, these powers were confined and
constrained by the powers given the other branches of the federal government. For example, the president cannot begin a war. He or she
needs Congress to declare it. But Lincoln could find precedent for his
precipitous action in the case of a domestic insurrection. For example,
President Washington did not seek congressional approval to put down
the Whiskey Rebellion in 1794–1795 and President John Adams did not
ask Congress for permission to suppress Fries Rebellion in 1799.[16]

Residual powers are not mentioned in the Constitution. Like Taney,
Lincoln was playing fast and loose with constitutional texts. In calling
out the militia he had exercised a power given to Congress in Article I,
Section 8, to "provide for calling forth the Militia to execute the Laws of
the Union, suppress Insurrections and repel Invasions." The same article
of the Constitution allowed that in times of civil insurrection, the writ of
habeas corpus might be suspended, but it employed negative rather than
positive language: "The Privilege of the Writ of Habeas Corpus shall not
be suspended, unless when in Cases of Rebellion or Invasion the public
Safety may require it." Taney read the text to assign the power to Congress.
Lincoln disagreed. To his thinking, the provision of the Constitution for
the suspension of the writ was triggered "when in cases of rebellion, or
invasion, the public safety does require it." His reading of the text was
purposive—looking to the reason suspension of the writ was included
in the Constitution rather than to the plain text that gave Congress the
authority to suspend it. Because the constitutional text was negative, it
could be read as a limitation on Congress rather than on the executive
branch. "Now it is insisted that Congress, and not the Executive, is vested
with this power. But the Constitution itself, is silent as to which, or who,
is to exercise the power; and as the provision was plainly made for a
dangerous emergency, it cannot be believed the framers of the instrument intended, that in every case, the danger should run its course, until
Congress could be called together; the very assembling of which might be
prevented, as was intended in this case, by the rebellion."[17]

Lincoln's purposive reading of the suspension clause, like his reading
of "more perfect union" in the first inaugural address, was something of

a stretch, but laying it alongside his view of his own duties in Article II, it made sense to him. It also answered Taney's charge that Lincoln was not conforming to the limited role assigned him in the Constitution. "The attention of the country has been called to the proposition that one who is sworn to 'take care that the laws be faithfully executed,' should not himself violate them." What choice did he have? "Of course some consideration was given to the questions of power, and propriety, before this matter was acted upon. The whole of the laws which were required to be faithfully executed, were being resisted, and failing of execution, in nearly one-third of the States. Must they be allowed to finally fail of execution, even had it been perfectly clear, that by the use of the means necessary to their execution, some single law, made in such extreme tenderness of the citizen's liberty, that practically, it relieves more of the guilty, than of the innocent, should, to a very limited extent, be violated?" Lincoln deliberately conflated the duty of the chief executive with the duty of a criminal magistrate. Here he appealed to natural law, though he did not cite it directly. Lincoln had recourse to natural law theories in his debates with Douglas, arguing that slavery was a wrong in natural law although it was abetted by state and federal law. In natural law, when the existence of the entire government, including the judiciary, was imperiled, the chief magistrate was permitted to resort to extreme measures.[18]

If the constitutional text did not fully support the logic of his actions, he sought also to rest them on the law of war. "To state the question more directly, are all the laws, but one, to go unexecuted, and the government itself go to pieces, lest that one be violated? Even in such a case, would not the official oath be broken, if the government should be overthrown, when it was believed that disregarding the single law, would tend to preserve it?" Necessity was a part of the law of war when failure to act would have led directly to defeat. Rather than treat Congress to a learned disquisition, which was neither his style nor appropriate for the occasion, Lincoln added, "But it was not believed [by Lincoln himself] that this question was presented. It was not believed that any law was violated."[19]

Modern scholarship offers no clear answer to whether the text of the Constitution incorporates the law of war. Certainly presidents have both adopted and rejected it depending on the situation they faced.

In September of that year, Lincoln had cited military necessity as legal grounds for seizing the property of enemies, but not for freeing the slaves of noncombatants. His distinction lay in his understanding of international law. That understanding changed a year later, again based on the justification of military necessity.[20]

Was Lincoln wrong, and Taney right? As a matter of law, Taney probably had the better case, but had Lincoln not acted as he did, sending a message to others of Merryman's stripe, Maryland might well have seceded. With Washington, DC, so nearby, that would have been catastrophic for the Union cause.

Lincoln had asked his attorney general, Edward Bates, for help in preparing a reply to Taney. Bates did not appear in court, nor did he submit his views in the form of a brief on the case. They thus had no more or less than the effect of an advisory opinion explaining and justifying Lincoln's conduct. There was no such legal animal as an advisory opinion in a case that was no longer before a court. It did, however, find its way into Lincoln's address to Congress. Bates's opinion was dated July 5, 1861, although it must have been shaped by a series of meetings with Lincoln after Taney issued his opinion.

Bates was a no-nonsense lawyer of considerable experience in government. First a Whig, then a Republican, briefly Lincoln's rival for the presidential nomination, always suspicious of Buchanan, a believer that the nation should be a white man's preserve, fiercely opposed to secession but slow to recognize the threat, Bates was an obvious choice for a cabinet post—state if it did not go to Seward, attorney general if it did. He understood that the law must be tempered with practicality, initially opposing the compromise plans, supposing that "firmness" would win over the Southern moderates. When Sumter was bombarded, however, Bates saw the attack, and secession itself, as a domestic insurrection.[21]

At Lincoln's request, Bates conferred with Senator Reverdy Johnson of Maryland, a former attorney general, then drafted his advisory opinion. It began, "It is the plain duty of the President (and his peculiar duty, above and beyond all other departments of the government) to preserve the Constitution and execute the laws all over the nation." This reversed Taney's ordering of the authority of the branches. "It is plainly impossible for him to perform this duty without putting down rebellion, insurrection, and all unlawful combinations to resist the general government." Then Bates replaced Lincoln's purposive constitutionalism with far simpler logic. "The duty to suppress the insurrection being obvious and imperative, the two acts of Congress of 1795 and 1807 come to his aid, and furnish the physical force which he needs to suppress the insurrection and execute the laws. These two acts authorize the President to employ for that purpose, the militia, the army, and the navy." Congress recognized this as early as the Whiskey Rebellion of 1794, after President Washington had assembled the militia and marched on the rebels in western Pennsylvania. The suppression of that rebellion (though an armed tax strike hardly bears such a name) was precedent for Lincoln. "The argument may be briefly stated, thus: It is the President's bounden duty to put down the insurrection, as (in the language of the act of 1795) the 'combinations are too powerful to be suppressed by the ordinary course of judicial proceedings, or by the powers vested in the marshals.' And this duty is imposed on the President for the very reason that the courts and the marshals are too weak to perform it." Taney, one supposes, had distinguished the alleged weakness of the civil courts in Maryland in April 1861 from the actual weakness of the federal court for the District of Pennsylvania in 1794. Bates continued with the flip side of the separation of powers argument. "If it be true, as I have assumed, that the President and the judiciary are co-ordinate departments of government, and the one not subordinate to the other, I do not understand how it can be legally possible for a judge to issue a command to the President to come before him ad subjiciendum—that is, to submit implicitly to his judgment, and, in case of disobedience, treat him as a criminal, in contempt of a superior authority, and punish him, as for a misdemeanor, by fine and imprisonment."

Bates's final argument was a little more novel and a lot more suspect—a variation of the political question doctrine that the Taney Court had invoked in 1849, when it refused to get involved in the aftermath of Rhode Island's "Dorr Rebellion." Bates explained, "Besides, the whole subject-matter is political and not judicial. The insurrection itself is purely political." This was a fast shuffle of the deck, for the entire basis of Lincoln's policy was that secession was a violation of the Constitution not of the Republican Party platform. Bates's command of fact was as strained as his logic. He opined that secession's "object is to destroy the political government of this nation and to establish another political government upon its ruins." Actually, the Confederate government hoped to avoid war and did not propose at any time to destroy the Union save for leaving it. Like Taney and Lincoln, Bates did not feel the obligation to conform his legal opinion to fact. Bates's conclusion followed from his premise: "The President, as the chief civil magistrate of the nation, and the most active department in the government, is eminently and exclusively political in all his principal functions."

It was his fear of the Democrats' exploitation of this very argument that motivated Seward's warning to Lincoln—in responding to the Sumter crisis, stay away from anything resembling politics; rest protection of federal property on legal, not political, grounds. Bates surely saw Seward's missives. Seward and Lincoln shared them with the cabinet. But Bates must have thought he had a more convincing case than Seward's. "As the political chief of the nation, the Constitution charges [the president] with its preservation, protection, and defence, and requires him to take care that the laws be faithfully executed." It was true that the president was a political figure. He ran on a political platform and he was an elected official. Bates continued that the federal judiciary was not political in the same sense, because it was not elective. Hence, he reasoned, because "the judiciary department has no political powers and claims none, and therefore (as well as for other reasons already assigned) no court or judge can take cognizance of the political acts of the President, or undertake to revise and reverse his political decisions."[22]

Taney did not reply to Bates, but had he, it could have been devastating. For Bates had conceded the very evil that Taney decried. Lincoln's acts were political; Taney's were not. Lincoln may have followed political dictates, but he violated legal ones. Taney had said that the president was not above the law, while Bates had written that whenever the president decided that his acts were political, they were not subject to legal scrutiny. But Taney did not require Lincoln to appear in court. There was no precedent for it, but there had been cases where it might have been an issue. For example, in the course of the treason trial of Aaron Burr, Thomas Jefferson had refused to appear before John Marshall at the Richmond, Virginia, circuit court, but Jefferson did send to the court the documents that Burr needed for his defense. As a general rule, presidents have to comply with writs asking for documentary evidence. Presidents must also testify in common lawsuits and criminal lawsuits when commanded to do so.[23]

Nor did Taney find Lincoln or any of the officers who carried out his orders to be in contempt of the court. His opinion was not dictum, however, because it disposed of a real case or controversy before him as a circuit judge. Lincoln's actions gave Taney the chance to reply to Lincoln's views of *Dred Scott* expressed at the Cooper Union meeting. In effect, the lawyers vied with one another at a distance rather than in court. Merryman was eventually released and though a grand jury indicted him for treason, he was never tried. Nor did he ever serve the Confederacy. Instead, he remained in Maryland and in later life served as the state treasurer. But the message was sent: those who openly interfered with the Union war effort would face punishment in military or civilian courts.[24]

Merryman was a Copperhead, a Northern pro-Confederate supporter. Historians still dispute whether the Lincoln administration's campaign to stifle Copperheads' dissent crossed over from legitimate suppression of insurrectionary activity to illegal oppression of free speech. Of course, he was not the only lawyer/politician to demand loyalty. As early as July 8, 1861, James Fox "Bowie Knife" Potter, a Wisconsin lawyer and judge who served one term in the Thirty-Seventh Congress, proposed that a committee be formed to ferret out anyone with "secessionist" attitudes in the federal government's departments. The proposal passed unanimously. (Challenged to a duel by a slave state congressman known for skill with a pistol, Potter suggested bowie knives instead. The challenge was dropped.) The Merryman episode was no exception as events proved. Indeed, he got off lightly.[25]

The suppression of free speech and press during the Civil War may seem the nadir of the legal profession's participation in the war. Lincoln and the US attorneys shut down or arrested newspaper editors whose writings were deemed to aid the Confederacy. Dissidents were harassed and sometimes jailed. Some, like Warren P. Isham of the *Chicago Times*, were accused of spying for the enemy. Others, like E. M. Fuller of the *Newark Evening News*, were denounced for interfering with the draft. There was precedent: the Federalist Party's Sedition Act of 1798 resulted in the arrest, trial, and conviction of Jeffersonian Republican editors for criticism of the Adams administration. The Sedition Act was intended to be a wartime measure, but the war against France that the Federalists (save Adams himself) wanted never came to pass and the Sedition Act was not renewed when the Republicans came to power in 1801 (although they did not repeal state versions of the seditious libel act). The instinct to use federal law to suppress unwonted press criticism of administration policy did not disappear, however, although just like the Republicans in 1798, the Civil War–era Democrats condemned the suppression of free speech and freedom of the press. In any case, the attempt to muzzle pro-Southern sympathizers in the North probably had little to do with the outcome of the war, and given that the jailed individuals were invariably Democrats, one suspects more than a little partisanship in their prosecution.[26]

Two cases marked the outer boundaries of presidential martial law power—those of Clement L. Vallandingham and Lambdin P. Milligan. Both began early in 1861 and continued in one fashion or another throughout the war. While the two men were not the only victims of hasty or ill-considered prosecutions—thousands were persecuted who ran the gamut from peace Democrats to active abettors of the Confederacy—the cases of both men were notorious at the time and remain so in scholarship.[27]

Vallandingham was an Ohio Democratic lawyer/politician and before the war served in the state legislature. He and Stanton were friends and political allies. But Vallandingham had a streak of intemperance that Stanton had learned to curb, and during the war, which the former man opposed, he used his place in the Ohio congressional delegation to accuse Lincoln of misconduct in office. As it happened, Vallandingham was proslavery and supportive of states' rights, arguing in Congress that federal forces had no business interfering with slaveholders' rights to their property, but those were not the grounds on which he berated the president. He thought Lincoln a tyrant and said so.[28]

On May 7, 1863, Vallandingham was arrested for violating a military order forbidding speech that gave aid and comfort to the enemy, even though he gave the speech in Ohio, far from the scenes of carnage. He was no longer a congressman, however, and did not have the protection accorded his speech by that station. A military tribunal convicted him and sentenced him to confinement for the duration of the war. Lincoln commuted the sentence and arranged for Vallandingham to be exiled to the Confederacy. (Vallandingham was not the only Confederate sympathizer so exiled; Governor Claiborne Fox Jackson of Missouri was similarly punished for setting up a "shadow" government of Confederate Missouri early in the war; spy Rose O'Neal Greenhow was exiled as well.) Petitions from the Ohio Democratic delegation and the Democratic governor of New York did not deter the president. The district court judge, Humphrey H. Leavitt, sitting in the Circuit Court for the District of Ohio, to whom a habeas corpus writ was directed, refused to honor it, disregarding Taney's reasoning in Merryman. "The court cannot shut its eyes to the grave fact that war exists, involving the most eminent public danger, and threatening the subversion in destruction of the Constitution itself. In my judgment, when the life of the republic is in peril, he misstates his duty and obligation as a patriot who is not willing to concede to the Constitution such a capacity of adaptation to circumstances as may be necessary to meet a great emergency, and save the nation from hopeless ruin. Self-preservation is a paramount law."[29]

The Supreme Court, in *Ex Parte Vallandingham* (1864), concurred, Chief Justice Taney joining the Court's opinion that it could not issue a writ of habeas corpus to a military tribunal. As Justice Wayne reasoned, "The appellate powers of the Supreme Court, as granted by the Constitution, are limited and regulated by the acts of Congress, and must be exercised subject to the exceptions and regulations made by Congress. In other words, the petition before us we think not to be within the letter or spirit of the grants of appellate jurisdiction to the Supreme Court."[30]

Milligan was an Indiana lawyer/politician with aspirations to high office in the Democratic Party. A believer in states' rights, he condemned Lincoln's conduct of the war. In particular, Milligan objected to the imposition of martial law in areas not adjacent to the Confederacy where the civil courts were still in operation. He also defended, sometimes successfully, Southern sympathizers prosecuted for their views. Federal officials believed that Milligan also associated with secret societies whose purpose was not to defend the Constitution, but to overthrow it. The extent of that collaboration was a matter of dispute. In the election cycle of 1864, with the issue of the war still in doubt, fears of wider conspiracy were abroad. Words could further disaffect those who were already opposed to the war effort, but Northern unionists feared conspiracy even more, for dissent was the tip of the iceberg, and conspiracies might have far more serious effects. As the report of one such conspiracy, the so-called Great North-Western plot planned by the Order of the Sons of Liberty, explained, "The investigation has elicited testimony of the most startling character, showing conclusively to the minds of all reasonable men who have given to it careful, earnest attention that there was a most formidable, deep and well-arranged conspiracy, which, but for timely discovery and judicious action, would have resulted most disastrously, not only to the particular cities and towns specified and doomed to destruction, but to the whole country." The near hysteria in this and other accounts shows that the suppression of Copperhead organizations had popular support, lest "who shall say that had the savage hordes of Jeff. Davis then been turned loose upon an unarmed community, to carry desolation and ruin as they should sweep over our fair States." Accused of attempting to create a new nation in the Midwest friendly to the Confederacy, in actuality the secret order was hardly secret and acted as an extreme element of the Northern Democratic Party during the election of 1864. A few of the Order were willing to engage in some sort of insurrectionary activity, however, and revelations of this gave to the Republicans in Indiana a campaign issue. The result was the military trial of the alleged conspirators, including Milligan. In this way partisan politics perverted the normal course of justice as much as wartime hysteria did in the North.[31]

On September 17, 1864, military authorities arrested Milligan at his home in Indianapolis. A military tribunal heard the case, even though the federal courts in Indiana were open. In fact, the US attorney for the District of Indiana had already brought indictments against Milligan before a federal grand jury. (The grand jury declined to indict him.) The army officers convicted Milligan of a grab bag of offenses, including conspiracy, insurrection, and violation of the laws of war, and sentenced him to be hanged. When the case was appealed to the US Circuit Court for the District of Indiana, Justice David Davis, a

Lincoln appointee, ruled that the case should never have gone before a military tribunal. On appeal to the US Supreme Court, in 1866, the justices, in a majority opinion that Davis authored, announced that military justice should not operate when the civil courts were open. Counsel for Milligan included Buchanan's unionist attorney general, Jeremiah Black, and lawyer/politician (and lately Union general) James Garfield. They insisted that the military commissions were unconstitutional in Indiana where the federal courts were open. Attorney General James Speed left the defense of the commissions to none other than Benjamin Butler, no longer wearing blue, but hired for the occasion. Butler defended the commissions as a wartime necessity, wherever they sat. Davis disagreed. "Milligan insists that said military commission had no jurisdiction to try him upon the charges preferred, or upon any charges whatever, because he was a citizen of the United States and the State of Indiana, and had not been, since the commencement of the late Rebellion, a resident of any of the States whose citizens were arrayed against the government, and that the right of trial by jury was guaranteed to him by the Constitution of the United States." In short, Milligan asked the Court to find that the laws of war did not apply in Indiana, where the war did not rage. Davis agreed. He explained that in time of war, passions had overruled good law. "During the late wicked Rebellion, the temper of the times did not allow that calmness in deliberation and discussion so necessary to a correct conclusion of a purely judicial question. Then, considerations of safety were mingled with the exercise of power, and feelings and interests prevailed which are happily terminated. Now that the public safety is assured, this question, as well as all others, can be discussed and decided without passion or the admixture of any element not required to form a legal judgment."[32]

In time of war, the laws were not silent, but military exigency warped some of them. The old problem, a kind of legal Gordian knot, of protecting those who would destroy the very institutions that provided protections, was not untied by these apparently contradictory rulings. One can only conclude that the lawyers on the bench and the lawyers representing the clients did what lawyers do best—find ways to resolve disputes according to law, if not precisely within the confines of existing law.

More recent assessments of the suppression of dissent, looking back through the lens of World War I's mass persecution of dissidents, have found the limits that the Civil War lawyers imposed on themselves and on the attempt to curb opposition to the war to be less extensive and less threatening than the Democratic Party and press of that day proclaimed. Our modern idea of a robust First Amendment protecting free speech and press did not exist in the 1850s and 1860s. At the same time, Lincoln was not a dictator and the constitutional protections of free speech and press were not ignored. Merryman, Vallandingham, and Milligan all posed very real threats to the defeat of the Confederacy, if not to the survival of the Union, but they did not face the punishment that other losers in civil wars did. None of them was executed, nor were families deprived of their property, nor did their cases open the door to mass incarceration or execution of opponents of the war aims. Lawyers understood that in a constitutional regime including a first amendment, there must be limits to the use of law to stifle dissent, but the precise boundaries of those limits depended on what kind of war the two sides thought they waged.[33]

# 4

## Was Secession a Crime?

IN LATE 1862, WITH the carnage of Shiloh and Antietam still vivid before their eyes, the Civil War lawyers wondered if there could be any end to the war. On December 16, 1862, as reports of the casualties of the battle of Fredericksburg arrived, Lincoln exclaimed, "If there is a worse place than hell, I am in it." One of the casualties was T. R. R. Cobb, fulfilling his prophecy, on the eve of battle, that he would never see his home again. Reporting the death, a friend wrote to Howell Cobb, campaigning in another theater of the war, "How valuable should be the liberties purchased with such precious blood." The butchery of the conflict only hardened the resolve of some of the lawyers in government, as Ohio senator and lawyer John Sherman wrote to his brother, William, engaged in the siege of Vicksburg, "There is no way but to go but on." Still, the carnage made all the more important the legal question of whether the waging of a civil war was a crime, and if so, what kind of crime.[1]

The wartime diary of Secretary of the Treasury Samuel Chase showed how complex the legal practicalities of this subject could be: "No state nor any portion of a people could withdraw from the Union or absolve themselves from allegiance to it, but that when the attempt was made, and the state government was laced in hostility to the federal government, the state organization was forfeited." So much for the political status of the seceding state—but what about the status of individuals who served the Confederacy? Were they domestic rebels or belligerents (foreign enemies in wartime)? If military action was not aimed at the seceding states because they could not secede, nor at the Confederate States of America because it did not exist, were those men who made war on the United States simply traitors? In the Vallandingham and Milligan cases, Lincoln and his cabinet members seemed to proceed on the basis that they were, and some among the multitude of Confederate officers and politicians, not to mention the civilians who aided and abetted the Confederate war effort, could theoretically at least be arrested and tried for crimes against the United States. But should they be?[2]

The lawyers faced the question of the criminality of rebellion in a series of federal cases and codes between 1861 and 1863. In the piracy, treason, and *Prize Cases*, lawyers and judges determined what kind of war the two sides waged at sea. In the latter year, Lincoln's administration approved and promulgated a code for Union officers and men in the field. Confederate legal officers responded. These efforts provided a template for what was criminal and what was not in the course of the war.[3]

In 1861, two circuit courts—one in New York City sitting for the Southern District of New York, the other in Philadelphia sitting for the Eastern District of Pennsylvania, tried Confederate privateers for piracy and sedition. Circuit courts composed of one Supreme Court justice and one district court judge handled all serious federal crimes in that district. Closely watched by federal and Confederate authorities, managed on the prosecution and defense sides by leading attorneys, with two High Court justices sitting on the bench, the two trials would tell the people of the North and South what kind of treatment captured soldiers and sailors could expect. Although these were trial courts, not courts of appeal, and thus the rulings and opinions of the judges did not extend beyond the parties at the bar, they did address the question of the criminality of the defendants. In particular, these prosecutions turned on whether the Confederacy was an independent nation and its naval agents operated under letters of marque, as permitted by international law, or the Confederate seamen were United States citizens, guilty of the crime of treason or piracy. The Federal Crimes Act of 1790 covered offenses at sea and "any river, haven, basin, or bay, out of the jurisdiction of any particular State." Or, as the defendants' counsel argued, were the men in the dock members of the military forces of a foreign nation with whom the United States warred?[4]

The trials for treason and piracy demonstrated how federal attorneys straddled the two concepts of rebellion and war. The two sets of facts introduced at trial varied. In the first case, Confederate naval officer T. Harrison Baker was the captain of the CSS *Savannah* when it took a Northern vessel for a prize, on June 2, 1861. The *Savannah* and her crew were themselves captured by a United States Navy vessel the next day and conveyed to New York City to await trial on charges of piracy. A month later, a US naval vessel overwhelmed a prize crew that the Confederate raider *Jeff Davis* had put aboard a Northern merchant vessel. Captain William Smith and his fellow Confederate crewmen were taken to Philadelphia to face charges of treason.[5]

Four months passed before the members of the two Confederate raiders' crews came to trial. By that time, formidable legal teams had assembled to conduct their defense. Although it was an unpopular step for him, prominent New York City attorney Daniel Lord offered to defend the *Savannah* crew. He had gone to Yale with the prize captain's father. Algernon Sullivan, founder of the prestigious New York City law firm of Sullivan and Cromwell, was hired by the Confederate government to join in the defense. Lincoln's attorney general Edward Bates hired a special counsel, William M. Evarts, to prosecute. Justice Samuel Nelson presided over the trial along with district court judge Samuel Betts. In the meantime, counsel for the *Jeff Davis*'s prize crew had assembled in Philadelphia, and trial in the circuit court commenced. Leading defense counsel was George S. Wharton, a prominent local attorney who would become one of the great benefactors of the University of Pennsylvania. Wharton was a Democrat and Buchanan had appointed him US attorney for the Eastern District of Pennsylvania. Opposing him was his successor as US attorney, George A. Coffey. When Coffey fell ill, Bates arranged for William Kelley, a Republican congressman from Philadelphia and an early supporter of Lincoln, to replace Coffey. Justice Robert Grier presided, along with district court judge John Cadwalader, whose role in the Merryman affair has already been discussed.[6]

In both cases jury selection proved critical. The right to a jury trial in criminal cases was guaranteed by the Fifth Amendment to the federal

Constitution. Jury selection actually began before the full panel was assembled in the courtroom and questioned by counsel, for, as the most recent study of nineteenth-century American juries suggests, members of jury panels in these sorts of cases reflected an "elite" of the community. Under questioning by the bench, jurors who indicated that they could not come to a fair verdict were dismissed. Jury selection took a few hours in both courtrooms, a not uncommon stretch of time for important trials in this era of American law. The entire process indicated the high regard that contemporaries accorded the jury trial. It was then, as now, an "ideal central to national belief." The essential fairness with which the two juries in these cases regarded the arguments of counsel and the presentation of evidence also reflected the high quality of the counsel on both sides. In both of them, the Civil War lawyers played a vital role in preserving the integrity of the federal judicial process. Of course, this was still early in the war. After the horrific losses the Union suffered in the next two years, such impartial juries might have been much harder to assemble, but a later code of conduct for Union forces during the war stated that even when a military tribunal met, "all civil and penal law shall continue to take its usual course."[7]

In cross-examination and summation, the defense sought to establish what it could not prove with documentary evidence—that the Confederacy was a nation and its sailors acted in conformity with the laws of war between belligerents. It argued that the taking of the prize ship was not piracy because the sailors acted under the reasonable assumption that the Confederacy was a legal government and they had "letters of marque" from Confederate president Jefferson Davis permitting them to seize Union shipping. It could have argued, in the alternative, that if the prosecution regarded the seamen as US citizens who had committed a crime against their own country, then the imposition of a blockade of Southern ports and the seizing of merchant shipping by the US Navy was itself illegal. One could only impose a blockade, according to the law of nations, on an enemy nation (which would have made the Confederacy's privateering legal under the law of nations). What was more, an informal exchange of prisoners of war, especially officers, was already in progress. If the Confederate officers had committed treason, how could they be exchanged? Was that not a tacit acceptance of the defense claim that the Confederacy was a separate nation fighting for its independence? Prisoner exchanges were common when sovereign nations fought, but not when domestic insurgents waged war on their own government or its people. No matter the fine ironies of the defense, the jury convicted the Philadelphia privateers the same day their defense closed.[8]

In New York City, Justice Nelson admitted into evidence documents that purported to show (that is, that could be read to show) that the Confederacy was a sovereign nation. Grier had either excluded or qualified such evidence in the *Jeff Davis* case. The charge of piracy against the *Savannah* crew offered a defense line that the indictment for treason had not. If the defense could convince the jury that the Confederacy was a sovereign nation, or at least that there was some genuine evidence to that effect, the defendants were not pirates. The jury in the New York case was divided—eight found the defendants guilty, and four disagreed. A new trial was ordered. Before that trial began, President Davis sent word to Lincoln that for every member of either crew executed, a randomly selected Union prisoner of war would be executed. Lincoln relented and exchanged all but two crew members, the two unfortunates having died in prison.[9]

Grier's and Nelson's varying stances on the admissibility of evidence had a direct impact on the outcome of the trials. Grier was a Democrat from Pennsylvania, one of two James K. Polk appointments to the Court. A unionist and a moderate on the subject of slavery, easygoing and much liked on the Court, he was more a politician off and on the Court than a jurisprudent. His opinions were short and to the point, often well crafted, and rarely groundbreaking. Perhaps his strong adherence to the Union affected his ruling.[10]

Justice Samuel Nelson, unlike Grier, was a veteran jurist, serving for many years on the New York State Court of Appeals before the lame duck Senate session in 1845 confirmed President John Tyler's nomination of him. During the crisis of 1860–1861, he served as an unofficial member of the Peace Commission, trying to find a way to repair secession short of going to war. He was, moreover, a close friend and ally on the Court of Taney, and he opposed Union military operations against the Confederacy, including the blockade. There is little doubt that these views influenced his rulings on the admissibility of the Confederate documents. Both Grier and Nelson were lawyer/politicians who found themselves on the bench and to it both brought their views of secession and their understanding of the law of evidence.[11]

A second set of seminal cases on the criminality of secession, beginning in 1862 and concluding the next year, illustrated the lawyers' and judges' view of the Civil War. The cases revolved around ships seized for alleged violations of the blockade. Imposed on April 27, 1861, by executive proclamation, the blockade was de facto evidence that genuine war had begun between the United States and, depending on whose argument one accepted, the rebellious denizens of the eleven seceding states or the Confederate States of America. Penalties for violation of the blockade were not criminal, however. Seizure and confiscation were civil penalties and represented an alternative to criminalization.

In the *Prize Cases* (1863), the Supreme Court split over the question of the legality of the seizure of blockade runners. In the process, the Court defined an alternative to criminal punishment for aiding and abetting the insurrection. Grier wrote the majority's opinion. Nelson dissented, along with Catron, Clifford, and, Taney.[12]

On April 19, 1861, Lincoln had issued a proclamation whose first part seemed to define the conflict as a domestic insurrection: "Whereas an Executive proclamation has been already issued requiring the persons engaged in these disorderly proceedings to desist therefrom, calling out a militia force for the purpose of repressing the same . . . with a view to . . . the protection of the public peace and the lives and property of quiet and orderly citizens pursuing their lawful occupations." Punishment for individuals and groups falling into this category would, one should expect, have been criminal. If the legal authority for the proclamation was Lincoln's duty to see that the laws were obeyed—the same duty that impelled him to suspend habeas corpus in the Merryman matter—the conflict must be read as a domestic insurrection. Under the Militia Act of 1795, he could call out the militia to suppress a domestic insurrection, but nothing in that act entailed a blockade. He then continued that "until Congress shall have assembled and deliberated on the said unlawful proceedings," he had imposed "a blockade of the ports within the States aforesaid, in pursuance of the laws of the United States and of the law of nations in such case provided."[13]

The reference to the law of nations only applied if the war were waged against a foreign enemy. One cannot, under the law of war, blockade one's own ports. The punishment of one's wartime enemies was not criminal, it was political, a version of civil law. If the authority for the blockade lay in the president's wartime powers as commander in chief, the laws of war did apply, but that meant that the Confederate raiders must represent a foreign enemy, and thus the Confederacy was a sovereign nation—a status that Lincoln never accorded the Confederacy. Were he to do this, its soldiers, sailors, and civilians could not be regarded as criminals. Under this version of the war, the punishment for violating the blockade applied not to the insurrectionists but to foreign nationals and neutral nations. Lincoln concluded: "For this purpose a competent force will be posted so as to prevent entrance and exit of vessels from the ports aforesaid. If, therefore, with a view to violate such blockade . . . and if the same vessel shall again attempt to enter or leave the blockaded port she will be captured and sent to the nearest convenient port for such proceedings against her and her cargo as prize as may be deemed advisable."[14]

At the same time as the criminal/civil nature of the proclamation was unclear, Lincoln's determination to strangle the Confederacy with a blockade was not. Secretary of the Navy Welles was initially hesitant to order it deployed (indeed, he did not have the resources to effectuate it fully), but he did his best to comply. Attorney General Bates worried that it would not be defensible in the Supreme Court, but he hired independent counsel from elite members of the bar to attempt it. So important to the war effort and so unclear in its legitimacy, one can see why the blockade and the so-called *Prize Cases* tested Lincoln's and his cabinet members' view of the contest itself. *Merryman* never went to the High Court, hence as precedent, even had Lincoln obeyed Taney, it would not have affected the entire land. But when the Supreme Court spoke, it spoke for every federal court. Truly much was at stake as the oral arguments opened in February 1863. For twelve days, top-notch lawyers vied to sway the justices, and while the vote on the Court may have been predictable, the fate of the nation hung in the balance.[15]

The cases arising under the blockade meant that the lawyer/politicians who sat on the High Court would get their chance to assess what kind of war it was. Until this time, the Court had not had its say on the legal nature of the war. To some extent, the political background of the justices would color their views. Today, the political affiliations of the justices may be clear to Court watchers and almost all of them came up through the ranks of the lower federal courts. In the 1850s and 1860s, the Court's incumbents were lawyer/politicians whose party affiliations, loyalty, and service were major reasons they were nominated. One might expect the older Democratic members to be somewhat suspicious of Lincoln's claims to exercise his wartime authority, and newer Republican members to be more friendly. Three members of the Court were new—Lincoln appointees from Republican ranks. Ohio's Noah Swayne was the first, arriving on the Court at the beginning of 1862, shortly followed by Samuel F. Miller, an Iowan, in July of that year, and then David Davis of Illinois, in October. These were relatively young men, free of the taint of proslavery and secessionist views, and they could be counted on to support the blockade, but three votes would not be enough to uphold the lower courts' decisions.[16]

Swayne, a Quaker from Pennsylvania, came by his dislike for slavery young. His parents were antislavery activists. He served a number of years as the US attorney for the federal district court in Ohio. By 1856, he was a Republican stalwart, and in 1860, he backed Lincoln. A robust figure of a man, he would also support a robust version of freed slaves' civil rights and liberties after the Civil War. Swayne served until 1881 and died in 1884.[17]

Born in Kentucky to a farm family that had come from North Carolina, Miller read law on his own and joined the Kentucky bar in 1847, at the age of thirty-one. He opposed slavery, but Kentucky did not. So he shifted his practice to Iowa, where he freed his slaves. An impressive physical figure in the courtroom, a wonderful storyteller, and a very sharp intellect, Miller became a leader in the antislavery movement and joined the Republican Party at its inception, in 1854. He sat on the Court until 1890.[18]

Davis was a veritable giant of a man at nearly three hundred pounds. He was born and reared in Maryland, where his family had slaves and property, but he went west to find his fortune; though he never became a rich man, he did establish a solid law practice in Bloomington, Illinois, followed by a judgeship. Davis was Lincoln's campaign manager in 1860, "the Achilles" of his campaign and close advisor during his presidency. He was the executor of Lincoln's estate. He remained a politico on the Court, thought about running for president himself, and resigned in 1877 to become a senator from Illinois. He died in 1886.[19]

Nelson and Taney were likely to find Lincoln's April 19, 1861, proclamation unconstitutional. Two other holdovers on the Court, John Catron and Nathan Clifford, could be counted on to join the chief justice. For his own part, though a states' rights Democrat, a defender of the legality of slavery, and a well-regarded Nashville resident, Catron remained loyal to the Union when Tennessee seceded. Though threatened with death by Confederate vigilantes, he continued to ride circuit in Kentucky and Missouri during the war and once Tennessee was largely in Union hands, he held federal circuit court there. But no mistake, as a Tennessee Supreme Court justice, Catron had regarded slaves as "a very dangerous and most objectionable population where [they] are numerous." Clifford was a Maine lawyer/politician who served in the state and national government (he was Polk's attorney general and a member of Congress). Buchanan selected him for the Court to replace Curtis. A loyal Democrat, though a moderate on the issue of slavery, he did not support secession but neither did he favor the war effort.[20]

Grier's would then be the deciding vote, and if party allegiance were all that mattered, he might have joined Taney. He was a Democrat. But he not only opposed secession; sitting on circuit in *US v. William Smith,* he had told the jury that the Confederacy was not a sovereign nation. "It does not follow that every band of conspirators who may combine together for the purpose of rebellion or revolution or overturning the government of which they are citizens or subjects, become ipso facto a separate and independent member of the great family of sovereign states. A successful rebellion may be termed a revolution; but until it becomes such it has no claim to be recognized as a member of the family, or exercise the rights or enjoy the privileges consequent on sovereignty." Given the lineup of the justices, it would seem that the blockade would be found constitutional and the confiscations upheld. But neither side regarded the issue of the criminality of the war, as opposed to the outcome of the case, as quite so easily resolved.[21]

The US attorneys brought (sued out) "libels" (the admiralty law terminology for condemnation) against blockade runners. The district courts, given admiralty jurisdiction by the Judiciary Act of 1789, found for the federal government, condemning the ships and cargos as contraband of war. The owners, by their counsel, appealed the decisions of the district courts to the US Supreme Court. The issue on its face was the legality of seizures based solely on a presidential proclamation. Beneath that issue of law lay the question of the criminality of the rebels and their supporters. If the war was an insurrection, they were liable to criminal prosecution; if it was a struggle between two sovereignties, then the Confederates were not liable to criminal prosecution, unless in the course of the war they committed acts that were criminal in themselves—for example, the murder of civilians. It was thus the implications and applications of the Supreme Court's decision to the issue of criminality that mattered as much as its actual opinion in the matter of the seizures and confiscations.

The facts varied in the four seizures joined under the caption the *Prize Cases* in the High Court. The *Amy Warwick* was a merchant vessel owned in Richmond that sailed from New York City to Rio de Janeiro before the war commenced, taking on a cargo of coffee in Brazil that was seized on its return voyage in July 1861. At that time, the ship sailed under US colors and its captain had no knowledge that hostilities had begun. The owners denied that they had any hostility to the government or laws of the United States; that the captain of the ship did not know about the blockade; and that the taking of ship and cargo was unlawful.

The *Crenshaw* was captured at the mouth of the James River in May 1861, trying to break the blockade. It was sailing to Liverpool, England, with a cargo of tobacco from Richmond. Its owner and its master knew that Virginia had seceded and was part of the Confederacy but averred that they had no part in that act and did not know about the blockade.

The *Hiawatha*, ironically in light of its name, was a British vessel, also sailing from Richmond to Liverpool in May laden with tobacco. Its owners were British and they challenged the capture on the grounds that notice of the blockade had not reached them, hence it could not apply to them. What is more, they were neutrals in the war, and their rights at sea should have been observed as a matter of the laws of war respecting neutral powers.

The *Brilliante* was a Mexican schooner and its owners and shippers were Mexican nationals. The ship was captured off the coast of

Mississippi, during its regular run from Campeche to New Orleans. Its captain claimed that he had waited offshore to learn from the US naval vessels whether he could approach the port and offload his cargo. He was seized instead.

The legality of the blockade was the central issue in all the district court cases. Judges Samuel Betts in the Southern District of New York and Peleg Sprague for the District of Massachusetts wrote fairly extensive opinions that were later published. Betts had been sitting since 1826, an appointee of John Quincy Adams. Prior to his appointment he had served in Congress and on the state's supreme court. Sprague had graduated from Harvard and had gone on to represent Maine in both the House and the Senate before accepting the judicial post from President John Tyler. Both judges upheld the blockade as a legitimate exercise of the president's wartime powers. The question remaining was what kind of wartime powers could the president assert in a civil war? Although the federal district courts had a lot of experience with prize cases, particularly during the European wars of the 1790s and 1800s, the War of 1812, and the South American independence movements in the 1820s, in those cases the issues were who among the backers of the privateers that took the prizes was entitled to the prize ships and their cargos or whether the privateers were actually pirates. In this sense, the admiralty jurisdiction of the federal courts did extend to crimes at sea and in the ports. But did this make blockade running a crime? Thus the issues that the cases raised were somewhat novel ones, what jurist Oliver Wendell Holmes Jr. would later call "hard cases."[22]

The oral and written arguments before the Supreme Court brought to the Old Senate Chamber where the Court sat some of the most brilliant counsel in the land. The US government did not have a solicitor general until Congress provided for that office in 1870. Instead, it hired Richard Henry Dana of Boston and William Evarts of New York City to argue the cases. The reporter of the cases for the High Court, none other than Jeremiah Black (having been refused a seat on the High Court by the Republican majority in the Senate), reproduced in full Dana's argument and that of James Carlisle, counsel for the *Brilliante*'s owners and shippers, "because they came to his hands in a form which relieved him of the labor which the others would have cost to re-write and condense them."[23]

Dana was not only a lawyer but also an antislavery reformer, writer, and by 1856 a Republican politician. He clearly agreed with Lincoln's prosecution of the war, including the blockade. The problem for him and the other government attorneys was that Lincoln could defend the blockade in international law (the law of war) only if he regarded the Confederacy as a belligerent. In other words, he could close Confederate ports if the federal government was at war with a sovereign power. But Lincoln and his administration never regarded the Confederacy in this light. It was, in his view, a collection of rebellious citizens of the United States. Attorney General Bates thought that the closing of ports was legal because Confederate authorities refused to collect and return customs duties, but a blockade of the entire coast of the Confederacy was unsustainable as a matter of law. Secretary of the Navy Gideon Wells agreed. But Seward had found a loophole in the form of British policy. Perfidious Albion, the epithet applied to Britain because of its treatment of the laws of war, had never bothered to consult international law when it confuted British interests, but in this case, the British ambassador said that only a blockade would legally restrain British trade with the Confederacy. In fact, Confederate leaders assumed that Britain would object to any blockade and would come to the aid of the Confederacy if a blockade were imposed. They were wrong. Britain remained neutral and, as a neutral, did not attempt to contest the blockade. So the cases of the four ships became a domestic matter rather than grounds for a second war, the United States against Great Britain.[24]

The order of argument was this: the appellant, counsel for the ship and its cargo, spoke first, followed by the counsel for the appellee, here the federal government. Dana's oral argument (Black's transcription was based on Dana's text of his oral argument) came in the first case, the brig *Amy Warwick*, and the second argument Black included in his headnote to the case was James Carlisle's for the Mexican bark *Brilliante*. Both men had heard the cases argued in the district courts; thus, there were no surprises when the arguments were brought in the Supreme Court. But oral argument did not appear in the reports of the cases below. Here, then, they are taken from the report of the case compiled at the end of 1862 and printed in 1863. I have arranged them as they would have appeared in the district court, however, with Dana for the government answered by Carlisle for the ships.

Dana had already argued the case of the brig *Amy Warwick* in the lower court. There and before the justices, Dana's premise was simple: the term "war" applied to both external and internal conflicts where the combat was widely extended and the significance of the combat was general. Nice distinctions about external and internal enemies and their rights had to be put aside when the very existence of the state was at stake. As Judge Peleg Sprague put it when the case had come to the District of Massachusetts, "But it is contended that although this property might be liable to confiscation if the contest were a foreign war, yet that it is otherwise in a rebellion or civil war. This requires attention. As the constitution gives congress the power to declare war, some have thought that without such previous declaration, war, in all its fulness, that is, carrying with it all the incidents and consequences of a war, cannot exist. This is a manifest error. It ignores the fact that there are two parties to a war, and that it may be commenced by either." Rather than going in all directions or studding his oral argument with rhetorical flourishes, Dana channeled Sprague. The counselor pressed the single point: "The case of the *Amy Warwick* presents a single question, which may be stated thus: At the time of the capture, was it competent for the President to treat as prize of war property found on the high seas, for the sole reason that it belonged to persons residing and doing business in Richmond, Virginia?"[25]

Dana then elaborated his argument that it did not matter how one termed the Civil War, that is, whether the Court saw it as a war against a foreign enemy or the suppression of a domestic rebellion. The neutral status of vessels attempting to run the blockade was no bar to their capture. His task was a challenging one, however, because in previous wars, Americans had insisted on these distinctions. In particular, during the Napoleonic Wars, Britain's refusal to respect the neutral status of American merchant vessels led President James Madison to focus on neutral rights when he asked Congress to declare war on Britain in 1812: "British cruisers have been in the continued practice of violating the American flag on the great highway of nations, and of seizing and carrying off persons sailing under it, not in the exercise of a belligerent right founded on the law of nations against an enemy, but of a municipal prerogative over British subjects. British jurisdiction is thus extended to neutral vessels in a situation where no laws can operate but the law of nations and the laws of the country to which the vessels belong."[26]

Dana hoped that he could overcome this and similar precedents by distinguishing the current wartime situation from its predecessors. That effort would test both his skill as an advocate and his command of the law. He chose to move slowly, sometimes repeating or elaborating a point rather than simply making it and moving on. How different this was from Lincoln's style of pleading, but then Lincoln never argued a case before the highest court in the land. Dana began with an old and reliable maneuver—concede at the outset what one would eventually have to concede, then distinguish it from one's own cause. "There are certain propositions applicable to war with acknowledged foreign nations, which must first be established," but "an examination of the reasons on which those propositions rest will aid in determining whether the propositions are also applicable to internal wars." The concession was that there was a difference between war with a foreign nation and an internal war. Then came the distinction: "The general rule may be stated thus: Property found on the high seas, subject to the ownership and control of persons who themselves reside in the territory of the enemy, and thus subject to the jurisdiction and control of the enemy, is liable to capture as prize of war." In other words, in war the enemy's property is always subject to seizure and confiscation.[27]

He then and after added what are today called "string" citations, lists of cases that he thought supported his point. He did not go into each of them, as they were fully reported in other sources. They would have appeared as well in his written brief, for after 1821 this was required by the Court. "The above cases will be found to sustain the following propositions which I suppose will not be controverted, as applicable to cases of war with a recognized foreign power, and therefore are not elaborated." If he had no intention of going into them, why cite them? The lure of legal pedantry to one side, a well-prepared advocate has to anticipate his opponents' arguments. Better to tell the Court that the cases favored Dana's argument.[28]

Further elaboration followed. "First, it is immaterial in such case, whether the owner of the property has or has not taken part in the war, or given aid or comfort to the enemy, under whose power he resides." Thus the question of neutral rights disappeared. It surely would reappear when the blockade runner was owned by a neutral entity, but again better to dismiss it here than have it unanswered. "Second. It is immaterial whether he be or be not, by birth or naturalization, a citizen or subject of the enemy." So long as the property was useful to the enemy, it was liable to confiscation. This was the general category of jurisdiction over the thing, not the person. No one proposed to jail or otherwise punish the crews or the owners of ships of foreign registry. "He may be a subject of a neutral sovereign. He may even be a special and privileged resident, as consul of a neutral power. Still, if property subject to his ownership and control . . . [i]ts capture is one of the justifiable modes of coercing the enemy." In the end, "These are immaterial inquiries." The only element that remained was "the property in the particular case, if not captured, or if restored, would in fact have benefitted the enemy, and that its capture would tend to the injury of the enemy."[29]

The bottom line was the last of the points. "The laws of war go by general rules. Property in a certain predicament is condemned, the general rule being founded on the experience and concession that property so situated is or may be useful to the enemy in the war, and that the rights of neutrals and the dictates of humanity do not forbid its capture." This was the same kind of reasoning as Congress used to justify the first of the Confiscation Acts in 1861—custom, international law, the precedent of taking and selling Loyalist property in the Revolutionary War, and simple necessity in time of war abridged the otherwise inviolate rules of private property. Note that the second Confiscation Act included slaves but was limited to that property that enabled the enemy to wage war. It was the efficacy of the confiscation— its relation to the object of winning the war that justified the taking of the enemy's property.[30]

Then Dana returned to the starting point of the argument: "Those reasons are . . . equally applicable to an internal war. WAR is simply the exercise of force by bodies politic, or bodies assuming to be bodies politic, against each other, for the purpose of coercion. The means and modes of doing this are called belligerent powers [emphasis in original]." War was war, and in war, the protection of the property of noncombatants and the rights of private ownership were secondary to the goal of victory. "The customs and opinions of modern civilization have recognized certain modes of coercing the power you are acting against as justifiable. Injury to private persons or their property is avoided as far as it reasonably can be. Wherever private property is taken or destroyed, it is because it is of such a character, or so situated, as to make its capture a justifiable means of coercing the power with which you are at war." Dana found that the "political power"—in this case, the executive charged with conducting the war—had the discretion to impose a blockade, confiscate property, and do whatever else necessity decreed.[31]

Dana had pushed the rock up a steep slope, but he was not quite to its top. Were the rules for waging a war against a foreign sovereignty "equally applicable to internal wars"? Yes, he answered. The underlying rationale for blockades in war was to cripple the enemy's ability to wage war. Surely that was the same in domestic insurrections. Dana had to tread carefully, for the application of his argument for the confiscation of blockade runners to the confiscation of slave property was not far from the surface of everyone's thinking. The Union needed the loyalty of citizens of the slaveholding border states. If they and their representatives came to believe that Lincoln and the Republicans were radicals waging war on slavery itself, they might seek a separate peace with the Confederacy. Lincoln was already engaged in suppressing pro-Confederacy politics in the border states. In Congress, conservatives and Democrats were trying to limit confiscation to articles used in combat.[32]

Dana knew what everyone else knew—he had to answer the concerns of the unionist slaveholders without addressing those concerns directly. He never did mention the confiscation of slaves, but his argument about the legality of the blockade extended itself logically to the legality of confiscating slaves as contraband of war. "This [war-making] power . . . compels obedience, and exacts allegiance from all inhabitants of the territory, without respect to their wishes. It compels each inhabitant to pay taxes and imposts upon his property, to aid in the war, and makes his property liable to contribution or confiscation."[33]

When he argued before the Court, Dana had already heard counsel for the shipowners assert that even if the rebellion were classed as a war, only Congress had the constitutional authority to declare war, and Lincoln had imposed the blockade before the special sessions of Congress convened. "War is a state of things, and not an act of legislative will." The president was required by law to act "to repel war with war, and make prisoners and prizes by the army, navy and militia which he has called into service and employed to repel the invasion." This was not only true when a foreign power had struck, but, "in case of civil war, the President may, in the absence of any Act of Congress on the subject, meet the war by the exercise of belligerent maritime capture. The same overwhelming reasons of necessity govern this position, as the preceding." Every district judge that had heard the prize cases agreed: "[Chief] Judge [James] Dunlop, in the District of Columbia; Judge [William] Giles, in Maryland; Judge [William] Marvin, in Florida; Judge [Samuel] Betts, in New York; Judge [Peleg] Sprague, in Massachusetts; [and] Judge [John] Cadwalader, in Pennsylvania." Cadwalader, readers will recall, was the brother of the general who held Merryman in close confinement. Dana did not have to add this list, but perhaps his iteration of the judges was meant to remind the Court that all of them, whatever their party affiliation, had found the blockade legal.[34]

James Carlisle, Washington, DC, counsel for the *Brilliante*, the last of the four cases, directly challenged the legality of the blockade, an argument that threatened the entire Union naval enterprise. Carlisle was a personal friend of Chief Justice Taney and had argued before him on previous occasions. He had also argued a number of prize cases in the district courts, including this one. Carlisle maintained that the Mexican ship was a neutral vessel, and the rights of the owners and shippers under international law could only be curtailed if their ship entered a war zone. His argument had a series of interlocking parts. (Note how much this structure resembled Seward's Memorandum.) This is called arguing in the alternative. The parts need not be logically connected; indeed, they can be wholly independent or even conflicting grounds for a favorable decision. First, there was "no actual breach" of the blockade because the ship was outside the blockade at the time that naval vessels seized it. Carlisle conceded that the ship had left the coast, but when it was taken it was not within the blockade. The master of the ship was trying to communicate with the naval vessel, seeking permission to return to Mexican waters, when it was boarded. He had no intention of violating the blockade. Note that this argument presumed that the blockade was legal and that the master of the *Brilliante* knew about it. "He swears that he had no intention to violate the blockade.

There is nothing to contradict him, but everything corroborates his declaration."[35]

The second argument rested on a brief review of American policy with respect to its own neutrality in other nations' wars and the structure of American federalism. "The condition of things was unprecedented. From the nature and structure of our peculiar system of government, it could have had no precedent." The same limitation arose from the Constitution itself: "The co-existence of Federal and State sovereignties, and the double allegiance of the people of the States, which no statesman or lawyer has doubted till now, and which this Court has repeatedly recognized as lying at the foundation of some of its most important decisions; the delegation of special and limited powers to the Federal Government, with the express reservation of all other powers 'to the States and the people thereof' who created the Union and established the Constitution." Might not his clients rest their case on these principles?[36]

A third argument drew from Carlisle's reading of Lincoln's intent. "Assuming the power to close the ports of the seceded States, he evidently did so with doubt and hesitation." Carlisle had no doubt heard—debates in Lincoln's cabinet were hardly confidential—that Welles and Bates had opposed the blockade. "Actually if the power be conceded to him, it cannot be denied that he might modify the strict law of blockade, and impose a qualified interruption of commerce. He might well have doubted whether, under the Constitution which he had sworn to support, a state of war could exist between a State, or States, and the Federal Union; whether, when it ceased to be insurrection, and became the formal and deliberate act of State sovereignty, his executive powers extended to such an exigency." The larger point Carlisle derived from this speculative foray into presidential thinking was that Lincoln did not have the authority under domestic law to impose a blockade and knew it.[37]

The oddity in Carlisle's argument, never expressed despite the fact that he surely was aware of it, was that the Confederacy had declared that a state of war existed between it and the United States of America as early as May 6, 1861. Then, the Provisional Confederate Congress passed an act recognizing the existence of war between the United States and the Confederate States. Given this, and the act's further provisions for letters of marque, captures and seizures of property, all before the US Congress's first confiscation act, could Carlisle have argued as he did that ships attempting to evade the federal blockade had no reason to assume its legality? When one side declares that war exists, even if the other side (in this case the Union) subsequently regards the conflict as a domestic insurrection, surely the laws of war permit a blockade. Even if Lincoln's call for volunteers to put down a rebellion in April preceded the Confederate legislation, passage of this legislation created the presumption that a war existed.[38]

Carlisle's next argument was based on Lincoln's categorization of the conflict as a domestic insurrection rather than a war against a foreign power, ignoring the posture that the Confederacy had taken prior to Lincoln's address to Congress, in July 1861. "The President, so late as his message of July . . . believed that the State sovereignties had been usurped by discontented leaders and a factious and inconsiderable minority. With the information laid before him, he declared that these seceded States were full of people devoted to the Union." If this were so, then he could not impose the blockade—that would be an act of war against his own people.[39]

Carlisle then turned to the text of the proclamation. The "disturbance to be by 'a combination of persons'" in Lincoln's proclamation "are not at all recognized as presenting a case for belligerent rights and obligations." Lincoln presumably knew this when, "naturally and prudently, the President did not assume to proclaim a strict blockade, with the extreme rights which obtain between belligerents, and with the corresponding rights of neutrals . . . . But he knew that this was not war. It was the suppression of insurrection." Lincoln even told the British, through Seward, that "to attribute anything of belligerent right to these 'combinations of persons' and these 'unlawful proceedings,' was an outrage and an offence to the United States. In effect, his position was that it was purely a municipal question; and of course, there could be no blockade, in the international sense, and no capture jure belli."[40]

Carlisle insisted that the proclamation "was made during that period when the President, casting about among doubtful expedients," and "the [legal] question here is, how can the United States, under the Constitution, be involved in war?" Carlisle provided the answer to his own question. "It is plain that there was no municipal law by which it could be justified. The President cannot make, alter, or suspend 'the supreme law of the land'; and this condemnation rests solely upon his authority." Was there then a basis in international law for Lincoln's policy? Lincoln thought so, but Carlisle responded, "Blockade is a belligerent right. There must be war, before there can be blockade in the international sense, giving jurisdiction in prize." But the proclamation and subsequent policy explicitly denied that the United States was at war.[41]

Carlisle had listened carefully to what Dana had argued for the government in the first of the cases. "The counsel for the United States, speaking for the President, take[s] very bold and very alarming positions upon this question. One of them testifies, in well-considered rhetoric, his amazement that a judicial tribunal should be called on to determine whether the political power was authorized to do what it has done. He is astounded that he should be required to 'ask permission of your Honors for the whole political power of the Government to exercise the ordinary right of self-defence.' He pictures to himself how the world will be appalled when it finds that 'one of our Courts' has decided that 'the war is at an end.'" By "one of our courts" Carlisle was here referring to Chief Justice Taney's opinion in *Ex Parte Merryman*, standing at the bar and facing the same chief justice. Taney must have been nodding, if not smiling, to hear Carlisle's adaptation of his opinion. "What place is this, where such thoughts are uttered? If the question were asked literally, and the dull walls of this old Senate Hall could comprehend and answer, they would give back in echoes the voices of departed patriots and statesmen—'this place is sacred to the Constitution of the United States.'"[42]

Black's transcription of Carlisle's oral argument did not include any form of diacritical marks, but one can imagine Carlisle's feigned indignation as he offered these oratorical passages. The justices did not have to be reminded of the separation of powers, or of the place of their Court in the structure of federal government, but Carlisle argued in the tradition that Lincoln, Seward, Chase, and Douglas had also mastered—a little high dudgeon did not hurt. Again, the justices were not a country jury and were not likely to be swayed, but Carlisle knew that many in the North had strongly approved Taney's tongue-lashing of Lincoln and viewed the blockades as another example of overweening executive discretion. "But what tribunal is this? Is it 'one of our Courts?' Does it sit 'by commission of the sovereign?' Who is its sovereign? and what is its commission?" The high dudgeon of Carlisle's condemnation of Lincoln's conduct recalled Taney's tone in *Merryman*. Whether meant as imitation or as homage to the chief, it was typical of the high style of antebellum Supreme Court oratory. Whether it persuaded anyone of anything was another matter entirely.[43]

It was the president and the proclamation that violated the law of the land, according to Carlisle. "This is a Government created, defined, and limited by a written Constitution, every article, clause, and expression in which was pondered and criticised, as probably no document in the affairs of men was ever before tested, refined, and ascertained." Nowhere in that document did the word "necessity" appear, nor did the framers contemplate giving to presidents dictatorial powers in time of insurrection or war. "The matter then comes back necessarily to the pure question of the power of the President under the Constitution. And this is, perhaps, the most extraordinary part of the argument for the United States . . . . It makes the President, in some sort, the impersonation of the country." Carlisle went even further: "This is to assert that the Constitution contemplated and tacitly provided that the President should be dictator, and all constitutional Government be at an end, whenever he should think that 'the life of the nation' is in danger. To suppose that this Court would desire argument against such a notion, would be offensive."[44]

The case was submitted on February 23 and the Court's decision was announced on March 10, 1863—a very short time by modern standards, but understandable given the exigencies of the war. Justice Grier wrote the majority opinion, with which Justices Swayne, Miller, Davis, and Wayne agreed. Nelson wrote in dissent, joined by the chief justice, Clifford, and Catron. The votes aligned with the politics of the members of the Court, but in the American judicial system, courts of law are not supposed to be political forums. Unlike the cut and thrust of politics in the legislative bodies and the highly partisan conduct of elected executives, "equal justice under law," the aphorism in the pediment of the Supreme Court building today, is assumed to reflect the ideal of judgment in the federal courts. Studies of actual cases reveal that this ideal, even were it applied in every case, cannot fully describe what happens in individual cases. Lawyers in actual cases choose among various lines of attack and defense. Judges in them apply a variety of sometimes conflicting precedents and interpret statutes in opposing ways. This "indeterminacy" in outcomes is present to some degree in every civil lawsuit and criminal prosecution. Most cases have very low political stakes and participants' roles are constrained by precedent, statute, and procedural rules that do not have a partisan bias. By contrast, the law in high-stakes cases like the treason and piracy cases, and the *Prize Cases*, was indeterminate precisely because so much rested on their outcome. The lawyers who argued them and the judges who decided them thus played two parts. One was the conventional role of advocacy and judgement according to law; the other was setting policy for the government. While the lawyers insisted that they were giving their clients the best counsel and the judges proclaimed the neutrality of their opinions, everyone watching the cases knew that their outcome would shape the fate of the warring parties.[45]

Grier began, "That the President, as the Executive Chief of the Government and Commander-in-chief of the Army and Navy, was the proper person" to announce the blockade "has not been, and cannot be disputed." Nor could anyone deny that "the right of prize and capture has its origin in the 'jus belli,' and is governed and adjudged under the law of nations." So long as the war actually existed, the blockade was legitimate. The only question remaining was "whether, at the time this blockade was instituted, a state of war existed which would justify a resort to these means of subduing the hostile force."[46]

It was then not uncommon, and remains so to this day, for the judge to borrow from counsels' briefs. Major portions and key ideas from Dana's brief animated Grier's opinion. "War has been well defined to be, 'That state in which a nation prosecutes its right by force.'" It was not "necessary to constitute war, that both parties should be acknowledged as independent nations or sovereign States. A war may exist where one of the belligerents, claims sovereign rights as against the other." A civil war was as much a war as a conflict between nations. "Insurrection against a government may or may not culminate in an organized rebellion, but a civil war always begins by insurrection against the lawful authority of the Government." One need not have a formal declaration of war (a hint that Grier did not buy the argument that Lincoln should have waited for Congress to meet). "A civil war is never solemnly declared; it becomes such by its accidents—the number, power, and organization of the persons who originate and carry it on." Belligerent status lay in the actions of the rebel, a set of facts that applied to secession: "When the party in rebellion occupy and hold in a hostile manner a certain portion of territory; have declared their independence; have cast off their allegiance; have organized armies; have commenced hostilities against their former sovereign, the world acknowledges them as belligerents, and the contest a war." A corollary to this proposition was that "the parties to a civil war usually concede to each other belligerent rights. They exchange prisoners, and adopt the other courtesies and rules common to public or national wars."[47]

Grier next turned to face head-on the blockade runners' cavil that Lincoln had overstepped his constitutional powers. "By the Constitution, Congress alone has the power to declare a national or foreign war. It cannot declare war against a State, or any number of States, by virtue of any clause in the Constitution," however, setting the Constitution against the clear language of the militia acts. Under these, "the Constitution confers on the President the whole Executive power. He is bound to take care that the laws be faithfully executed . . . . [H]e has no power to initiate or declare a war either against a foreign nation or a domestic State." One might question whether this was the intent of the framers of Articles I and II, "But by the Acts of Congress of February 28th, 1795, and 3d of March, 1807, he is authorized to called out the militia and use the military and naval forces of the United States in case of invasion by foreign nations, and to suppress insurrection against the government of a State or of the United States." Common sense told Grier, "It is not the less a civil war, with belligerent parties in hostile array, because it may be called an 'insurrection' by one side, and the insurgents be considered as rebels or traitors."[48]

Like Dana, Grier elevated common sense to a guide to the law of war. "The law of nations is also called the law of nature; it is founded on the common consent as well as the common sense of the world. It contains no such anomalous doctrine as that which this Court are now for the first time desired to pronounce, to wit: That insurgents who have risen in rebellion against their sovereign, expelled her Courts, established a revolutionary government, organized armies, and commenced hostilities, are not enemies because they are traitors; and a war levied on the Government by traitors, in order to dismember and destroy it, is not a war because it is an 'insurrection.' "[49]

There was a more difficult question: "What is included in the term 'enemies' property?' Is the property of all persons residing within the territory of the States now in rebellion, captured on the high seas, to be treated as 'enemies' property' whether the owner be in arms against the Government or not?" Again, the precise denotation of the term did not matter to Grier so much as the context of the usage. The seizing of an enemy's property "is a necessary result of a state of war." The doctrine applied on the high seas as it did on land. The opposite assumption, "that where a civil war exists, the party belligerent claiming to be sovereign, cannot, for some unknown reason, exercise the rights of belligerents, although the revolutionary party may," made no sense.[50]

Nelson's dissenting opinion in the *Prize Cases* was somewhat more learned than Grier's and rested squarely on what Lincoln before the war had called "the old Constitution" of limited federal powers and strict separation of the powers of the branches of government. In this sense, the very same set of cases, under the very same laws, resulted in an opinion the exact opposite of Grier's. Nelson shunned the references to common sense and practicality that Grier's opinion and Dana's brief featured. He countered that presidential powers were limited rather than enlarged by the laws of war in the law of nations. "It has been said that the proclamation, among other grounds, as stated on its face, is founded on the 'law of nations,' and hence draws after it the law of blockade as found in that code." Lincoln could cite the laws of war as empowering him to order the blockade, but if he did, then the rights of the neutral vessels should not have been abridged. "This view of the proclamation seems to have been entertained by the Secretary of the Navy, under whose orders it was carried into execution." Citing Welles's hesitancy was more or less window dressing, as Welles served at the pleasure of the president, and his views were not legally cognizable, but Nelson was hunting about for grounds to reinterpret the application of the Proclamation. Thus far, he nibbled at the edges of an argument rather than biting deeply.[51]

Nelson clearly felt more confident if he could avoid the practical question (that is, the relation between the blockade and the ultimate triumph of the Union). He found a precedent that undercut Dana's argument. Reasoning from precedent was the essence of common law, that is, letting a prior decision on a case with a similar fact pattern under the same laws determine the outcome of the present case: "The question [of notice to a neutral vessel in time of war that a blockade exists] is not a new one in this Court." Nelson cited Chief Justice John Marshall's opinion in *Maryland Insurance Company v. Woods* (1810), that when an American vessel comes upon an English blockade of its French enemy's possession in the Caribbean, "that . . . vessel cannot be placed in the situation of one having notice of the blockade until she is warned off. It gives her a right to inquire of the blockading squadron, if she shall not receive this warning from one capable of giving it, and, consequently, dispenses with her making that inquiry elsewhere." This precedent, according to Carlisle, applied to the *Brilliante* while it lay at anchor in Biloxi Bay. "We are of the opinion, therefore, that, according to the very terms of the proclamation, neutral ships were entitled to a warning by one of the blockading squadron and could be lawfully seized only on the second attempt to enter or leave the port."[52]

Nelson was not known as a natural law jurist, but he understood Carlisle's argument about the laws of war well enough. And he agreed with Carlisle: "Another objection taken to the seizure of this vessel and cargo is, that there was no existing war between the United States and the States in insurrection within the meaning of the law of nations, which drew after it the consequences of a public or civil war." The distinction between domestic and foreign wars that Dana and Grier called unrealistic Nelson thought crucial to the case. "The legal consequences resulting from a state of war between two countries at this day are well understood, and will be found described in every approved work on the subject of international law." Even a civil war may be waged as if it were such a foreign war, but Congress had not declared war when the Proclamation was published, and even when Congress met, it did not declare war. "For we find there that to constitute a civil war in the sense in which we are speaking, before it can exist, in contemplation of law, it must be recognized or declared by the sovereign power of the State." That power "by our Constitution is lodged in the Congress of the United States—civil war, therefore, under our system of government, can exist only by an act of Congress, which requires the assent of two of the great departments of the Government, the Executive and Legislative." Lincoln's authority as commander in chief and his oath to preserve and defend, and his duty to see that the laws were obeyed, could not be exercised without the explicit consent of Congress. His discretion did not extend to the proclamation of a blockade any more than he could declare a war, foreign or domestic, on his own authority.[53]

Nelson now turned to the ultimate source of authority on the Constitution—its framers—just as had Lincoln in his Cooper Union address. Using originalism to construe the meaning of the fundamental laws was not an invention of Attorney General Edwin Meese or Justice Antonin Scalia in the 1980s. It was a well-established constitutional heuristic in the nineteenth century. "The framers of the Constitution fully comprehended this question, and provided for the contingency." The framers gave to Congress the power to call forth the militia and to declare and prosecute a war. "From their experience with the monarchical tyranny of George III, they rightfully were wary of giving the president untrammeled military authority."[54]

Nelson conceded that "ample provision has been made under the Constitution and laws against any sudden and unexpected disturbance of the public peace from insurrection at home or invasion from abroad." Once the war was set in motion, "the whole military and naval power of the country is put under the control of the President to meet the emergency. He may call out a force in proportion to its necessities, one regiment or fifty, one ship-of-war or any number at his discretion." But Lincoln could not declare the existence of any war on his own authority. "The [militia] Acts of 1795 and 1805 did not, and could not under the Constitution, confer on the President the power of declaring war against a State of this Union, or of deciding that war existed, and upon that ground authorize the capture and confiscation of the property of every citizen of the State whenever it was found on the waters." That authority belonged only to Congress. Nelson's conceptualization of a strict and limiting separation of powers, like Buchanan's in his December and January messages to Congress, limited the executive to executing the will of another branch. "This great power over the business and property of the citizen is reserved to the legislative department by the express words of the Constitution. It cannot be delegated or surrendered to the Executive. Congress alone can determine whether war exists or should be declared; and until they have acted, no citizen of the State can be punished in his person or property, unless he has committed some offence against a law of Congress passed before the act was committed, which made it a crime, and defined the punishment." Nelson invented a term for the excessive and illegal use of presidential power against the seceding states. "So the war carried on by the President against the insurrectionary districts in the Southern States, as in the case of the King of Great Britain in the American Revolution, was a personal war against those in rebellion," but Lincoln, in a constitutional system, did not have the residual powers that the king had.[55]

Giving the forceful condemnation of presidential excess in the body of his opinion, Nelson's conclusion was curiously modest. It did not have the righteous wrath of Taney's opinion in *Merryman*, certainly, which may be why Nelson, rather than Taney, wrote the dissent (although another reason was that Taney, who had been ill for the past half dozen years, was no longer up to the task). For Nelson, the conclusion was obvious: "Upon the whole, after the most careful consideration of this case which the pressure of other duties has admitted, I am compelled to the conclusion that no civil war existed between this Government and the States in insurrection till recognized by the Act of Congress 13th of July, 1861; that the President does not possess the power under the Constitution to declare war or recognize its existence within the meaning of the law of nations, which carries with it belligerent rights, and thus change the country and all its citizens from a state of peace to a state of war; that this power belongs exclusively to the Congress of the United States, and, consequently, that the President had no power to set on foot a blockade under the law of nations, and that the capture of the vessel and cargo in this case, and in all cases before us in which the capture occurred before the 13th of July, 1861, for breach of blockade, or as enemies' property, are illegal and void, and that the decrees of condemnation should be reversed and the vessel and cargo restored."[56]

By conceding that Congress had the authority to order a blockade, even against domestic rebels, Nelson perhaps inadvertently did something that Dana and the other government lawyers wanted: he made the suppression of the rebellion legal. Carlisle and Taney may not have agreed, but there could be no doubt after the piracy and *Prize Cases* that blockades and confiscation were constitutional.

Even more important, both the majority and the minority opinions could be read to say that criminal prosecution of some of the Confederates for their conduct was licit. Just what that conduct might be was not clear in the opinions, but in another part of Washington, DC, in the office of the Department of War, lawyers were working on that very question.

In 1862, Secretary of War Stanton and Henry Halleck, a West Point graduate, lawyer, and politician who served as head of the army, asked continental law scholar and Columbia University professor Francis Lieber to compose a code for the conduct of the war in the field. The idea for codes for the conduct of war is almost as old as organized warfare itself, but written commentary on international law, including treatment of the enemy in time of war, first appeared during and after the religious wars of the seventeenth century. The general thrust of these was the limitation of the despoliation of the enemy, particularly noncombatant or civilian populations. The problem was not the enforcement of these strictures but the prevention of illicit conduct. The code would define what acts were permissible in the federal conduct of the war. By implication, the code would also indicate what acts by Confederate troops and officers were permissible, and which would merit criminal prosecution by military tribunals. Not so hidden away was the question of the treatment of prisoners of war. Their liability to criminal penalties was increasingly important, as more and more men on both sides found themselves in this condition. This code went into force in 1863 and remains the basis of US martial law. Once again, by this intervention, lawyers helped make the Civil War far more civil than most domestic insurrections.[57]

In 1855, Halleck had left a military career behind to establish himself as one of California's leading real estate and mining lawyers. In the course of his lawyering, he had occasion to cross swords with Stanton, the two of them representing opposing mining interests. But both men were strong unionists and this brought them together in 1862, Halleck as the newly appointed head of the armed forces and Stanton as secretary of war. Stanton did not care for Halleck, thinking him an unscrupulous litigator (much the same opinion that Stanton's critics expressed of him), though Halleck's success in the western theater of the war in 1862 had by far exceeded what the Army of the Potomac had done under its commander George B. McClellan. Over time, the two strong personalities of Stanton and Halleck would clash in Washington as they had in court, but they learned to work together in the prosecution of the war.[58]

From his Columbia office in New York City, Prussian immigrant Francis Lieber offered his services to Halleck, as a "personal friend." A republican advocate in his home country's monarchical system, he had left Prussia for England in 1825 and then the United States two years later. He began his career as an educator in Boston and later in Columbia, South Carolina, where he taught history and philosophy. In 1856, he returned to the North and joined the faculty at Columbia University. By this time Lieber was recognized as the foremost academic authority on the subject of jurisprudence, the science of the law, in the United States. For example, Lieber's 1838 treatise on statutory interpretation, *Legal and Political Hermeneutics, or Principles of Interpretation and Construction in Law and Politics*, was the first of the modern tracts on the subject. A strong unionist and vigorous opponent of slavery, Lieber pressed Halleck to take up the subject of a code for the treatment of noncombatants and prisoners of war. Halleck tried to fend off the insistent professor, but by the end of 1862, clearly some form of martial law code was necessary. In February 1863, the fruits of Lieber's labors arrived on Halleck's desk, went to Lincoln, and on April 24, 1863, the president approved the "Instructions for the Government of Armies of the United States in the Field"—General Order 100.[59]

Lieber's view of law was positivistic. That is, law was the command of the state that must be obeyed. But he assumed that all legal writings gave their full meaning only after interpretation by the appropriate audience. "Interpretation of some sort or other is always requisite." In that effort, the code maker must offer a compendium of "true and safe principles of interpretation." He recognized that in a country with so many elective and appointive legal officers and lawyers, it would not be easy to arrive at easily applied rules. "The freer the country the more necessary becomes interpretation." Writing a code for the conduct of a civil war in a common law–based legal system like America's would not be easy.[60]

Add to this republican Tower of legal Babel the problems of applying eighteenth-century European ideas to a nineteenth-century American civil war, and Lieber's achievement becomes all the more noteworthy. The standard work on the subject was already a century old. Emmerich de Vattel's *Law of Nations* (1757) belonged to the Enlightenment, a time of reform and liberalization of law. Vattel concluded the third book of his *Law of Nations* with a section on civil wars that seemed to apply to the conduct of the civil war in 1863. "It is a question very much debated, whether a sovereign is bound to observe the common laws of war towards rebellious subjects who have openly taken up arms against him?" Punishment of former rebels was not the conduct of a good or wise sovereign. "Although it be his duty to repress those who unnecessarily disturb the public peace, he is bound to show clemency towards unfortunate persons, to whom just causes of complaint have been given, and whose sole crime consists in the attempt to do themselves justice." No one would deny that "subjects who rise against their prince without cause deserve severe punishment: yet, even in this case, on account of the number of the delinquents, clemency becomes a duty in the sovereign."[61]

As Lieber prepared a code for the conduct of Union army forces during the war, he surely had open on his desk a copy of Vattel. Lieber did not slavishly copy the Swiss diplomat, quite the opposite, but as an international law authority Lieber was writing not only for Halleck but for other international law scholars. Thus one has to understand Lieber's thinking both as jurisprudence and as advice to the Lincoln administration. Lieber was a proponent of total war—a war that would crush the Confederacy so thoroughly that it would never rise again. He was, thus, not an advocate of Vattel's notions of humane warfare, but he could not discard them entirely. For example, Vattel had argued that the property of private citizens in territory engaged in civil war should not be confiscated by the victor. Lincoln's blockade proclamation, strongly supported by Lieber, was the very opposite of Vattel's view. But Lieber included conditions, exceptions, and qualifications in his code to accommodate if not follow Vattel's view. What became General Order 100 thus had a dual quality, part academic, part martial.[62]

The General Order 100 had ten sections and 157 articles ranging from courts martial to the treatment of prisoners of war. The recruitment and deployment of African American troops by the federal government had made the question of who could be a prisoner of war a vital question. As Article 49 of Section III provided: "A prisoner of war is a public enemy armed or attached to the hostile army for active aid, who has fallen into the hands of the captor, either fighting or wounded, on the field or in the hospital, by individual surrender or by capitulation. All soldiers, of whatever species of arms; all men who belong to the rising en masse of the hostile country; all those who are attached to the army for its efficiency and promote directly the object of the war, except such as are hereinafter provided for; all disabled men or officers on the field or elsewhere, if captured; all enemies who have thrown away their arms and ask for quarter, are prisoners of war, and as such exposed to the inconveniences as well as entitled to the privileges of a prisoner of war." The concept was an old one, growing out of endless rounds of war on the European continent, and by 1863 it had been refined to a relatively simple formula: "A prisoner of war is subject to no punishment for being a public enemy, nor is any revenge wreaked upon him by the intentional infliction of any suffering, or disgrace, by cruel imprisonment, want of food, by mutilation, death, or any other barbarity."[63]

Prior to the promulgation of General Order 100, prisoners of war were exchanged. That process, unwieldy from its inception, ended in December 1862, when Jefferson Davis published Order 111: "(section 3). That all negro slaves captured in arms be at once delivered over to the executive authorities of the respective States to which they belong to be dealt with according to the laws of said States. (section 4). That the like orders be executed in all cases with respect to all commissioned officers of the United States when found serving in company with armed slaves in insurrection against the authorities of the different States of this Confederacy." In effect, provisions for prisoners of war in General Order 100 were an answer to Davis's decree. Nevertheless, Lincoln ended the exchange of prisoners of war, an act that resulted in the death from disease and starvation of many thousands of US and Confederate troops held in prisoner-of-war camps. The cost of this rule-of-law decision by Lincoln, and the racially motivated illegality of Davis's stance to which Lincoln responded, was a noteworthy incivility in an otherwise civil Civil War.[64]

General Order 100 anticipated a plan for postwar reconstruction. Section II concerned the "public and private property of the enemy": "A victorious army appropriates all public money, seizes all public movable property until further direction by its government, and sequesters for its own benefit or of that of its government all the revenues of real property belonging to the hostile government or nation. The title to such real property remains in abeyance during military occupation, and until the conquest is made complete." There was little new in this, as it seemed to recapitulate the Confiscation Acts. But Lieber inserted exceptions to these confiscations, and they told the military that this civil war did not criminalize Southern society and so authorize across the board confiscation as a criminal penalty for living in the Confederacy. "As a general rule, the property belonging to churches, to hospitals, or other establishments of an exclusively charitable character, to establishments of education, or foundations for the promotion of knowledge, whether public schools, universities, academies of learning or observatories, museums of the fine arts, or of a scientific character such property is not to be considered public property." The same was true of certain kinds of property. "Classical works of art, libraries, scientific collections, or precious instruments, such as astronomical telescopes, as well as hospitals, must be secured against all avoidable injury, even when they are contained in fortified places whilst besieged or bombarded." Although they might be removed and stored, "in no case shall they be sold or given away, if captured by the armies of the United States, nor shall they ever be privately appropriated, or wantonly destroyed or injured." In general, "The United States acknowledge and protect, in hostile countries occupied by them, religion and morality; strictly private property; the persons of the inhabitants, especially those of women: and the sacredness of domestic relations. Offenses to the contrary shall be rigorously punished."[65]

There was an exception to the list of exceptions that went directly to the legality of the confiscation of privately owned slaves. "Slavery, complicating and confounding the ideas of property, (that is of a thing,) and of personality, (that is of humanity,) exists according to municipal or local law only." Thus far, Lieber had laid no basis for the taking of slaves from persons not in rebellion. He added that "the law of nature and nations has never acknowledged it," that is, that one man could absolutely own another. The next sentence followed logically: "Therefore, in a war between the United States and a belligerent which admits of slavery, if a person held in bondage by that belligerent be captured by or come as a fugitive under the protection of the military forces of the United States, such person is immediately entitled to the rights and privileges of a freeman." Had Lieber just said, in passing, that the freedmen had civil rights and liberties, including the right to vote? He never explained, but events would prove him prescient.[66]

As a necessity or as the concomitant to punishing those guilty of inciting a civil war, the entire and permanent liberty of the confiscated slave may have been a defensible legal concept. In all wars, the notion that private property is untouchable vanishes. But the emancipation of the slaves of noncombatants did not rest on natural law jurisprudence or the Constitution, a point made by opponents of the view that all Confederates' slaves might be regarded as the contraband of war. Lieber's response to this view rested not on settled law but on an inference from one reading of natural law. "To return such person into slavery would amount to enslaving a free person, and neither the United States nor any officer under their authority can enslave any human being. Moreover, a person so made free by the law of war is under the shield of the law of nations."[67]

Lieber had begun this project in the summer of 1862. Between that time and the promulgation of Order 100 in April 1863 the Civil War lawyers in Lincoln's administration, led by the chief executive, had profoundly changed the nature and perhaps the purpose of the war. They had announced the freedom of all slaves in rebellious territory in the Emancipation Proclamation of January 1, 1863. Given this, Lieber's code could hardly have called for the postwar return of the slaves to their former masters.[68]

One student of the laws of war, Stephen Neff, has called the Lieber code "something of a masterpiece." Some credit for it should be shared among Lincoln, Halleck, Stanton, and the Department of War's solicitor William Whiting as well as Lieber. The code's implementation, however, depended on Joseph Holt, formerly of Buchanan's cabinet who now served as the advocate general—the chief lawyer—of the US Army. Holt was a Kentucky Democrat turned Republican, and though closely tied to the secessionists in his state, was by 1862 an "intransigent Unionist," and last but not least, a slaveholder who came to denounce slavery as a "ghastly offense" against "human rights."[69]

Holt made clear his intent to throw the weight of the advocate general's office behind the confiscation of slaves, and then the Emancipation Proclamation. The problem that Holt faced was that the Confederacy was a wartime enemy, but when military necessity did not dictate confiscation, the Lieber code barred unnecessary or revengeful destruction of life and property. On the border between these legal precepts lay the "incidental" damage the army might inflict on civilians and reprisals for violations of the laws of war. Today the former would be called and dismissed as "collateral" damage, but Union commanders took care to justify such damage as either necessary or purely accidental. In fact, they were required to submit such reports to Halleck when he was in charge and continued to do so even when Halleck served as General Ulysses S. Grant's subordinate. Reprisals, military responses to wrongful acts by the enemy, were "inherently" unlawful under the laws of war, in part because they struck at those who were not responsible for the initial wrong and in part because they might be out of proportion to the original wrong. The code nevertheless allowed them when no other means was available to suppress future unlawful acts by the enemy. The code did not cover other means of revenge, for example, the taking of hostages, the punishment of individual civilians for unspecific acts (like loyalty to the Confederacy), and outlawry (treating combatants as though they were common criminals). In fact, all of the above happened in border guerrilla conflicts, like that in Missouri, during the war.[70]

Regular courts and courts of military commission followed both federal criminal law and the Lieber code in instances of guerrilla warfare. In Missouri, for example, recruiting for the Confederate army and spying virtually shuttered the civil courts in 1861, as they recorded only one civil case and no criminal cases. But the next year 204 cases were initiated or continued, a total (averaging the two years) that was roughly comparable to the yearly dockets for the rest of the war. Although military provost marshals arrested suspects and answered only to the district military commanders rather than the federal courts' judges, regular criminal proceedings resumed against those suspected of conspiring against the federal government as well as those who did not pay taxes, hijacked postage stamps, and committed other less mundane offenses. In 1862 there were thirty prosecutions; in 1863, fifty-eight prosecutions;

in 1864, seventy-five prosecutions; and 1865, thirty-six prosecutions. These were based on grand jury indictments, though not all went to trial as the defendants disappeared into "the bush."[71]

Sometimes, as in the case of William T. Sherman, senior officers decided that General Order 100 must be loosely interpreted in light of the extent and ferocity of the rebellion. A West Point graduate and briefly a lawyer before the war, once again in uniform, Sherman decided that Confederate sympathizers were unregenerate law breakers. "All their people are armed and at war," he wrote to his brother Senator John Sherman in August 1862. Thereafter he promised to scourge the land of rebels, though his rhetoric was far worse than his and his subordinates' actual conduct. In any case, he was always providing legalistic explanations for his departures from the code, as he did in a letter to the mayor of Atlanta two years later, ordering its citizens to leave the city or face the consequences. "You cannot qualify war in harsher terms than I will. War is cruelty, and you cannot refine it; and those who brought war into our country deserve all the curses and maledictions a people can pour out. I know I had no hand in making this war, and I know I will make more sacrifices to-day than any of you to secure peace. But you cannot have peace and a division of our country."[72]

Sherman's prewar legal career was short, but during and after it he evinced an almost autocratic faith in law and order. Other senior officers, themselves lawyers before the war, held court during it. These provost marshal courts, as in Missouri, had ill-defined but great discretion. Some of their duties were administrative—overseeing recruiting, for example. Other duties pertained solely to the army—such as capturing and dealing with deserters. Much of their story belongs to the postwar period, but in one case, that of Rose Herera, one can see how martial law, the legal spirit, and a lawyer's outlook influenced Major General Nathaniel Banks, commander of Union forces in occupied New Orleans at the end of the war. A former governor of Massachusetts and Democrat turned Republican, Banks "had never done well as a lawyer" though he did practice and thought highly of the profession. In the provost marshal's court for the city, he heard former slave Herera's suit to hold her former mistress, Mary DeHart, in jail for kidnapping Rose's three oldest children and spiriting them away to Cuba after federal forces occupied New Orleans. Banks faced a predicament for there was no federal law of kidnapping (except at sea), and a civil court, to which Rose had first appealed, found no grounds in Louisiana state law for detaining Mary. Nor was there any clear violation of military orders regarding the occupation of the city or the freeing of its slave population. The state had passed legislation ending slavery, but Mary had acted before that law was passed. The emancipation proclamation did not apply, because in January 1863, when Mary took the children to Cuba, New Orleans was in Union hands, no longer part of the rebel South. But Banks felt that there was an equity, a justice, in the law that Mary had willfully violated. He found grounds in Louisiana's slave law, an ironic place to look surely, that forbade the selling of a slave mother's infant (under the age of ten) children away from her. On this he based his judgement. Mary was to return to Cuba and bring the children back.[73]

In cases like this, lawyers in blue had to apply an uncertain law to unclear cases under the most straitened circumstances. That they were able to do just that showed how strong the rule of law tradition was, even in times of violence. Not every decision favored the slaves or former slaves, nor did every union lawyer/soldier see the world as Banks and Sherman did. But important lawyers in Washington had come to the conclusion that the emancipation question lay at the center of the war—and any peace that followed.

# 5

# An Emancipation Proclamation

LINCOLN AND THE LAWYER/POLITICIANS in Washington, DC, with the exception of a handful of abolitionists in the Republican Party, had not at first regarded slavery as the crucial issue it would become. By contrast, from the outset of the war the abolitionists had seen in secession a way to end slavery. As lawyer, reformer, and fiery orator Wendell Phillips had told a Boston audience in December 1861, "Indeed, the only way, the only sure way, to break this Union, is to try to save it by protecting slavery." They recognized that the protection of slavery was the reason Southerners voted for secession, but the purpose of the war was to suppress a domestic insurrection by the free population of the Confederacy. Still, because slavery was at the center of the controversy and because slaves could be found on or near every potential battlefield, the Civil War lawyers had to develop a policy to deal with it. While the majority of the Republicans were willing to pass confiscation acts and rescind the Fugitive Slave Act of 1850, they resisted anything as radical as the abolition of slavery. The press of events, however, would force their hand.[1]

Prior to the war, Benjamin Butler was a successful lawyer and politician in Massachusetts. He had no pronounced views on slavery itself, though by the 1850s he was a Free Soil Democrat and campaigned for Buchanan. Almost by accident he was one of the first of the lawyer/politicians to formulate a policy for the disposition of slaves. At the inception of hostilities, Butler commanded the Union forces on the

James River's Fort Monroe, across the Hampton Roads from Newport News, Virginia. To him came a number of slaves who rowed themselves across Mill Creek from the Confederate fortifications on which they had been working. At first, Butler was unsure of what to do with the escapees, and higher command offered little help. He believed that the "holding of slaves" was sanctioned by law, and he was not opposed to slavery in peacetime. He decided to regard the runaways as the contraband of war, in part because they were aiding the war effort of an enemy, in part because he needed their labor for his own fortification. It was a policy that was soon adopted by the Union in other theaters of the war and Congress included it in the First Confiscation Act of 1861.[2]

On August 3, 1862, a sweltering day in the capital relieved only the by promise of late afternoon rain, Lincoln summoned his cabinet. The mood was somber. General George McClellan's Peninsula offensive had ended in failure and retreat. The war looked endless to Salmon Chase. Now was the time, he thought, to raise the question on all their minds—what to do about slavery. "I expressed my conviction for the tenth or twentieth time," he recorded in his journal, "that the time for the suppression of the rebellion without interference with slavery had long passed." His solution rested on the way in which the administration had chosen to wage the war. "We had elected to operate on the principles of a civil war, in which assuming that the whole population of every seceding state was engaged against the Federal Government, instead of treating the active secessions as insurgents and exerting our utmost energies for their arrest and punishment." That is, instead of treating the individual secessionists as traitors, the enemy was the entire white population of the Confederacy. Chase offered as proof of the correctness of that approach that "the bitternesses of the conflict had now substantially united the white population of the rebel states against us." Without saying so, Chase was telling Lincoln that his long-held belief in the unionist sentiments of a majority of Southerners could no longer be sustained, and that meant that slave property of all Confederates could be confiscated. "The loyal whites remaining, if they would not prefer the Union without slavery, certainly would not prefer slavery to the Union," hence they would not object, in the end, if reunion cost them their slaves. Chase did not believe that and rapidly moved on to his major point, "that the blacks were really the only loyal population worth counting, and that, in the Gulf States at least [where Union forces controlled the coastlines], their right to freedom ought to be at once recognized." He had an ally. "Mr. Seward expressed himself as in favor of any measure likely to accomplish the results I contemplated," but he preferred that they be "without proclamations." Lincoln was not quite convinced, and though "pretty well cured of objections to any measure except want of adaptedness to put down the rebellion," he did not think that the time had come "for the adoption of such a plan as I proposed."[3]

As Seward conceded and Lincoln recognized, slavery was the most comprehensive and difficult-to-resolve legal question that secession and the Civil War raised. Slavery was not mentioned by name in the federal Constitution, and before the war, abolitionists insisted that omission meant that slavery was unconstitutional. In *Dred Scott*, the High Court rejected that view. Slavery was a matter of domestic (state) law and would remain so. Taney's opinion could even be read as implying that Congress could not bar slaveholders from bringing their slaves into the territories. Although candidate Lincoln had little good to say of that decision or of slavery itself, he understood that it was the law of the land. Thus President Lincoln's first efforts with regard to slavery, declaring slaves who contributed to the Confederate war effort contraband of war, and later by offering federal compensation to slave owners who freed their bondmen and women, did not address the general emancipation of slaves. He next turned to what became the Emancipation Proclamation, resting it on a complex argument about presidential powers in wartime.[4]

The discussion in the cabinet meeting on August 3, 1862, came when Lincoln was already leaning toward emancipation as a wartime expedient. Announced on September 22, 1862, and applying only to those portions of the country still in rebellion on January 1, 1863, the proclamation did not free many slaves. For example, it did not apply to slavery in the loyal border states, or even to those parts of Confederate states by then in federal hands, like New Orleans. Yet even in New Orleans, it was assumed by many that "By the Emancipation Proclamation of the President, Slavery is everywhere abolished—the institution is legally extinct—the title is defective, and cannot be made good. To such an extent is this the case, the acknowledgment of the independence of the

Confederate States to-day would not restore the negro to slavery, for the still acknowledged supreme law of the land has declared that such an institution does not exist." Former Supreme Court justice Benjamin Curtis, no friend to slavery himself, also saw it as a first and giant step toward ending slavery and condemned it along with the block-ade because he thought that Lincoln's wartime powers did not include the legal authority to take private property from noncombatants. The question was joined by Harvard law professor Joel Parker, William Whiting in the Department of War, and Edward Bates, among others. Not so hidden in this virtual exchange of legal briefs was the ques-tion of whether the president intended the abolition of slavery—that is, whether freeing the slaves of a wartime enemy would become a wider and permanent freeing of all slaves when the war was over.[5]

Before that fateful September, Lincoln's hesitation to act beyond confis-cation of runaway slaves might or might not have been due to "antebel-lum legal culture," as the foremost student of the emancipation project, Eric Foner, has written. Pressured by Chase in the cabinet and Senator Charles Sumner of Massachusetts to make the contest become one of "freedom and slavery," Lincoln still hesitated. Caution had marked Lincoln's every step thus far in the war, and the opposition to a more general emancipation policy that smacked of abolitionism infuriated his administration's Democratic allies. But caution had its limits and its exceptions. Chief among the latter was Benjamin Butler, now in command in New Orleans. Closely watched by Lincoln and his cabi-net members, Butler told Chase that he did not need executive action to free slaves from their Louisiana masters. "The Acts of Congress," meaning the confiscation acts, were in his mind tantamount to ending slavery, notwithstanding quibbles about and by unionist planters whose slaves found refuge in Butler's city.[6]

Butler (like Chase, Seward, and members of Congress like James Ashley and James Wilson) was ahead of the president. Through the spring and summer of 1862, opposition to both limited emancipation and general emancipation had come from those very individuals who had defended slavery before the Civil War—Southern unionists and Southern sympathizers in the Northern Democratic Party. Whether or not they served the Union in a political or a military capacity, their views matched those of the Southerners who had pledged their loyalty to the Confederacy. Not all subscribed to Alexander Stephens's "cornerstone" notion that a true democracy could only be built on the backs of slaves, but they opposed any radical alteration of the nation's social and legal system.[7]

For example, in April 1862, when discussions of a proposed second confiscation act spread throughout the North, New Hampshire's Joel Parker, a professor of law at Harvard Law School, warned that confiscating slaves who came into Union lines was not the same as freeing them. His *Constitutional Law, with Reference to the Present Condition of the United States*, insisted "there is no more authority to declare, by a general law, that the slaves of all rebels shall be free, than there is to declare, summarily, by a similar law, that all rebels shall be hanged, without a trial." Established law demanded that no property be confiscated without individual legal proceedings—a stifling legalism that suffused Lincoln's cabinet in that month. Parker added that should the "duty" that the slave owes to his master be temporarily terminated by the conditions of war, after the war the slave was legally bound to return, or be returned, to his master through the operation of the Fugitive Slave Act of 1850.[8]

In a pamphlet widely reprinted and widely read, Boston lawyer (and after publication, War Department solicitor) William Whiting weighed in to defend the president's war powers. Whiting had been a student at Harvard Law School and studied international law with Justice Joseph Story there. Whiting began by explaining that slavery in 1862 was not the same as slavery in 1787. In 1787, slavery was national. In the Civil War era it was sectional. In 1787, there was no significant abolitionist movement. In 1860, the South was almost alone in clinging to its peculiar institution. Most of the Northern states, along with Britain and France, had abolished slavery. Where it existed in the United States, the privilege of owning slaves was qualified, not absolute. That privilege was lost when slaveholders raised rebellion. If the legal destruction of this privilege was the price of saving the Union, leaders of the Union should have no qualms about destroying slavery. The rebellious slaveholder had brought it on himself. On other grounds, if the defense of the Union were abetted by freeing four million men and women, then "justice and humanity" would be served as well. The Constitution contained within it all that was necessary for the preservation of a perpetual union. This included the taking of private property including slaves for public use, a step the Confederacy had already taken, Whiting noted. The freeing of slaves on land who aided the rebellion was the same as the seizing of ships on the seas—a clear reference to the constitutionality of the blockade proclamation. The former were not fugitives from labor and so did not come under the rubric of the 1850 act. Instead, the president, when he deemed it necessary and appropriate to "weakening the enemy," had entire discretion on how and where to free slaves. Whiting insisted that nothing in the law of nations forbade this step (the inverse of Carlisle's argument that nothing in the law of nations permitted it). Indeed, Britain had done just that in the Revolutionary War and the War of 1812—surely one of the oddest of the many inversions of history and law in the Emancipation Proclamation debate.[9]

More important to Lincoln than doubts about the legitimacy of confiscation were the growing manpower needs of the army. Year-long volunteers might remain and a draft might augment the numbers in arms, but recruitment of free blacks and former slaves was one answer he could not ignore. Along with more conservative Republicans in Congress, Lincoln pressed for a new Militia Act that would allow the service of confiscated slaves. Congress passed the act along with a second and more far-reaching confiscation act in mid-July. But Lincoln was already thinking about a more thoroughgoing blow to recalcitrant rebels: the emancipation of slaves who were not presently within Union lines, but resided in the Confederacy. Chase pushed Lincoln in this direction. So did former slave and now leading abolitionist Frederick Douglass. Bates was initially hesitant, but signed on. Seward advised Lincoln to wait until the Union armies had a victory. The defeat of Robert E. Lee's Army of Northern Virginia at Antietam Creek served the purpose. Lincoln announced the preliminary Emancipation Proclamation on September 22. It was to go into effect on January 1, 1863, unless the Confederacy conceded defeat and its states renounced their insurrection.[10]

The Emancipation Proclamation had the same origins and presumably the same legality as the original Blockade Proclamation. But the Supreme Court had not yet ruled that the blockade's first months, based solely on Lincoln's wartime powers, was constitutional. Emancipation might be regarded as an extension of the second Confiscation Act, but Congress did not take the opportunity to go as far as the Emancipation Proclamation proposed to go. For a time, a parallel proposal to arrange for a massive colonization of freemen in Africa, with on and off support from Lincoln, sputtered and then died. That notwithstanding, from the outset Lincoln made clear that the authority to emancipate lay within the wartime powers of the presidency, and that the purpose of the proclamation was the successful prosecution of the war. Though criticized by one later scholar for being "loaded down with lawyerish language" and another with being too "legalistic"—certainly accurate judgments of its prose—that in fact was its great strength. With his choice of language, Lincoln demonstrated his commitment to a lawful war. Moreover, by "using the language one lawyer puts to another," Lincoln, the foremost of the Civil War lawyers, had taken a step unthinkable under the old Constitution to which, in his inaugural address, Lincoln had pledged himself.[11]

Even though Lincoln had seemed to vacillate on the subject of emancipation in the weeks before he read the preliminary draft to the cabinet, no one who listened to him closely on the subject during those weeks could miss the tendency or direction of his thinking. He had given his assent to the Second Confiscation Act, and given even the narrowest deployment of the act, slaves were going to be freed. According to Harold Holzer, perhaps Lincoln's foremost modern biographer, "Certainly by the spring and early summer of 1862 he had set the table, commencing to issue a series of veiled albeit mixed messages about his future plans." After the cabinet meeting on August 3, he told Vice President Hannibal Hamlin, an abolitionist, and members of his cabinet Seward and Welles of his plan for an Emancipation Proclamation. If he was cautious, that was a lifelong trait. If he wanted to keep everyone in doubt, it was a rhetorical strategy that had long served him well. Compensated emancipation was always on the table, but never close to his plate. It would have been prohibitively expensive. If it also involved some form of economic bonus to freed slaves to migrate—all the worse for a nation already in debt for the war. Occam's razor here cut cleanly: no expenditure or effort was needed to proclaim the freedom of slaves in those areas still in rebellion.[12]

Still, one who preferred to read the proclamation narrowly might argue it was merely a gloss on the Second Confiscation Act. The latter, passed and signed on July 17, 1862, over two months before the proclamation, provided for the confiscation of the property, including slaves, of those in rebellion against the United States. There needed to be a trial and conviction of individuals who violated the law, but the slaves taken as a punishment for the offense did not have to have been used to support the Confederate war effort directly. In effect, the act emancipated the slaves of those convicted of rebellion. This was congressional confiscation rather than executive action. Lincoln might have asked Congress to frame a third act saying more or less what the Emancipation Proclamation said, but it might not have gained the approval of the more conservative Republicans and the Democrats. By imposing it himself, he avoided that possibility. He also demonstrated a personal commitment to emancipation that merely signing an act of Congress would not necessarily have shown.[13]

The "stating part" of the proclamation indicated Lincoln's authority for it: "I, Abraham Lincoln, President of the United States of America, and Commander-in-Chief of the Army and Navy thereof." No question could remain about the war powers origin of the emancipation. The purpose of the proclamation then followed: "Hereafter, as heretofore, the war will be prosecuted for the object of practically restoring the constitutional relation between the United States, and each of the States, and the people thereof, in which States that relation is, or may be, suspended or disturbed." Surely within Lincoln's powers as commander in chief and his oath to enforce the laws was his power to restore the Union. He included the proposal for compensated emancipation of slaves within the Union. "That it is my purpose, upon the next meeting of Congress to again recommend the adoption of a practical measure tendering pecuniary aid to the free acceptance or rejection of all slave States, so called, the people whereof may not then be in rebellion against the United States and which States may then have voluntarily adopted, or thereafter may voluntarily adopt, immediate or gradual abolishment of slavery within their respective limits." He also included recognition of the colonization project: "And that the effort to colonize persons of African descent, with their consent, upon this continent, or elsewhere, with the previously obtained consent of the

Governments existing there, will be continued." Nothing thus far in the proclamation strained his relations with the unionist Democrats, constitutional conservatives, or border state politicians, or exceeded the provisions of the Second Confiscation Act.[14]

Then Lincoln went beyond that earlier legal ground into territory that more radical Republicans and abolitionists had urged on him all along. "On the first day of January in the year of our Lord, one thousand eight hundred and sixty-three, all persons held as slaves within any State, or designated part of a State, the people whereof shall then be in rebellion against the United States shall be then, thenceforward, and forever free." Unlike the Second Confiscation Act, which referred to individuals in rebellion, the proclamation referred to territory. The term "forever free" answered the question of postwar status of the slaves. The instruction was directed to military personnel: "The executive government of the United States, including the military and naval authority thereof, will recognize and maintain the freedom of such persons, and will do no act or acts to repress such persons, or any of them, in any efforts they may make for their actual freedom." His office would determine which of those states was still in rebellion. All officers in military or naval service were to effectuate the proclamation (a tacit recognition that some of the officers were still resisting accepting slaves). No officer was to return a runaway to a former master, unless that master could prove that he had not taken up arms against the United States (shifting the burden of proof to the claimant, a reversal of provisions of the Fugitive Slave Act of 1850). "And I do hereby enjoin upon and order all persons engaged in the military and naval service of the United States to observe, obey, and enforce, within their respective spheres of service, the act, and sections above recited." When the war was over, the federal government would compensate loyal slave owners for the loss of their bondmen.[15]

Had it been issued in peacetime, presidential emancipation would have violated the Fifth Amendment to the Constitution. It provided "nor shall private property be taken for public use, without just compensation." Setting aside the "for public use" clause (the proclamation did not say that slaves freed under it were taken for public use, although in fact Union commanders routinely put runaway slaves to work before the proclamation was issued), nothing in the proclamation promised compensation to slave owners for their losses. In *Dred Scott*, Chief Justice Taney had relied on this text to find unconstitutional the Missouri Compromise and other acts of Congress that deprived slave owners of their property in federal territories without compensation. Unionist slaveholders in Confederate lands were not eligible for compensation for their freedmen and women, although they might seek compensation for other property taken by Union forces under the two confiscation acts. All the proclamation did was turn slaves in Confederate lands from property into persons—but this was a giant step. Compare the emancipation of slaves under the proclamation to the self-emancipation of slaves in, for example, the Haitian Revolution, and one can see how the Civil War lawyers had transformed the potential bloodbath of a slave uprising (the very event that Confederate leaders so feared) into an orderly process under fixed law.[16]

Neither of the Confiscation Acts addressed the permanent state of those slaves taken from an offender. That question was addressed by the one addition to the draft proclamation that the cabinet, principally Seward, had insisted on: the status of the slaves must not depend on the incumbent president. It could not be a personal or political condition. It must be a matter of law. Lincoln had originally included the phrase "present incumbent" in the document, potentially limiting the emancipation to his own term. Given that no one knew how long the rebellion and the war would continue, or if Lincoln would be reelected in 1864, the revision of the proclamation to drop "present incumbent" in favor of "forever free" set the federal government on the course to end slavery as a matter of law.[17]

Once again opposition to the preliminary proclamation came from the usual suspects: Southern unionists, proslavery Democrats, and even some members of Lincoln's own party. Postmaster General Montgomery Blair of Maryland (a slave state) insisted that the nation must remain white and the freedmen must emigrate or be colonized. Initially, Attorney General Bates agreed, but he later recanted. Much of this opposition lay in the deep ground of racism—the belief that people of color were inherently inferior. For those who opposed secession and supported the war solely to restore the Union, there was no contradiction in opposing the end of slavery.[18]

The question confronting Lincoln and his cabinet lawyers at the time was not how deep racism ran in the foundations of the country; it was the legality of the proclamation. Had the outcome of the *Prize Cases* already been determined, defenders of the emancipation program could have claimed a species of judicial support—for, like the blockade, emancipation was tied to wartime exigency. In both cases, the extraordinary exertion of presidential power would have been justified by the realities of war and the necessity of victory. But the preliminary Emancipation Proclamation, though coming over a year after the Blockade Proclamation, was moving parallel to rather than coming after the *Prize Cases*. The Second Confiscation Act was authority of a sort, but not precisely on point. In the end, it was on Lincoln's authority as commander in chief in time of domestic war, on his wartime powers, that the legality of the proclamation would rest.

There were three possible readings of the legitimate extent of Lincoln's use of war powers, each with a myriad of shadings: the first that he had overstepped those powers; the second that one must view each extraordinary measure within its military and political context (in effect that constitutional limitations on Lincoln's powers must not interfere with the successful prosecution of the war), and the third that the nature of the Civil War required that the other branches of government and public opinion defer to the president's own interpretation of the extent of his powers. All these interpretations of the legality of the proclamation were in play at the time. At stake as well was the relation between the president and the other branches of the federal government. Under the separation of powers doctrine reflected in the three distinct articles of the Constitution addressing the Congress, the presidency, and the Supreme Court, the powers and duties of each were distinct, but there were areas of discretion in each and the framers understood that each could check and balance the others. Thus presidential "legislation" and presidential imposition of criminal prosecution in the proclamations might be condemned as crossing over into the domain of the other branches. From the debates over emancipation in the cabinet and the text of the proclamation one may surmise that Lincoln understood this criticism and was trying to blunt it by exercising his war powers narrowly in this matter. After all, he described it as "a fit and necessary war measure for suppressing said rebellion." And so it was received in friendly quarters like the Republican *Providence* [Rhode Island] *Journal*. Its editor opined that taking slaves away from rebels was just like taking their houses and their arms. But such easy comparisons suggested that even among friends, Republican opinion regarded the slaves as property rather than persons—the very same distinction on which Southern proslavery thought rested. It was clear that the full implications of Lincoln's wartime emancipation policy were not understood by all those who supported it.[19]

It was precisely because Lincoln regarded the proclamation as law and his correspondence and message to Congress in December 1862 as political that the apparent contradiction between them disappears. The "old Constitution's" version of federalism—with its deference to the "domestic institutions" of the various states—was the legal obstacle Lincoln faced as he framed the proclamation. By rooting emancipation in the precise language of the Militia Acts rather than in the sweeping rhetoric of his other messages, Lincoln sought to ensure it would be read as a legal document. Short of saying something along the order of "the proclamation is legal, my comments on the issue otherwise are political," Lincoln's handling of the text made precisely that point. To be sure, Lincoln needed political support and public opinion to make the policy work—but political support and public opinion did not make (or unmake) the policy's legality.[20]

Lincoln's announcement of the emancipation policy on September 22, 1862, offered slaveholders in Confederate lands a carrot—return to the Union by the beginning of the new year, and slave property would not be touched. He probably knew that not many in the rebellious South would be able to take advantage of this offer, although some slaveholders might leave the Confederacy and journey, with their slaves, to slave states still in the Union. The delay was a political move to dampen criticism of the policy in the North.

Lincoln and the cabinet anticipated a chorus of protest against the emancipation plan within the free states. One potential source of this dissent was the Northern Democracy. Like Edward Bates, many of these Democrats were strong supporters of the Union and rejected all legal defenses of secession. At the same time, as debates in Congress over a proposed amendment to end slavery the next years would prove, some of these same Democrats agreed with Chief Justice Taney that free blacks could not be citizens. This was no longer a theoretical constitutional question when Lincoln proposed the Emancipation Proclamation. Secretary Chase in particular wanted the issue clarified, in part because he had been so vociferous in condemnation of Taney's *Dred Scott* obiter dictum that blacks could never be citizens. He turned to Bates for an advisory opinion. The resulting document had no force as law and was clearly choreographed within the cabinet before Bates caused it to be published on November 29, 1862. Bates took the question to be this: "Is a man legally incapacitated to be a citizen of the United States by the sole fact that he is a colored, and not a white man?" He found no clear answer in the law books and the records of the courts, ignoring Taney's views entirely. (One must bear in mind that Taney's opinion was not accepted by a majority of the justices—hence his view of the incapacity of colored men to be citizens was not a legal precedent.) Instead, the subject was "little understood" even after eighty years of American governance. "The Constitution of the United States does not declare who are and who are not citizens," except in a reference to "natural born citizens." The implication was that the Constitution recognized a kind of birthright citizenship. The Constitution also permitted citizenship through naturalization, and no one was denied naturalization because of race. So much for national citizenship. Although there was much "loose and indeterminate language" in various opinions on the subject of state citizenship, one fact was clear: the states determined who could be citizens. Massachusetts, for example, defined citizenship as every male resident of a town having a freehold and paying taxes. Similar definitions in North Carolina and Illinois did not exclude blacks, except that Illinois barred free blacks from voting. All denied certain rights to women but clearly regarded them as citizens. The conferral or denial of the right to vote did not confer or deny the status of citizenship. Finally, there was no intermediate status between citizenship and noncitizenship. Yes, there was a group of people whose "physical qualities" distinguished them as African in ancestry. Many of these men were "held in bondage." That created some "artificial difficulties" in determining who was and who was not a citizen, but not in who could be a citizen. Instead, "in the United States it is too late now to deny the political rights and obligations conferred and imposed by nativity." Slaves, one could argue, were not citizens, but "color" could not deny a man the rights of citizenship. Such a position was viewed with "incredulity, if not disgust" in every other civilized nation.[21]

Democrats in the North who still opposed the idea of black citizenship after emancipation found an ally in an unexpected place. Almost immediately after the publication of the preliminary proclamation a formidable dissent came from Benjamin Robbins Curtis, former US Supreme Court justice. Curtis was in private practice when he wrote, having resigned from the Court in 1857 after a serious personal confrontation with Chief Justice Taney over the *Dred Scott* decision. Curtis wanted his dissent published alongside Taney's opinion and the chief justice refused, charging Curtis with misconduct. Curtis resumed private practice in Boston. A Whig in politics but not a Republican, he opposed secession and initially supported Lincoln. Again, in traditional Whig fashion, he thought that Congress should take the lead in making national policy and the president merely enforce the will of Congress. Thus by 1862 he had become disillusioned with the president's extensive use of his discretionary wartime powers. The preliminary Emancipation Proclamation was the last straw. It drove Curtis, he said, to make his criticism public.[22]

Curtis thought the war "just and necessary," denied that he was a party man, and dismissed any thought that he was disloyal. But the proclamation was expression of "transcendent" executive power that cast a "portentous cloud" over the rights of persons far from the scenes of military activity. The proclamation would annul state laws long in effect by which generations of men and women had organized and understood racial relations. Curtis read social conventions into the law in a way that anticipated Justice Henry Billings Brown's reading of Jim Crow in *Plessy v. Ferguson* (1896): the law could not and should not attempt to interfere in long-standing racial customs. Just as Brown later warned that any attempt to interfere in those relations would be bad for both races, so Curtis implied that any attempt to interfere in slavery would be bad for society as a whole. Curtis, as he had shown in his *Dred Scott v. Sanford* dissent, was not proslavery, but this essay showed that his innate social conservatism, read into the law, forbade rash or overly general revolution in social relations. "What about our future," he asked, when all those slaves were freed? Curtis did not suppose that

Lincoln intended to incite race war in the South, but that did not matter to the legal question—for if Lincoln could, as a matter of executive fiat, reorder so well entrenched an institution as slavery, where was the limit to his powers? What might he do when the conflict was finished? Would the people of the country remain free? Curtis here was not talking about those bondmen and women freed by the proclamation; he was talking about freedom in the pre–civil war sense, in the same way that Revolutionary-era slaveholders talked about Britain enslaving Americans. But Lincoln's "usurpations were not irreversible . . . . Let this gigantic shadow, which has been evoked out of the powers of the commander-in-chief, once be placed before the people, so that they can see clearly its proportions and its mien, and it will dissolve and disappear like the morning cloud before the rising sun."[23]

As Curtis correctly noted, the proclamation was neither a piece of legislation nor a court decision. The debate on it raised the question of whether, even in time a war, a president could make something that had the force of statute law. The Crown certainly could, a point that Carlisle had conceded in *Prize Cases* oral argument, closely followed by his insistence that the president was not a king, and acting like one only made him a tyrant. But the president had already made law concerning the conduct of the war with the blockade, a step that took property from private citizens not engaged in waging war. Recall, however, that when Curtis wrote, the High Court had not yet ruled on the first seizures of blockade runners.

Curtis had feared that Lincoln's wartime exercise of power would become a permanent feature of what later historians called the imperial presidency. In one respect Curtis was correct: emancipation would be permanent. Although the question was not answered by the preliminary announcement of emancipation, European liberals, who now fully supported the Union cause on that basis, joined Chase, Sumner, and Seward in assuming it would. Lincoln confirmed that expectation in his Reconstruction Proclamation of December 8, 1863. "Whereas, it is now desired by some persons heretofore engaged in said rebellion to resume their allegiance to the United States, and to reinaugurate loyal state governments within and for their respective states: Therefore— I, ABRAHAM LINCOLN, President of the United States, do proclaim, declare, and make known to all persons who have, directly or by implication, participated in the existing rebellion, except as hereinafter excepted, that a full pardon is hereby granted to them and each of them, with restoration of all rights of property, except as to slaves." With this offer, the postwar fate of slavery in the rebellious South was sealed.[24]

Unlike Lincoln, Jefferson Davis had no qualms about using his wartime powers to make law, as his order of December 24, 1862—responding to the proclamation, one assumes—demonstrated. Davis's blast was evidence of what the war would have resembled had the lawyers not had a hand in curbing its violence. Davis prefaced that response with an executive bill of attainder (a criminal sentence without a trial by someone other than a judge) prohibited by the federal Constitution and most state constitutions: "Now therefore, I Jefferson Davis, President of the Confederate States of America, and in their name do pronounce and declare the said Benjamin F. Butler to be a felon deserving of capital punishment. I do order that he be no longer considered or treated simply as a public enemy of the Confederate States of America but as an outlaw and common enemy of mankind, and that in the event of his capture the officer in command of the capturing force do cause him to be immediately executed by hanging; and I do further order that no commissioned officer of the United States taken captive shall be released on parole before exchange until the said Butler shall have met with due punishment for his crimes." The mélange of criminal and civil law, the ignorance of international law of war (for, after all, Davis claimed to represent an independent nation, not a band of rebels), and the guilt by association are appalling examples of the counterfeit of law. He then added to the list of Butler's crimes: "The slaves have been driven from the plantations in the neighborhood of New Orleans till their owners would consent to share the crops with the commanding general, his brother Andrew J. Butler, and other officers; and when such consent had been extorted the slaves have been restored to the plantations and there compelled to work under the bayonets of guards of US soldiers," a mischievous caricature of the fact that slaves in New Orleans were not covered by the proclamation because the city and its environs were no longer in Confederate hands. Judah P. Benjamin, who signed the order as secretary of state, had a hand in drafting it, but nothing could modify Davis's unlawyerly temper.[25]

To lawyers in Davis's cabinet, unlike Davis himself, the proclamation's full implications were immediately understood. Virginia lawyer/politician James Seddon occupied a post in the Confederate government roughly equivalent to Edwin Stanton's in Lincoln's administration, the fourth of five to hold that position in Davis's cabinet and the longest incumbent. He watched the emancipation project unfold from the preliminary announcement in September 1862 through its elucidation in the General Order 100 issued to the federal troops in April 1863. On June 24, 1863, writing to a federal agent for prisoner exchange, Seldon issued a response to the Emancipation Proclamation. It was less a reasoned brief than an explosion of dismay at the "confused, unassorted, and undiscriminating" nature of the emancipation policy that despoiled the "unarmed citizen" of his personal property. Honor in war, he thought, demanded that no combatant promote "servile insurrection," a kind of savagery that justice and humanity, as well as the laws of war, forbade. He supposed that when slaves in the Confederate territories learned that Lincoln had freed them, they would surely turn on the masters and mistresses with pent-up fury. Such animus among the slaves and distress among the free would forever end slavery in the South. In any case, the war that the Union waged had no basis in the federal Constitution, just as emancipation had no basis in the laws of war. Seddon even referred to the *Dred Scott* decision, for "the Highest judicial tribunal has determined that slavery and the slave trade are not contrary to the law of nations, and the voluntary removal of slaves to a state where slavery does not exist does not prevent" the reenslavement of the slave when he returned to a "slave state." No one answered his diatribe, or more accurately, it had already been answered.[26]

Seddon, like Davis, was horrified by the prospect of millions of freed slaves in the heartland of the Confederacy, but a handful of Confederate lawyer/politicians recognized that the war was unwinnable so long as it was a war to save slavery. One of these men, wearing the gray uniform of a Confederate major general, prepared a response. Like Seddon's letter, its focus was the future of slavery in the Confederacy, but unlike official policy toward slaves, Patrick Cleburne proposed the unthinkable. He had seen the loss of Vicksburg to Grant's forces and feared that the Confederacy was doomed unless it made full use of its black manpower—the same wartime exigency that led Lincoln to the

Emancipation Proclamation. He prepared a memorial (a formal version of a memorandum) for his commanding generals, which General Johnston prudently tabled, but a critic of the memorial sent it on to Richmond, where it landed on Jefferson Davis's desk as just about everything concerning the war did. Davis rejected it out of hand, ordered Secretary of War Seddon to tell Cleburne's superiors that all copies of it be destroyed, although a year later, after Cleburne had died from battle wounds, Davis proposed a watered-down version of the policy.[27]

Cleburne was born in Ireland in 1828, served in the British occupation army of Ireland during the potato famine, and relocated to the Arkansas side of the Mississippi, a land of opportunity for those who had the capital or the brains to benefit from the cotton boom there. He never owned slaves and quietly expressed his opinion that slavery was wrong (perhaps influenced by his experience in Ireland). After a short career as a druggist, he passed the bar and began his legal practice in 1856, riding circuit and arguing cases for cotton nabobs. Typical of lawyers in this era, he entered a partnership and then supported his partner Thomas Hindman's bid for the Senate. Arkansas was Democratic country, and with Hindman's help, Cleburne was an emerging force in the state's Democratic Party. A popular lawyer/politician, he was elected a captain, then a colonel, then commander of the state's volunteers after Arkansas seceded on May 6, 1861, and he saw action in the western theater until his death in 1864.[28]

Cleburne's memorial to the commanders of Confederate forces in the Army of Tennessee, dated January 24, 1864, but undoubtedly composed earlier, offered a striking counterpoint to Lincoln's far shorter proclamation. It combined the persuasive rhetoric of a lawyer arguing to a jury with the precision of a senior officer reporting to his superiors. Cleburne did not refer to Lincoln's assertion of war powers as a model for Confederate leaders, but the similarity was so obvious that it needed little explanation. Cleburne laid out the military situation of the Confederacy in stark terms, then added, "The subject is so grave, and our views so new . . . that we feel it a duty both to you and the cause" to argue for arming the slaves. "We have now been fighting for nearly three years, have spilled much of our best blood, and lost, consumed, or thrown to the flames an amount of property equal in value to the specie currency of the world . . . . Our soldiers can see no end to this state of affairs except in our own exhaustion; hence, instead of rising to the occasion, they are sinking into a fatal apathy, growing weary of hardships and slaughters which promise no results."

Cleburne then expressed a concern the very opposite of Lincoln's. Lincoln saw the iniquity of slavery. Cleburne recoiled at the threat of enslavement of the white population of the Confederacy, an ironic counterpoise to Lincoln's thinking. "If this state [of defeat in the field] continues much longer we must be subjugated." Building to his suggested remedy required another dose of courtroom melodrama. At the same time, Cleburne very accurately predicted what defeat would bring: "It means that the history of this heroic struggle will be written by the enemy; that our youth will be trained by Northern school teachers; will learn from Northern school books their version of the war." A solution lay not on the field of battle but in the law. "Slavery, from being one of our chief sources of strength at the commencement of the war, has now become, in a military point of view, one of our chief sources of weakness." Cleburne urged the recruitment of able-bodied slaves to counter Lincoln's. "Slavery is a source of great strength to the enemy in a purely military point of view, by supplying him with an army from our granaries; but it is our most vulnerable point, a continued embarrassment, and in some respects an insidious weakness."

Runaway slaves left the Confederacy's fields without workers. Civilians' fear of their slaves sapped the whites' morale. "We propose . . . that we immediately commence training a large reserve of the most courageous of our slaves, and further that we guarantee freedom within a reasonable time to every slave in the South who shall remain true to the Confederacy in this war." In a choice between "the loss of independence and the loss of slavery, we assume that every patriot will freely give up the latter—give up the negro slave rather than be a slave himself." Remove the barrier of antipathy to slavery in England, and its people would immediately give aid to the Confederacy. Remove the issue of slavery and all in the North who saw the Confederacy as built on slavery would change their minds and come to the peace table. "The idea that it is their special mission to war against slavery has held growing sway over the Northern people for many years, and has at length ripened into an armed and bloody crusade against it. This baleful superstition has so far supplied them with a courage and constancy not their own. It is the most powerful and honestly entertained plank in their war platform." Without this, the self-important moralism of the war party in the North would crumble. "The measure we propose will strike dead all John Brown fanaticism, and will compel the enemy to draw off altogether." Finally, and not least, "it will take from his negro army the only motive it could have to fight against the South, and will probably cause much of it to desert over to us."

Cleburne's proposal meant a profound change in the law. Obstacles to that change abounded. He knew that "the Constitution of the Southern States has reserved to their respective governments the power to free slaves for meritorious services to the State." The Confederate constitution's strong states' rights provisions did not allow its central government to take such a step. That would have been the very type of interference with a state's domestic law that the South Carolina Declaration of Causes decried. But like Lincoln's proclamation, Cleburne's memorial hinted that Jefferson Davis's war powers were sufficient grounds for the freeing of the slaves. Winning the war trumped the letter of the law. Lincoln could count on the lawyers in his cabinet to support his assumption of wide-ranging war powers. Cleburne hoped that the Confederate government in Richmond could do the same. Further changes in the law of slavery would be required. "We can do this more effectually than the North can now do, for we can give the negro not only his own freedom, but that of his wife and child, and can secure it to him in his old home. To do this, we must immediately make his marriage and parental relations sacred in the eyes of the law and forbid their sale." Cleburne's proposal thus went beyond Lincoln's; indeed, it anticipated the Thirteenth Amendment to the federal Constitution. "If, then, we touch the institution at all, we would do best to make the most of it, and by emancipating the whole race upon reasonable terms, and within such reasonable time as will prepare both races for the change, secure to ourselves all the advantages, and to our enemies all the disadvantages that can arise, both at home and abroad, from such a sacrifice."[29]

Cleburne's closing recommendation fell on deaf ears. By contrast, Lincoln's proclamation gave hope to abolitionists in and out of the government that a general emancipation was possible. An amendment to the federal Constitution was the next logical step. Cleburne had not proposed such an amendment to the Confederate Constitution's Article I, Section 9, Clause 4: "No bill of attainder, ex post facto law, or law denying or impairing the right of property in negro slaves shall be passed"; he recognized that it was unlikely to pass muster under the provisions of the Confederate Constitution—that is, ratification by two-thirds of the states' legislatures or by conventions in two-thirds of the states. But with missing members from eleven slave states, the US Congress might well pass an amendment ending slavery. Ratification in the free states was highly likely, and if and when the war ended, the federal government could make ratification by the former Confederate states a condition of the restoration of the Union.

As limited as it was, the Emancipation Proclamation hinted at the most extensive revision of the founders' Constitution and the greatest intrusion of federal power in the lives of ordinary men and women—slave and free—in the history of the nation to that time. The draft of the amendment, occurring at the same time as the proclamation, raised some of the same concerns, but it was understood to be temporary and did not affect so many people as emancipation. For example, in the year before the war "about one fifth of the white families owned fifty-five hundred slaves in Augusta Country, Virginia. Slaves were worth about six million dollars in the county, making its farmsteads the most valuable, per capita, in the state. Slavery lay at the heart of Augusta County's economy." The prospect that emancipation would be permanent, that is, that slaveholders in the Confederacy would never regain ownership of property worth nearly $3 billion, and that three million men and women, and their progeny, would be freed, profoundly changed the economic character of the nation. Before secession, the slaveholding South was considerably richer than the largely agricultural North. With emancipation, the per capita wealth distribution of the two sections would also change dramatically, as the prospective freedmen and women would have little property, while the slaveholder would lose about $2,000 (in modern figures) per slave.[30]

Seen in these terms, emancipation was a government-mandated redistribution of wealth unparalleled in the nation's experience. The funds raised by the excise taxes under the Internal Revenue Act of 1862 and the brief experiment with an income tax in the United States during the war paled by comparison. The excise taxes were regressive but were limited to luxury items, and the income tax applied only to those whose incomes exceeded $600 per year. Rising from 3 percent across the board to 7 percent, the income taxes raised a maximum of nearly $70 million in the final year of the war.[31]

The idea that law could effectuate such a redistribution of wealth was, like emancipation itself, a wartime expediency. The Union simply needed the funds to carry on its military operations. But the constitutional implications of such expediencies outlived their implementation. For example, slavery existed, or did not exist, as a function of state law. By supervening state law in this most important legal area, emancipation hinted at a profound shift in federal-state relations. Northern Democrats' opposition to emancipation rested precisely on this ground—the federal government's enumerated powers, the defining limits of strict construction of the Constitution, and states' rights federalism did not include emancipation. Lincoln did not refer to Alexander Hamilton's idea of loose construction of the Constitution, but Lincoln's program furthered the goals of a strong national government that the Hamiltonians had pursued in the 1790s. At that time, the Jeffersonian Republicans had opposed Hamilton on states' rights grounds. Lincoln's Republicans reversed those polarities. Emancipation was the opening wedge of this reversal.

In the course of pondering what to do with slavery when the war ended, Lincoln naturally considered the allied question of what to do with the rebelling Confederates when hostilities ceased. The end of the war in military terms would be the surrender of Confederate forces and the dissolution of Confederate governmental power. But what about the end of the war in civil terms? Lincoln's solution was a first cousin to the Emancipation Proclamation. On December 8, 1863, he issued a Proclamation of Amnesty and Reconstruction. Internal and external evidence linked it to Emancipation. Lincoln himself said, "Whereas, with reference to said rebellion, the President of the United States has issued several proclamations, with provisions in regard to the liberation of slaves; and Whereas, it is now desired by some persons heretofore engaged in said rebellion to resume their allegiance to the United States, and to re-inaugurate loyal state governments within and for their respective states," he regarded the two issues as tied together. If taking property on such a scale seemed a drastic punishment in the minds of Confederates, reconstruction would be mild. One must remember as well that Lincoln had married into a slaveholding family and knew firsthand its suffering as a result of the rebellion. He continued, "To all persons who have, directly or by implication, participated in the existing rebellion, except as hereinafter excepted, that a full pardon is hereby granted to them and each of them, with restoration of all rights of property, except as to slaves, and in property cases where rights of third parties shall have intervened, and upon the condition that every such person shall take and subscribe an oath, and thenceforward keep and maintain said oath inviolate; and which oath shall be registered for permanent preservation." Excepted from the general amnesty were former Confederate senior officers, members of the Confederate government, those who had violated the laws of war with respect to Union prisoners of war (in particular soldiers and sailors of color), and those who had held federal judicial and legislative office or commissions in the US Army or Navy and resigned to serve the Confederacy.[32]

The plan itself included a structure for returning the states to the Union as well as pardoning the former rebels. When 10 percent of its 1860 voting population had taken the oath, the voters of a state could select new members of the state government and submit a revised constitution barring slavery—again the connection to the Emancipation Proclamation—for reinstatement. Presumably, that government could then send senators to Congress and arrange for elections to the House of Representatives. That formula was as terse and legalistic in its language as the Emancipation Proclamation. Its legal authority rested on Lincoln's executive powers under the Constitution, not quite the same powers that had allowed Lincoln to issue the Emancipation, but close enough. Under the Constitution, the president has the power under Article II, Section 2, to grant reprieve and pardon to those who commit crimes against the United States. There was no limit on this pardoning power for crimes like treason, if Lincoln chose to regard the rebels as traitors. Lesser offenses like taking federal property were included. Lincoln wanted Congress to accede to this view, and early responses from recaptured territories in the rebelling states seemed to show that the plan had promise of speedy effectuation, but there was resistance in Congress to what seemed to radicals the very lenient terms Lincoln offered.[33]

The legal core of the amnesty was an oath of allegiance. Lincoln knew that oaths (and affirmations for those whose religion forbade them from taking an oath) were a vital part of all legal proceedings in antebellum America. His adoption of the oath was thus simple and brilliant, but hardly novel. Testimony in court and depositions and affidavits taken outside of court were all sworn to under oath. Persons seeking to become naturalized citizens under the 1790 act of Congress took an oath to support the Constitution of the United States. The president and all officers of the federal government took oaths of office, the most visible of which came when the president was inaugurated. Lincoln swore under oath to preserve and defend the Constitution, a point that he emphasized in his first inaugural address. Oaths were solemn promises to perform or not perform whose power lay in religious faith as well as legal practice. The violator of an oath put his immortal soul in peril. For this reason, in old English law, accused felons were not allowed to testify under oath, lest their lies forfeit their souls as well as their bodies. All of the officers of the US Army, the federal judges, and the members of Congress who resigned their commissions and then raised rebellion against the United States had violated their oaths. That was one reason they were excluded from the amnesty.[34]

Lincoln's plan for Reconstruction was the carrot he offered to those in rebellion; emancipation and confiscation were the sticks with which he punished the rebels. Both were legalistic; in using both, he offered the promise of renewal of rule of law when the rebellion was quashed. Neither ended the war, however, and as it entered its third winter, Congress contemplated the dilemma on which the rebellion was founded: what to do with slavery.

# 6

## "A New Birth of Freedom"

WHEN THE NEW THIRTY-SEVENTH Congress met in December 1863, Ohio representative James M. Ashley introduced legislation that would have ended slavery forever. Ashley was a member of the Ohio bar, though he did not practice law, and an ardent and early abolitionist. He was a founding member of the Republican Party whose antagonism to slavery was sincere and formed early. He was joined by Senator John Hale of New Hampshire whose December proposal would have ended slavery by congressional act. Hale was a lawyer/politician, like Ashley, and like the Ohio man also a stout antislavery activist. Neither man proposed a constitutional amendment. A number of bills followed from Republican congressmen, premised on the hitherto forbidden ground that Congress could abolish what the Constitution had condoned. Some of these bills rested on the logic that the rebellion could be more effectually ended if slavery were abolished, but the Confiscation Acts and the Emancipation Proclamation had already arrived at that position. All of the bills failed, as most Republicans still clung to the tattered pieces of the old Constitution.

The debate over the fate of slavery when the war ended resumed in earnest in February 1864 and continued for another year. Republicans agreed that the Constitution must be amended. In March, Illinois senator Lyman Trumbull reported out of the judiciary committee the language that would be the basis for the next year's debate: that "neither slavery nor involuntary servitude, except as a punishment for a crime whereof the party shall have been duly convicted, shall exist within the

United States, or any place subject to their jurisdiction." The one echo of the old Constitution was the plural possessive, "their" rather than the collective, national "its"—for the United States. A second section did what the Republicans had hesitated to do when the session of Congress began: "Congress shall have the power to enforce this article by appropriate legislation." It was the final and most significant wartime passage of arms of the Civil War lawyers.[1]

One might wish that the debates that followed featured the same quality and care that the best antebellum lawyering had shown; but waged in a presidential election year, with the outcome of the war no longer in doubt but its end still not in sight, partisanship seemed more important than close legal argument. Intra-party rivalries, personal factions, and cross-aisle differences all seemed to come to a head in the year-long debate over the amendment. That is not to say, however, that a careful reading of the debates in Congress would not enable one to follow the legal threads spun in the debates over the Emancipation Proclamation.[2]

Ashley was never a big Lincoln fan, though he had campaigned for the president and wanted to work with him. As 1864 opened, Lincoln did not have a formal role in the proposal for ending slavery once and for all, but his thinking was "evolving" in parallel with the movement for the end of slavery. He no longer considered colonization as a corollary of emancipation, for example. Nevertheless, he had not yet thought through the legal requirements of equality for the freedmen. Whether this was not in his mind (recall that he had explicitly stated that the black man was inferior to the white man) or it was a bridge too far to cross in the winter of 1864, Lincoln was not yet ready to tackle those questions. When he referred to "a new birth of freedom" in his November 1863 Gettysburg Address, he did not link it to abolition. Indeed, such matters had receded once again into the background of his thinking.[3]

The second of the lawyers in Congress to champion the amendment was James F. Wilson of Iowa. Born in Ohio, Wilson, like Ashley, was a defender of civil rights before there was a civil rights movement. A Republican state legislator, he entered the House of Representatives in 1861 and remained there until 1869, serving as the chair of the House

Judiciary Committee during Reconstruction. He left Congress in 1869 but was elected by the Ohio state legislature to the US Senate in 1883 and served in it for two terms. On March 19, 1864, he offered his thoughts on a thirteenth amendment to the Constitution on the floor of the lower house.[4]

Wilson proposed that slavery be forever prohibited in the United States, except as punishment for a crime, and that Congress have the authority to pass legislation to enforce the amendment. He conceded "that a proposition in the Congress of the United States to so amend the Constitution of the Republic as to weaken or destroy slavery is a novel thing . . . . It was long the custom in this body whenever slavery became excited and angry, to try to appease its wrath by offering it some new hold on the life of the nation." Wilson was no doubt referring to the "gag rule" barring the acceptance of antislavery petitions in the House of Representatives from 1835 to 1844 and in the Senate from 1836 to 1850. The result, he thought, was that slavery enslaved the nation itself "and a most cruel task-master it proved. Its political career was an incessant, unrelenting, aggressive warfare upon the principles of the Government, the objects for which the Constitution was ordained." Slavery "defiled everything."[5]

Why was slavery now so evil when the framers had allowed it to flourish? "This issue is no reflection on the wise and good men who laid the firm foundations and fashioned the sublime architecture of our Constitution." The framers simply had no idea of the corrupting influence of slavery on the Republic. The proof of this invincible ignorance was secession itself. "It is impossible to believe that the master workmen who gave to us this best of human Governments, in the least degree suspected that they were transmitting with it the seeds of dissolution." But they had built into the Constitution the means for the protection of republican liberty. The Amending Clause "is the safety-valve of the Constitution, so constructed and guarded as to prevent hasty and inconsiderate action, and utterly destructive of every pretense for forcible revolution." This was a backhanded comment on the Confederacy's refusal to wait for an amendment protecting slavery, although in the secession winter of 1861 Wilson would hardly have supported such an amendment. Wilson found the legal basis for the amendment in the Preamble to the Constitution, each of whose parts Wilson applied to emancipation. "The last, the grandest, the most sublime of the objects declared by the people in the ordination of the Constitution is, 'to secure the blessings of liberty to ourselves and our posterity.'" This clause alone provided a basis for the amendment. Wilson did not know or did not realize that the author of the Preamble at the constitutional convention was Gouverneur Morris, an outspoken opponent of slavery. At the same time, little in Wilson's speech suggested that he favored anything more than emancipation. Abolitionism of this species was hardly a call for legal equality for the freedman.[6]

Indeed, the purpose of Wilson's proposed amendment seemed to be to punish the rebels after the war had ended. That, at least, must have been what the Democrats in the House heard, because they said nothing in response, and the matter lapsed. In the Senate, where Republicans had a far larger majority of seats (none of the twenty-two seats of the Confederate states were filled), the amendment was revived. Lyman Trumbull of Illinois had taken part in Lincoln's deliberations on emancipation, and he was the first to raise the question again. But Trumbull, "highly skilled" in the courtroom, facile with the law, and "cold and calculating" in his role as chair of the judiciary committee, was a moderate, and he too seemed to regard the amendment as a way to ensure that "slave power" would never regain its former strength in Congress. (The amendment would change the basis for representation, ending the two-thirds rule. What was more, if given the right to vote, former slaves were not likely to elect their former masters.) Henry Wilson made a similar speech, talking so long that the galleries emptied.[7]

What the proponents of the amendment did not say was as important as what they did say. None of them argued that the Thirteenth Amendment's raison d'etre was to give constitutional sanction to the Emancipation Proclamation. Plainly, they were not looking backward. Neither were they looking forward, for neither man discoursed on the civil rights of the freedmen and women. It is hard to derive meaning from silence, but the absence of these matters demands some analysis. One may simply conclude that by the late winter of 1864, with the war still raging, no one questioned the military necessity of the Emancipation Proclamation, hence no one thought it needed further legal foundation. But the proposed amendment was not a wartime measure—that is, its impact would only really be felt when the

Confederacy had collapsed and all its territory had become part of the Union once again. Thus the legal impact of the end of slavery would arise as part of the reconstruction of the nation rather than during the Civil War. In other words, the legal questions would present themselves once slavery was no longer legal. These would be questions of the civil and political rights of the newly freed men and women. Only when the thinking of proponents of the amendment turned to these questions, questions of the peacetime impact of emancipation, would the speeches focus on legal matters.

The next impetus for the amendment came from an unexpected source—Senator Reverdy Johnson of Maryland. On April 5, 1864, he gave a long and detailed speech in favor of the amendment. Johnson was one of the foremost lawyers in the nation, much sought after for complex cases. He had represented John Sanford in *Dred Scott* and had won for his client. He supported the war effort, however, and in the Senate was a leader of the Union Democrats. For a lawyer/politician from a slave state to reject the states' rights position on slavery was something of a body blow to his party. The newspapers reported that his speech was booed by fellow Democrats. Republicans flocked across the aisle to shake his hand.[8]

Johnson was not an ideologue of any stripe. His approach to political issues was akin to his approach to legal cases. He was a conservative thinker. In *Dred Scott*, according to opposing counsel (George Ticknor Curtis, Benjamin Curtis's brother), Johnson offered "a forcible presentation of the southern view of our Constitution . . . . I believe that he held those opinions with entire sincerity." "Our Constitution" meant the "old Constitution" that Lincoln and Stevens lauded in the year before secession. Johnson was not apologetic in his advocacy of the amendment, however, and saw it as a necessary next step after the war. His advocacy did not ignore the concerns that Thomas Cobb had raised about relations between the two races, but the war had changed the legal status of slavery. "To manumit at once nearly four millions of slaves, who have been such by hereditary descent during their lives, and who because they were such, it being one consequence of their condition, have been kept in a state of almost absolute ignorance, is an event of which the world's history furnishes no parallel. Whether it will be attended by weal or by woe, the future must decide. That it will not be followed by unmixed good or by unmixed evil, is perhaps certain." In light of how divisive slavery had been, and would remain after victory, general emancipation was simply a matter of right, whatever its consequences. Johnson did what Lincoln did in his Cooper Union Address—use history—to claim that the framers expected slavery to end.[9]

Johnson's constitutionalism was thus different from Taney's in *Dred Scott*. Taney argued that the founders' views of African Americans controlled how the Constitution could be read. The framers could not conceive of citizenship for blacks, so he could not conceive of it. Johnson felt that changing conditions mandated a different reading of the founders' intentions. He was thus an originalist in a different way—using the past as a set of standards rather than a rigid rule. One might call this conservatism with a conscience. Johnson thought slavery morally wrong, but that was a private opinion, and "in the public situations . . . in which I have been heretofore placed, as well as in the one which I now hold, I have deemed and do deem it my duty to recognize the binding and paramount authority of the Constitution as it is."

Johnson nevertheless was convinced that slavery had an expiration date, and the war had hastened that date. He recalled that in 1847 he had listened as John C. Calhoun told the Senate "that republican freedom could not exist without African slavery, and proclaimed his attachment to the Union and to the Constitution upon the ground," an opinion Johnson opposed then and now. He disagreed with those who claimed that Congress could end slavery by legislation, or that the president could end it by fiat (he still opposed the Emancipation Proclamation), or that (as in *Dred Scott*) the courts could end it—but those were the precise reasons that he wanted Congress to pass the amendment. Fending off questions about the status of slaves if the war had ended before the amendment was in place, Johnson gave as fine an oral argument as was ever presented before the Court, a precisely legal argument in which he managed to support the amendment without recanting any of his earlier views. The clincher was a powerful counterargument: "But even if [permanent emancipation] could be done by either [Congress or the president] as far as the slaves in the rebellious States are concerned, it would fall far short of the object which in common with a large majority of the Senate, and, as I believe, of the country, I have at heart; for can either the executive or Congress under the war power emancipate the slaves in the loyal States?"[10]

Some of the Democrats had resisted earlier calls for the amendment by arguing that slavery should still be a matter for each state in the Union to decide for itself. For the federal government to interfere by pressing the amendment on the states would violate the basic tenets of federalism. Johnson brushed away this strong version of states' rights doctrine and the old Constitution. "To a limited extent the States are sovereign . . . but if [these opponents mean] to contend that the United States are not also in the same sense and to another extent equally sovereign, [they are] mistaken." To say "the only true sovereignty was that which belongs to the States . . . in my judgement, there never was a greater political heresy." The Constitution rested on "we the people," not we the states (in fact, on Gouverneur Morris's rewriting of the Preamble's original draft in the Committee on Style and Arrangement, but no matter). Calhoun's version of states' rights was put on death watch, ironically, by his South Carolina successors when they seceded.[11]

When opponents of the amendment insisted that slavery was left to the states in the Constitution, Johnson replied with a hypothetical—a type of legal rhetoric still common in first-year law classes: could the framers have banned slavery in the original document? If they could, then Congress could amend the Constitution to ban it now. Johnson then argued as Wilson had two months earlier: reread the Preamble and see that all of its clauses would be served by ending slavery.[12]

Johnson did not, however, excoriate the slaveholder or, except for a few passing remarks, argue that slavery itself was an abomination. To do so would have accused, by implication at least, some of his fellow congressmen who at that time owned slaves. His target was the Confederacy. "The conspirators who are now almost exclusively governing the South, or to speak more accurately, tyrannizing over the South, have for more than thirty years been plotting and anxiously looking to the accomplishment of the treason, the destruction of the Union." And his target was the ideology that underwrote slavery. "The moral and religious mind of the country has become nauseated by the teaching that scripture authorizes and approves slavery, and sanctions its perpetual existence, and that it authorizes such slavery as exists in

the Southern States, and does it because its victims are not of the same
color of their masters!" Slaves wanted freedom. "How do they prove
that in that particular we differ from the black man? Do we not see
that he is willing to incur every personal danger, which promises, if
successfully met, to throw down his shackles and to make him stand
upon God's earth, upon that earth created for all, as a man and not as a
slave?" Lincoln's sentiments exactly.[13]

On April 6, a day after the news reports of Johnson's speech sped
out from Washington on the telegraph lines, news came to the Senate
that Maryland voted to end slavery with a revised state constitution.
This is the course of action that would have placated opponents of the
national amendment like Garrett Davis of Kentucky, though it is hard
to see how Kentucky, with its strongly proslavery unionist government,
would follow Maryland's example.[14]

The most convoluted legal question the amendment proposal raised was
also the most open-ended—could an amendment to the Constitution,
as provided in Article V of the Constitution, itself be unconstitutional?
Surely an amendment that abolished the Union would be unconstitutional because it would conflict with the amending power. Democratic
opponents of an amendment ending slavery argued that such a step
would enlarge and extend the powers of the federal government (given
its final form allowing congressional action to enforce it). Presumably
an amendment that abolished Article V, in effect saying that there could
be no amendments, would so violate the spirit of the framers' work that
it too would be unconstitutional. An amendment that altered a state's
representation in the Senate (without that state's consent) would so violate the Great Compromise at Philadelphia (upper house representation
equally distributed among the states, lower house representation based
on population) that it would have been unconstitutional, as provided
in Article V. Were there other amendments that would on their face be
unconstitutional? Could an amendment abolish freedom of worship or
freedom of the press in the First Amendment? Or would the passage of
an unconstitutional amendment simply be a way to accomplish a revolutionary change in fundamental law without having a revolution? [15]

There were a number of ways in which the amendment altered the
body of the Constitution. Recall that it did not mention slavery at

all, grounds for some abolitionists to claim that the document was amenable to antislavery. In parallel if ironic fashion, the Thirteenth Amendment also did not mention the Three-Fifths Clause in Article I or the Rendition Clause in Article IV (requiring states to return to one another individuals bound to labor who had fled), but clearly it would render these portions of the Constitution inoperative. Older views of the Fifth Amendment would be altered. If slaves were property, the proposed Thirteenth Amendment would take that property from its (formerly lawful) owners without compensation. According to opponents of the emancipation amendment, these changes so violated the framers' intent that they effectually destroyed the Constitution. They certainly altered the old Constitution profoundly. Not only did the amendment end slavery but it also shifted the boundaries of federal-state relations. Following the still potent ideology of states' rights, opponents argued that the Constitution had, by its silence, left slavery to the states. If the federal government, by amending the Constitution, took that authority away from the states, the amendment took from the sovereignty of the states and added to the purview of the federal government. In fact, much that would come from Congress after the war did exactly that through another amendment, the Fourteenth. In this sense, the debate over the Thirteenth Amendment and federalism anticipated the debate over the Fourteenth Amendment.[16]

Allied to the federalism question was the legal status—the extent and nature of the civil rights—of freedmen and women. The Thirteenth Amendment was the first of the amendments to include a formal enforcement clause: "Congress shall have power to enforce this article by appropriate legislation." Did that clause mean that the amendment added civil rights legislation to the enumerated powers of Congress? Even if the second clause of the amendment provided for congressional legislation on civil rights, what were those rights? Were they absolute? In whose hands would the elaboration of those rights lie—the federal government (and Congress) or the state governments? Would the putative end of slavery by amendment rather than ordinary congressional legislation imply that Congress did not think it had the constitutional authority to impose on the states equal treatment of freedmen and women? If the status in law of the men and women freed by ratification of the amendment were left in the hands of the states, would various states have different regimes, just as they had different views on slavery and freedom before the war? Strong abolitionists assumed that equality under the laws would follow freedom; indeed, it was a natural concomitant of freedom. Twice the Senate voted down Garrett Davis's motion to bar all blacks from voting and holding office. Still, most conservative Republicans and most Democrats thought that freedom was no more than that—the end of bondage. But the details were legal questions left for later.[17]

On April 8, over the objections of Davis, the Senate passed the draft of the amendment reported out by the judiciary committee. According to newspapers, the galleries of the chamber were packed with spectators, including many women. The draft was largely the work of Lyman Trumbull. Charles Sumner had tried to add language as a preamble that "all persons are equal before the law" but the committee did not choose to follow his proposal. Instead, the proposed amendment read: "Section 1. Neither slavery nor involuntary servitude, except as a punishment for crime whereof the party shall have been duly convicted, shall exist within the United States, or any place subject to their jurisdiction. Section 2. Congress shall have power to enforce this article by appropriate legislation."

Democrats George R. Riddle and Willard Saulsbury of Delaware, and Davis and Lazarus Powell of Kentucky (states in the Union that still legalized slavery) adhered to doctrines of states' rights constitutionalism that were Democratic orthodoxy before the war. Davis's remarks, on March 30, denied that slavery was the cause of the war; instead, it was Massachusetts' "meddling with slavery," though South Carolina was as guilty. If anything was going to be abolished, it should be those two states. In a more serious vein, he argued that "if we are to have union, liberty, and peace, the indispensable condition is that the great fundamental principle, that the states are to have the entire and exclusive control of their own local and domestic institutions and affairs, must be held inviolable by the general government." Interference with these domestic institutions (including "the right of Kentucky" to retain slavery) would lead to "intolerable despotism." Powell warned that once slaves were free, they would pollute society and politics. He correctly foresaw that Republicans would press for legal equality for the freedmen. Saulsbury added that God had placed the white man over the black man, and God ordained slavery. They, along with four other Democrats, voted against the resolution. Leaving the chamber, Saulsbury was reported to have muttered, "I now bid farewell to any hope of the reconstruction of the Union." By contrast, Missouri senators John B. Henderson and B. Gratz Brown voted for the amendment, even though Missouri was a slave state. Henderson was a slaveholder himself, but he had explained why he voted as he did—slavery had caused the war. Henderson also sounded a caution for the Republicans—he remained a Democrat and looked forward to the time when his party in Congress would be joined by Democrats from the former Confederacy.[18]

That the vote, 38 to 6, was largely along party lines may suggest that law, as law, did not compel any senator's opinion, and that Johnson's speech, while widely reported in the newspapers, did not switch many votes. Only Johnson and James Nesmith of Oregon among the Democrats voted aye. When some Democrats spoke in opposition, they reproduced an even more virulent racism than Alexander Stephens's. When Republicans spoke in favor, save for the handful of true abolitionists in Congress like Charles Sumner and Zachariah Chandler of Michigan, they stressed how slavery had damaged the nation. The two sides were thus talking past one another. Two Democrats from non-slaveholding states, Thomas Hendricks of Indiana and James McDougall of California, and four Democrats from slaveholding states, George R. Riddle and Saulsbury of Delaware and Lazarus W. Powell and Davis of Kentucky, voted nay. All six men were lawyers; two had served as attorneys general and two as governors of their states. None owned or traded slaves, or had strong personal connections to the slave South, save those one would expect from Democratic politicians before the war. All were opposed to secession, but all warned against the problems that would supposedly follow freeing the slaves, including the ultimate horror of miscegenation. All six were the voices raised most loudly against the amendment, another clue to the key skills of advocacy that the practice of law conferred on its professionals in these debates.[19]

This said, one should not ignore the legal and constitutional content in the vying orations. The Democrats cleaved to the old Constitution. It protected slavery, and they did too, not necessarily because they agreed with Saulsbury's extreme racial views. Some saw in the amendment the first step not mandated by the needs of the war to create a new kind of federalism not envisioned by the framers (though in fact Alexander Hamilton, Gouverneur Morris, and a few other strong nationalists at the Philadelphia Convention might have approved both the amendment and a stronger central government). Such a revised federalism would have permanently and profoundly shifted the boundary between the federal government and the state governments' authority beyond the limits of the enumerated powers. Democrats who opposed the amendment were constitutional conservatives, a pose that coincided with the defense of slavery but did not rest on it.[20]

At the inception of the war, the Republicans overwhelmingly pledged their adherence to the "old Constitution." Secession violated it. What one may call the new Constitution, though its text was not altered until the ratification of the Thirteenth Amendment, was thus not the product of a conscious effort, a kind of conspiracy, by the Republicans to assign to the federal government functions that had been the exclusive preserve of the states. It was the result of a series of contingencies, what historian Bernard Bailyn in another context has called "a contagion" of unanticipated responses to unanticipated developments. Over the course of the war, initial perceptions were transformed in meaning, and these new perceptions "propelled" the Union lawyer/politicians toward a new conception of the role of government itself. The "intellectual dynamism" of such a process cannot be underestimated. Men like Trumbull and Johnson had no idea that they would propose an amendment to the Constitution when they first faced the prospect of secession, nor did they then see slavery as the worm in the bud of the Constitution.[21]

The reluctance of Democrats in the House to supply their portion of the necessary two-thirds for passage provided further evidence of the fact that views of slavery had contributed to the rise of the Republican Party in the first place. Aware of the need to win some Democratic votes in the North, Lincoln said nothing about the amendment during the electoral contest. He did approve the inclusion of the amendment in his party's 1864 platform and repeated that support when he accepted his party's nomination. Still, had not Lincoln been reelected in November 1864, enabling his lobbying effort for the amendment, it might not have passed at all. Lincoln was determined now that it would pass and lent his considerable weight behind it.[22]

Lincoln's December 6, 1864, annual message to Congress set the tone for this effort. He did not lead with the proposed amendment; indeed, mention of it came near the end and he contented himself with a single longish paragraph. Reading it, one senses that he was mentally and physically near the end of his tether. He pleaded without any of the clever riposte one found in his debates with Douglas, the sharp legal acumen of his First Inaugural, or the solemn gravity of his Emancipation Proclamation. He was factual, but did not rehearse the facts in an argumentative way. Perhaps he knew that Congress was as tired as he was and had spent a year debating the amendment. "At the last session of Congress a proposed amendment of the Constitution abolishing slavery throughout the United States passed the Senate but failed for lack of the requisite two-thirds vote in the House of Representatives. Although the present is the same Congress and nearly the same members, and without questioning the wisdom or patriotism of those who stood in opposition, I venture to recommend the reconsideration and passage of the measure at the present session."[23]

Lincoln did not dwell on the recalcitrance of the opposition party, though he wagged a finger at it—for the incoming Congress would have an even larger Republican majority. "Of course the abstract question is not changed; but [the] intervening election shows almost certainly that the next Congress will pass the measure if this does not. Hence there is only a question of time as to when the proposed amendment will go to the States for their action. And as it is to so go at all events, may we not agree that the sooner the better?" Why agree, when for a year the bulk of the Democratic membership had refrained from agreement? In characteristic fashion, he made his point by negation: "It is not claimed that the election has imposed a duty on members to change their views or their votes any further than, as an additional element to be considered, their judgment may be affected by it. It is the voice of the people now for the first time heard upon the question."[24]

Finally came an appeal to high-minded patriotism: "In a great national crisis like ours unanimity of action among those seeking a common end is very desirable—almost indispensable. And yet no approach to such unanimity is attainable unless some deference shall be paid to the will of the majority simply because it is the will of the majority." The vote in the election was not a plebiscite on the amendment. It was a vote on the expected victory, and thus, like the vote in 1860, it was largely sectional. Linking the vote to support for the amendment was a leap of logic uncharacteristic of Lincoln's previous addresses. He was reaching in tying the two together: "In this case the common end is the maintenance of the Union, and among the means to secure that end such will, through the election, is most dearly declared in favor of such constitutional amendment."[25]

The Emancipation Proclamation and the election of 1864 galvanized Lincoln scholars. The Fourth Message to Congress seems to have energized none of the students of his words. It should have been triumphal. It should have proclaimed liberty throughout the land for whites and blacks. It should have linked together all of Lincoln's efforts to end slavery, from his return to politics in 1854, through his long battle with Stephen Douglas and Roger Taney over *Dred Scott*, to his Inaugural Address, the Emancipation Proclamation, and the election of 1864. It did none of this, even though, as he admitted, Congress had yet to place the capstone in the arch of freedom. Perhaps one reason the Fourth Message failed in this respect was its lack of legalism. Writing and speaking as a lawyer for the bondsman, Lincoln's words reached upward and outward. In his December 1864 message, he did not sound like a lawyer at all. On the same day, however, he submitted the name of Salmon P. Chase to the Senate for the now vacant post of chief justice of the United States. The Senate confirmed the nomination at once, unanimously. Chase was the most persistent of the antislavery voices in the cabinet, and the nomination was a valedictory of sorts for the abolitionist movement. Perhaps Lincoln had passed the mantle of liberator to Chase and was simply relieved to have done so.[26]

The next month's debates in the House were not without drama, but they added little substance to the legal arguments. The new Congress would not take its seat until the end of the year, and the debate evidenced how tired the wartime members were. Democrats opposed to the amendment cited it as evidence of a plan to destroy the sovereignty of the states and prevent genuine reunion. A few played the racist card—the amendment would lead to the eventuality of black equality, plunging the nation into the depths of miscegenation. Even without this claim, legal racism was a central theme of the Democratic opposition to the amendment. Legal racism rejected any claim that free or freed people of color had to have equality before the law. Republicans replied by lauding the heroism of the black Union soldiers, but except for a few genuine radicals like Charles Sumner, they stopped short of promising civil rights for the freedmen. Democrats still insisted that the amendment would be an unconstitutional enlargement of the powers of government. Republicans replied that state legislatures would have the final say, conforming to the original intent of the framers. Repeatedly, Lincoln interceded personally, a moment captured in Steven Spielberg's prize-winning movie *Lincoln*. Seward, long an abolitionist, was even more active, organizing a lobbying campaign to gain the votes of New York Democrats. But Congressman Wilson and Senator Johnson had been right, just as Lincoln was right. The time had come to end the national nightmare of chattel slavery. That it ended by law was a product of a civil war waged under law by lawyers.[27]

Lincoln had the last word on this project of final freedom in his Second Inaugural Address, on March 4, 1865. What he did not say was as important as what he did say. At the start of the war, "one-eighth of the whole population were colored slaves, not distributed generally over the Union, but localized in the southern part of it. These slaves constituted a peculiar and powerful interest. All knew that this interest was somehow the cause of the war. To strengthen, perpetuate, and extend this interest was the object for which the insurgents would rend the Union even by war, while the Government claimed no right to do more than to restrict the territorial enlargement of it." An able summary of the difference of political opinion in 1860, this was also a statement that confirmed the legality of slavery where it already existed. The war changed everything. "Neither party expected for the war the magnitude or the duration which it has already attained. Neither anticipated that the cause of the conflict might cease with or even before the conflict itself should cease." Thus far, Lincoln abjured any accusation that he was an abolitionist at the start of the conflict. "Each looked for an easier triumph, and a result less fundamental and astounding." But slavery was an offense against God and man. "If we shall suppose that American slavery is one of those offenses which, in the providence of God, must needs come, but which, having continued through His appointed time, He now wills to remove, and that He gives to both North and South this terrible war as the woe due to those by whom the offense came, shall we discern therein any departure from those divine attributes which the believers in a living God always ascribe to Him?" But if God judged, Lincoln would not. "It may seem strange that any men should dare to ask a just God's assistance in wringing their bread from the sweat of other men's faces, but let us judge not, that we be not judged." Lincoln was plainly looking ahead to some kind of reconstruction based on reconciliation of whites in the North and whites in the South—"a just and lasting peace among ourselves." The "ourselves" could be read to omit the newly freed. Certainly Lincoln did not suggest any other more inclusive reading of the term.[28]

With the opportunity to trumpet the triumph of a national law of freedom, Lincoln had resorted to divine rather than federal law. He made no mention of the amendment, instead appealing to the judgement of the Lord. Given the chance to sum up the greatest legal achievement of the age, he reverted to divine providence and the will of a living God. If slavery was a theft of labor, and the cause of the terrible war, why leave judgment aside? Surely Lincoln was thinking about Reconstruction, and his peroration, "with malice toward none and charity for all" offered a generous peace to those still at war with the United States. His proposal to pardon the rebels, along the same lines, met with unanimous disapproval in the cabinet. Perhaps he was still trying to "consider all sides," as a highly sympathetic biographer has suggested. But to regard the "astounding outcome" of the war as the work of a just God rather than the imposition of law and order on a rebellious population was hardly accurate. Nor did it echo "the abolitionists' view of slavery as a national evil deeply embedded in all the institutions of society."[29]

Lincoln's prophetic magnanimity did not appease Northern Democrats or mollify Confederates any more than it paved the way to genuine equality for the freedmen. Newspaper reports of the address were respectful but "puzzled." What exactly did it mean? Used to somewhat muddled legalisms, readers did not understand the fuzzy sermonizing. Perhaps, and this is the most likely explanation, Lincoln was so weary, physically, psychologically, and intellectually, that he was no longer the wily lawyer. He believed that the end of the war and his own demise were so profoundly intertwined that a just God would end them both. Still, silence on the future of civil rights suggested that the legal revolution already wrought by the sacrifice of so many in the field had a long way to go even in Lincoln's mind.[30]

The assassination of President Lincoln lent an almost sacral authority to his and the Civil War lawyers' achievements. They moved toward a new conception of civil rights and equality hesitantly; they had begun a transformation of the shape and purpose of the federal government in that direction. The fulfillment of that transformation, a veritable revolution in constitutional ideas and institutions, may still not be complete, but they had begun it. An institution—slavery—had been so firmly a part of American law that before the war no one, save a few abolitionists, could have expected its demise four years after secession. The amendment was ratified by the former Confederate states as a condition of their readmission to the Union. For some on the winning side at the time, and some historians later, the Thirteenth Amendment was seen in "narrow" terms, as the complement to the Emancipation Proclamation, and essentially a wartime measure. For others, it was the beginning of a genuine revolution in civil rights, citizenship, and equality.[31]

It may be argued that amendments to the Constitution have a special significance in American law that goes beyond their manifest content. Because they require the concurrence of two-thirds of both houses of the national government (or a constitutional convention) and three-fourths of the state legislatures (or conventions therein), they are expressions of the national will. Grouped together, the Thirteenth, Fourteenth, and Fifteenth, the so-called Reconstruction amendments, approached a virtual constitutional convention (as opposed to the explicit provisions of the Constitution for such a gathering). If this is so, the framing and the passage of the Thirteenth Amendment marked a kind of popular mandate, a gravitational shift in public opinion on slavery. On August 13, 1863, Gideon Welles noted in his diary that the question of slavery after the war "required deliberate and wise thought and consideration . . . . [W]ere the rebellion suppressed the disposition of the slavery question was, in my view one of the most deliberate and important that ever devolved on those who administer the government." The Emancipation Proclamation was "justifiable as a military necessity," but the fate of slavery itself was a different question.

In 1865, no longer a question of wartime needs of one section of the country or a particular administration waging a particular kind of war, the end of slavery via constitutional amendment was a wholly different type of legal act from the Emancipation Proclamation. The amendment may have had a logical connection to the Emancipation Proclamation in that the former was unthinkable without the war and had evolved from the notion that the rebels must be punished; but as the idea of the end of slavery took form, it became that "new birth of freedom" that Lincoln promised in the Gettysburg Address. Welles now knew that the end of slavery would "shatter" the slaveholding world. He was right. The Thirteenth Amendment transformed the end of slavery from an incident of war into the purpose of the war and a justification for all the suffering on both sides that later generations could, in time, appreciate. The old Constitution did not die; as a disgraced but not silenced Vallandingham wrote after the war, "If we cannot have the Constitution as it is" the defenders of states' rights never surrendered their goal of determining just how far the "constitution as it ought to be" would empower the new regime of rights. They found strong support among their former adversaries, like Michigan judge and jurist Thomas M. Cooley. In his youth an adherent of the Democratic Party, by the time the South seceded he had decided that slavery had no place in America, but neither did legislation that deprived anyone of their basic liberties. If states deprived freedmen of their civil rights, it would be up to the legal profession in courts of law, not the legislature, to protect whatever rights the freedmen had gained. The old Constitution's shadow still darkened the political discourse of rights, though lawyers could provide relief for the nation's newest citizens.[32]

# Epilogue

## The Lawyers' Reconstruction

FROM THE PRECEDING CHAPTERS, it is clear in what ways one might claim that the Civil War was "of" and "by" the lawyer/politicians who sat in seats of power. During the period from 1860 through 1865, lawyers played key roles in every branch of government, and lawyers' decisions and acts shaped the conduct and outcome of the war. In what sense can one say that the Civil War was also "for" lawyers? How did it affect their lives and how did they benefit, if that is the right word, from it? The answer is a complex and perhaps controversial one that can only be roughly sketched here.

For the lawyers in the field and the loved ones at home, the war had revealed feelings that had never before been experienced. The horror, the camaraderie, the anxiety and the suffering, the dying and the acceptance of death were everyday burdens for those who fought and those who waited, sometimes in vain, for the soldiers to return home. Some lawyers in uniform retained their ideals to a degree that might seem surprising to us in our more cynical age. Shortly before he fell in the Shenandoah Valley fighting, former Virginia attorney general William Baylor wrote home that he was still battling for the old Constitution of states' rights that Virginia assigned for its decision to secede. For General Sherman, resting from the capture of Vicksburg, the law was as compelling a motive for fighting as for Baylor: "the Constitution, laws of Congress, and regulations of the executive departments, subject to the decisions of the Supreme Court are the laws which all must obey without stopping to inquire why. All must obey." Ohio's Albion Tourgée was an abolitionist before the war, and nearly losing an eye during the early fighting did not dampen his commitment to equality before the law. He went on to become a courtroom stalwart in the fight against Jim Crow. Fidelity to law, the victory of a higher law over disunion and disorder, demanded further service. For the lawyers in government posts and in the field who survived, the war brought a greater appreciation of the value of peace and order. As George Murphy, a Virginia lawyer serving with a cavalry troop in the Shenandoah wrote in his diary near the end of the war: "God grant this gloom may soon be dispelled with the bright rays of the sun of an eternal and honorable peace." With that peace would come the most revolutionary change in American law since the creation of the Republic—the end of slavery. And it would not have happened without the guiding hand of the Civil War lawyers.[1]

After the conclusion of hostilities, many lawyers who served in the field returned home to try to restore their local political careers and their private practice. Others stayed where they had served and began new lives. Some simply stayed in place throughout, shifting their allegiances as time and circumstance dictated. Commander Maxwell Woodhull, of the USS *Cimarron*, operating on the St. John's River in the Atlantic Coast of Florida during the war, had this to report of one such wily counselor. "This Mr. [Samuel L.] Burritt is a lawyer by profession, and rather a prominent man in these parts . . . . He is represented to me as at the outbreak of the Rebellion having been a Secessionist. After your conquest of this part of the country he took quite a showy part as a Union man. Since then he has returned to his 'secessionist proclivities.' And now, to guard against accidents, he is trying to be a 'go-between,' in other words, a 'waiter on Providence.'" Men like Burritt saw themselves, and others saw them, as prominent members of their communities. Thus it was natural that the men of the 3rd Ohio Volunteers would elect prominent lawyer J. Warren Kiefer of Springfield, Ohio, lieutenant colonel of the regiment, and that a year later, when a civilian board for the Fourth Military District in the state needed a commander for the newly formed 110th Volunteer Infantry, they would name Kiefer its colonel. After the war, Kiefer returned to his law practice and was elected to Congress. Hiram Steele, who practiced law and taught school in St. Johnsbury, Vermont, heeded the call to the colors and was elected captain of Company K of the 10th Vermont Volunteers. Mustered out of the service in 1865, he practiced law in Louisiana, becoming the assistant attorney general of the state. Andrew J. Kuykendall of Vienna, Indiana, was a "prominent lawyer-politician" who resigned his seat in the legislature to lead the 31st Illinois, after which he switched his party affiliation from Democratic to Republican and won a seat in Congress, where he remained after hostilities ended.[2]

Many of the Union's senior officers had been lawyers, and among those who returned to public life after their service were Chester A. Arthur, a member of the New York bar and later a president of the United States. Benjamin F. Butler was elected a member of the Massachusetts congressional delegation after he resigned his commission. Norton P. Chipman, a new member of the bar from Iowa when the war began and a delegate from the District of Columbia at its close (during which he was chief prosecutor of Henry Wirz, the notorious commandant of Andersonville Prisoner of War Camp), ended his legal career in California, where he sat on a state appellate court. Charles Devens, before his command a defender of fugitive slave aiders and abettors in Massachusetts, was after it a state supreme court judge and then attorney general of the United States in the Rutherford B. Hayes administration. James A. Garfield of Ohio, the US attorney for the District of Ohio when he entered the service, became, like Chester A. Arthur, a future president of the United States. Rutherford B. Hayes, another Ohio lawyer, Union officer, and future president, had a successful legal practice before the war and a controversial stint in the White House after Reconstruction. Robert Todd Lincoln interrupted his legal studies (resumed after the war) to take a commission in the US Army. John Alexander McClernand, an Illinois lawyer/politician, followed divisional command with a judgeship. Last, but hardly least, Daniel E. Sickles, a New York lawyer/politician and member of Congress who served in the Army of the Potomac until he was grievously wounded at Gettysburg, later served in diplomatic posts and once again in Congress.[3]

Some lawyer/politicians left government service and reentered private life and statewide politics. Bates resigned in the last year of the war, and returned to his family, his practice, and state politics where he labored against radical Reconstruction. Joseph Holt continued as judge advocate general under President Ulysses Grant, keeping himself as clear of the corruption in that administration as he could, and worried that Reconstruction, to which he had committed himself, was a lost cause. Gideon Welles stayed on in the District of Columbia through 1868, and then returned to his native Connecticut. There he edited and published his diaries, defending Lincoln and the war effort and giving aid and comfort to the reform wing of the Republican Party. William Evarts, special counsel to the attorney general before the creation of the Department of Justice (and the solicitor general's office in it), returned to his lucrative New York City civil practice. These men had guided the course of the war and shaped the peace. Now they reaped its rewards.[4]

For other lawyers in federal government service, the Civil War was a permanent interruption in both private and public life, and service did not benefit them when the guns were again silent. Lincoln's reward was a bullet in the brain from an assassin. William H. Seward barely escaped an attempt on his life. His stamina was never the same thereafter. Edwin M. Stanton found himself a virtual outcast in the Andrew Johnson cabinet and his return to private life was marked by debt. Of the members of Lincoln's cabinet, only Salmon P. Chase benefited directly from his service, joining the Supreme Court as chief justice, but he never really enjoyed the center seat and faced setback after setback in his ambition for the presidency.[5]

At first, leading Confederate lawyers faced postwar exactions. Jefferson Davis languished in federal custody awaiting trial for treason that never came while his wife, Varina, put together a legal team to defend him. Alexander Stephens also paid a steep price, confined for months following his arrest. Other Southern wartime lawyer/politicians never gained rewards for their contributions to the lost cause. Robert Toombs and Judah Benjamin had to flee the country because they had served the Confederacy, Toombs angry that he had to sell his family plantation to live in Europe and Benjamin furious and embarrassed that he had to leave Richmond ignominiously and lamenting on his deathbed that he would never again see his beloved South. One supposes that Counselor Samuel Burritt simply returned to Jacksonville, took the oath of allegiance (necessary to practice in federal courts), and surveyed what remained of his former extensive mercantile property and legal practice.[6]

Confederate lawyers seemed to have little hesitation in returning to their prewar professions. Kentucky's Confederate brigadier general Joseph Lewis left the field of martial combat and rejoined the field of legal combat shortly after the war ended. Asa Biggs, who resigned from his federal district court post in North Carolina because "whenever any State in her Sovereign capacity . . . shall solemnly so decide she has the right for sufficient cause (of which she must be the judge, as upon her alone rests the heavy responsibility for such a fearful act) to voluntarily and peaceably secede from the Union, which she voluntarily entered: . . . thereupon, a citizen of such State is absolved from his allegiance to the United States." Biggs would accept an appointment as a Confederate district court judge, but after the fall of the Confederacy, he continued in private practice until his death in 1878. After the general pardon of 1871 issued by President Johnson, Stephens reentered national politics, returning to Congress. But some Confederates, like lawyer and senior officer Jubal Early, never accepted the illegality of secession, simply regarding the war as a trial by combat in which the federal cause had been triumphant. Such wager of law, a feature of medieval legal practice, ended the matter in his mind. Other Confederate lawyers, like Stephens and Albert Bledsoe, sought in constitutional apologia a defense of their own conduct. Stephens's *Constitutional View of the Late War between the States* offered a series of "colloquies" whose content was familiar to anyone who had followed the arguments for secession before the war. Thus, Jefferson Davis had, in the years before secession, tried to preserve the Union, and when that failed, sought to lead the Confederate states out of the Union peacefully when the principles on which it was founded were abandoned. (Obviously Stephens's defense of Davis applied to Stephens himself.) Bledsoe conceded that "the subjugation of the Southern states and their acceptance of the terms dictated by the north" extinguished any constitutional right to secession. But even that concession echoed the prewar compact theory and its celebration of states' rights. The North had won in the field, not in the law, and that victory was irreversible. As he continued in his turgid treatise, *Is Davis a Traitor?* (1866), the compact theory of federalism was a legitimate constitutional interpretation. Indeed, from "the moment of the formation of the federal union there commenced a struggle for power which has not ceased to be directed against the Slave States."

The "passion" of the North was poised against the reason of the South until the war came. "It arose, like some monstrous abortion of night and darkness from the bottomless depths of a factious contempt for all law and authority." After the cannons were stilled, lawyers like Stephens and Bledsoe still believed that legal arguments were relevant explanations of the Confederate cause. They mattered.[7]

Despite the fulminations of some officials like Stephens and Bledsoe, the former Confederate bar played a vital role in bringing the nation together after the Civil War. They did this by returning to the core business of lawyering—bringing and defending lawsuits and representing clients in dispute resolution. Howell Cobb reopened his law office and reported to his wife in December 1865 that the first fees had arrived: "If constant attendance and close attention to business will bring in more we shall get it." Stephens was no sooner released from custody than he returned to the state court circuit in Georgia. Cobb and Stephens benefited with the reopening of the federal courts in the South. In the docket books of these courts, the signatures of former Confederate members of the bar accompanying their oaths of allegiance were duly recorded by district court clerks. Some of these signatures were bold, a one-line statement that the Confederate bar was back; other signatures, frail and barely legible, bore testimony to the travails of rebellion. The lawyers' return to their offices and the courtrooms was good *for* them. Northern lawyers and Southern lawyers could once again do business with former correspondents across sectional lines. Lawyers could feel pride that lawyering settled issues without muskets and cannons, and that the public looked up to them out of uniform.[8]

For lawyers in both the North and the South, civil rights acts and enforcement statutes created new kinds of legal business, suing and defending clients, making lawyers indispensable to all kinds of laypeople in a way that lawyers had not been before the war. Between 1864 and 1876, congressional legislation would provide for novel causes of civil action, removal of cases from state courts, habeas corpus reform, and additional excise taxes, among other initiatives. In addition, suits based on three "Reconstruction Amendments," along with a surge in debt relief filings, would keep federal courts and lawyers in those courts busy during this period.[9]

During the war, Republicans did not spend much time or thought on what means would be necessary to ensure that the emblements of freedom would include equal rights for the freedmen; but after the war Senators Lyman Trumbull and Henry Wilson collaborated on the Civil Rights Act of 1866. It defined national citizenship (anyone born in the United States was a citizen of the United States and the state in which he or she resided), replacing the older idea of state-conferred citizenship. The act also provided "reasonable protection to all persons in their constitutional rights of equality before the law, without distinction of race or color, or previous condition of slavery or involuntary servitude, except as a punishment for crime, whereof the party shall have been duly convicted." President Andrew Johnson vetoed the act, but Congress passed it over his veto. The act not only defined the civil rights of the newly freed but also provided for enforcement in federal as well as state courts. So, too, the Prejudice and Local Influence Act of 1867 allowed removal of a case to a federal court when a party could establish, to the satisfaction of the federal judge, that "he has reason to, and does believe that, from prejudice or local influence, he will not be able to obtain justice in such state court." All three acts expanded the diversity jurisdiction and the dockets of federal courts.[10]

The Habeas Corpus Act of 1867 was another of the remedial statutes whose potential for public interest litigation was clear because it shifted civil rights enforcement into federal courts. Congress had restored the writ in 1866, and the new act amended the Judiciary Act of 1789 to give all federal courts the authority to issue writs of habeas corpus to state officials. Two years after he proposed the legislations, Trumbull explained that its purpose was to help the freedman unlawfully jailed in the unreconstructed South. In fact, it did aid freedmen and women detained and sold for vagrancy to prison farms in the South, one of the many ways in which Southern black codes reenslaved former slaves. The necessary link between the petitioner and the federal judge was the lawyer, often working without compensation to effectuate the public interest. The federal judge did not have to accept the local officials' account of the detention but could inquire into the facts on his own. Black lawyers like George Lewis Ruffin understood the new public interest law, and in both public forums and party meetings, he supported this legal innovation that shifted the boundaries of federal and state criminal jurisdiction in profound ways that persist to this day.[11]

The Fourteenth Amendment, proposed on June 13, 1866, and ratified by the required three-fourths of the states on July 9, 1868, kept lawyers even busier. The amendment's Section I reads, "All persons born or naturalized in the United States, and subject to the jurisdiction thereof, are citizens of the United States and of the State wherein they reside. No State shall make or enforce any law which shall abridge the privileges or immunities of citizens of the United States; nor shall any State deprive any person of life, liberty, or property, without due process of law; nor deny to any person within its jurisdiction the equal protection of the laws." In one sense, it merely constitutionalized portions of the Civil Rights Act of 1866, but some students of the period have argued that the ratification of this amendment so fundamentally changed the shape of national law and federalism that it created a second constitution. Certainly it is true that suits based on the Equal Protection and Due Process Clauses of the Fourteenth Amendment substantially enlarged the powers of both the federal courts and state courts deciding cases on the basis of the amendment. The amendment is the source of a huge body of judicial opinion and legal scholarship as well as truckloads of litigation.[12]

With business in the courts growing, Congress's lawyers reordered the shape of the federal judiciary to ease access to counsel. The Judiciary Act of 1869 restored the Court to nine members and established nine separate judgeships for the US circuit courts. It also allowed judges to retire without losing their salary. Lyman Trumbull reported it out of the Senate Judiciary Committee on February 3, 1869, assuming that its way through Congress was paved with political as well as jurisprudential good intentions. The rebellion was over and reform of the courts was long overdue. It was popular among litigants and litigators; at the same time the naming of new judges by a Republican president and a Republican majority in the Senate would reward loyalty to the party and the Union in the South.[13]

Congress mollified lawyers with local practices who might have been upset by the Judiciary Act of 1869 with the Conformity Act of June 1, 1872. It provided that the civil practice and procedure in federal district and circuit courts (other than in equity and admiralty matters) must conform to the practice and procedure used by the state courts for similar civil cases "as near as may be" at the time. The Process Acts had linked federal to state procedure as the latter stood in 1792, and in many states procedure had been revised since that time. The act did not apply to rules of evidence that the federal courts had adopted or Congress had imposed on federal courts. The Federal Rules of Civil Procedure, which became effective in 1938, superseded the Conformity Act.[14]

With legislation like the Conformity Act, Congress clearly viewed the lawyers as important agents in knitting the nation together. But not all of these acts were concessions to lawyers in state practice. Some broadened federal practice. A striking illustration was the Jurisdiction and Removal Act of March 3, 1875: "An Act to determine the jurisdiction of circuit courts of the United States, and to regulate the removal of causes from State courts, and for other purposes." While it might seem on its face a part of the integration of the new circuit judiciary into the fold, that appearance was deceptive. It granted the US circuit courts what Chief Justice John Marshall in *Osborn v. Bank of the United States* (1824) had foretold: the jurisdiction to hear all cases arising under the Constitution and the laws of the United States, as long as the matter in dispute was worth more than $500. The statute also made it possible for plaintiffs and defendants in cases before state courts to remove a case to a US circuit court whenever the matter involved a question of federal law or if any members of the parties were from different states. The last of the civil rights acts of the era, passed in 1875, afforded those individuals barred from public accommodations on the basis of their race to bring suit in federal courts. This act, like its predecessors, was not some expression of empty idealism or ritual posing; it was the capstone of the plan to use the federal courts to ensure the gains of Reconstruction. By adopting an expansive interpretation of federal jurisdiction, in the long run the act fundamentally changed the role of the federal courts in the federal system, the most sweeping extension of judicial power since the short-lived Judiciary Act of 1801.[15]

Although one may suppose that lawyers' caseloads would naturally increase had there been no Civil War, and indeed the growth of business activity, the rise of corporate finance, and the expansion of industrial production all created demand for lawyers, the postwar surge in business in the nation's courts was also affected by Congress's resetting the agenda of the federal courts. As federal courts were just reopening in the former Confederacy, the yearly counts of cases filed tell the tale. Civil cases to which the United States was a party numbered over eight thousand in the year 1870, many of them coming out of the postwar legislation. Private suits in the federal courts were nearly twice as numerous in 1873.[16]

Despite the fact that the resumption of federal court sessions represented the triumph of the Union over the Confederacy, Southern lawyers had no hesitation turning to federal courts for civil relief during Reconstruction. In fact, compared to the prewar district courts' dockets, postwar private litigation was booming. In the Northern District of Georgia, for example, after the resumption of federal authority, the March 1867 minutes recorded 71 civil cases and fourteen federal crimes, most of the latter failure to pay fees under federal statutes. There was also one patent infringement case. A year later, the court spent three weeks hearing 151 civil suits and 121 federal criminal indictments for violation of the Revenue Act of 1867. Typical was the indictment of Thomas Harris for "distill[ing] without paying the special tax." Most of those indicted under the Revenue Act confessed and paid the fines. There were also three indictments of men who had defaulted on bonds that mail clerks were required to post.[17]

The Bankruptcy Act of 1867 was welcomed in the South and brought many propertied white people, represented by the bar, to the federal courts seeking relief for debts incurred during secession. In 3,180 filings—all but 404 voluntarily filed by debtors, from the Southern district of Mississippi, South Carolina, and the eastern district of Tennessee—white Southerners gained the aid of the federal courts. Southern sympathizers in the Eastern District of Missouri benefited from the act; within the first year of its operation there were 581 filings. Bankruptcy petitions flooded into the federal court for the Northern District of Georgia. The act's relatively high level of exemption of personal property from discharge to creditors stabilized a Southern economic system made fragile by wartime expenditures, reattached the interest of Southern lawyers to the federal courts, and reintegrated the Southern economy into Northern credit markets.[18]

Reconstruction congressional acts had a similar impact on Northern courts' dockets. In the Circuit Court for the District of Massachusetts, for example, the caseload was 472 filings in 1857, 508 filings in 1858, 557 filings in 1859, and 627 filings in 1860. These represented the usual array of civil suits for debt, along with personal injury suits against the Boston and Maine and Boston and Worcester Railroad, and suits against the City of New Bedford, the capital of the whaling industry. The war years dampened the caseloads and reversed the growth of the docket, with 496 filings in 1861 and 489 filings in 1862. But the upward trend reappeared at the end of the war, the court hearing and determining 963 cases in 1865 and a whopping 1,229 cases in 1866, many of them the same revenue cases the Northern District of Alabama faced. The Bankruptcy Act brought another bumper crop of cases: 1,062 in 1867 and 1,145 in 1868 into the Massachusetts district court. Recourse to the federal courts was national, not sectional.[19]

While federal removal and other provisions of the congressional act may have shifted the boundary of judicial federalism, new duties for the federal courts in the Reconstruction Era did not precipitate conflict with the state courts. State courts' dockets rose as fast as those of federal courts. In these years, litigants crowded the state courthouses. The boom years in California brought 196 cases to its highest court during the July and October terms of 1860, but in the same terms for the year 1875, the number of suits in the California Supreme Court was 380. The war years had slowed litigation in Illinois—a mere 179 cases came to its supreme court between 1863 and 1866—but by 1871 the docket swelled to over 275 cases a year. The Indiana Supreme Court heard over 900 cases in the year before the war, but by 1871, that number had grown to nearly 1,500 cases a year. The Supreme Court of Kansas was burdened with only 101 cases in 1866, but by 1872 the load had risen to nearly 400 and four years later it topped 481. The provisions for removal of some cases to federal courts did not deter former Confederates from appealing suits to their own supreme courts. Before war came, at the June 1859 and January 1860 meetings of the Alabama Supreme Court, 238 cases were filed. The December 1876 session of the court heard 232 cases. The Mississippi Supreme Court heard and determined 128 cases in the year before the war; by 1876, with Reconstruction ended (through extra-legal means to be sure), its supreme court heard 321 cases. The same pattern held in North Carolina, whose supreme court adjudicated 321 cases in its 1859–1860 sittings, and over 600 in 1876.[20]

If the business of the courts and the busyness of the lawyers in the aftermath of the war is any indication, Reconstruction imposed from above, that is, by the Republican majority in Congress, and received below by federal and state courts, was a boon for the legal profession. It would be too cynical to say that the purpose of the Republican lawyers in Congress was to provide succor for members of their profession who had been denied clients and causes during the war years. But a thing is what it is, and from all indications, it is reasonable to say that postwar legislation was as much for the lawyers and their clients as for the freedmen and women.

# Conclusion

## The Lawyers' Civil War
## in Retrospect

IN HIS 1866 COLLECTION of poetry, *Battle-Pieces*, Herman Melville looked back on the fields of carnage and saw a justification for the war: "Hallowed by hearts, and by the laws, we here who warred for Man and Right." The Civil War had been "a victory for law." Surely it was this for Lincoln, though he did not see the end of it. It was his character, courage, sense of duty, and above all his respect for the Constitution and its law that buoyed the nation's spirits when they ebbed and swelled with them when the final triumph of law and order was near. And through it all, his sense of the quality of mercy and his willingness to pardon, using the presidential pardoning power even for those who raised arms against the nation, proved the poet right.[1]

But what was so evident to Melville in 1866 was not as clear in the midst of the conflict. Lincoln's self-doubt more than once discouraged his devoted secretary John Nicolay, writing in his diary on August 23, 1864, "Everything is darkness and doubt and discouragement." Chief Justice Taney, who held office until the last year of the war, never seemed to realize the stakes of the conflict or the monumental legal changes it was bringing. After one cabinet session, Gideon Welles, who had early given up his law practice to accept administrative assignments in various Democratic presidencies, lamented that none of the lawyers there seemed to have a clear vision of the way ahead. "Discussions were desultory and without order or system, but in the summing-up and conclusions the President, who was a patient listener and learner, concentrated results, and often determined questions adverse to the Secretary of State, regarding him and his opinions, as he did those of his other advisers, for what they were worth and generally no more. But the want of system and free communication among all as equals prevented that concert and comity which is really strength to an administration." But even Welles, along with Chase, Seward, and Lincoln all understood, tacitly at least, that the questions they discussed most every day that they met were legal ones. Everyone in that heavily draped office knew the law and believed that it limited and directed their decisions.[2]

In countless exchanges among the lawyers in the president's office, on the floor of the Congress, and in the courtrooms of the United States, lawyers confronted the crisis as lawyers, believing—as they said—that in law there were solutions to the most basic of human problems. This was their legacy. As Oliver Wendell Holmes Jr., perhaps the greatest American jurist of his time and a combat veteran of the Civil War, wrote in 1909, "If we are lawyers, our memories and our reverence" for the past were part of the project of judging. Resolving disputes is what lawyers did, and the most lasting achievement of the lawyers in the Civil War era was turning that terrible conflict into a new and lasting regime of law. That regime was not always a sympathetic one. Realism in the law replaced grand ideas of natural law goodness. Thus, though his wartime letters reveal a young man moved to tears by the mutilation and death of his comrades, in later life the war and the law fused in the thinking of veterans like Holmes. The war annealed his view of the world, changing the diffuse idealism of the antebellum college student into the hardened cynicism of a Gilded Age law professor and judge. As he wrote in his seminal collection of essays on the common law in 1881, "The life of the law has not been logic; it has been experience. The felt necessities of the time," the history and the public policy, these—the felt realities, were the stuff of law for the lawyer/soldiers of the Civil War Era.[3]

The basis for any lasting regime of law was the federal Constitution, to which the former Confederate states once again pledged loyalty. A consensus at the start of the crisis that the Constitution limited the powers of the federal government fractured by the end of the conflict into two clusters of beliefs, one clinging to the old Constitution, with its states' rights foundation, its limitation of all government, and its narrow idea of (whites only) liberty, and the other cluster opening, gradually, even hesitatingly, to a broader view of governmental roles and guarantees of civil rights and equality to all. Former Confederates and their allies in the North "assumed that the regulation of the freedmen would be left to the individual states" while advocates of the civil rights acts and the Reconstruction amendments glimpsed a Constitution that ensured equal protection for all. Were these older views the "fixed standard on which constitutional government and the rule of law depend" or were they relics of a social order that the war had tested and found wanting? Had the Republicans "never desired a broad, permanent extension of national legislative power" and thus "framed the most limited, conservative reconstruction possible"? Or did the passage of civil rights acts and Reconstruction amendments fundamentally change the old federalism? Lawyers' elaboration of these two views over the long course of American constitutional theorizing and government activity goes on to this day.[4]

At the very least, the lawyer/politicians of the Civil War provided what the generals and the soldiers could not—legitimacy. From the beginning of the conflict to its conclusion, both the Union and the Confederacy believed that the law was on their side, and that it was important that the law be on their side. In a nation conceived in law, the Civil War lawyers provided reassurance that the sacrifices of the war were governed not by chance, but by the rule of law. When abstract words like freedom, liberty, union, and rights did not always have clear applications, or meant different things to different people, the Civil War lawyers gave concreteness to abstractions. In times of trial, such specificity lent comfort and gave purpose to human action. A Civil War of the lawyers, by the lawyers, and for the lawyers helped to preserve, as one of those lawyers wrote, a "nation, conceived in Liberty, and dedicated to the proposition that all men are created equal."

Is this too starry-eyed a conclusion? Perhaps. After the Civil War, the idealism of the antebellum era reformers waned. Rule of law had triumphed in the suppression of secession, but the violence of White Leagues and lawless vigilante organizations like the Ku Klux Klan proved that the rule of law did not extend to the Southern countryside. "If Reconstruction offered hope of meaningful change in the Reconstruction

South," that change did not come in the courts. Against such evil, even the best intentioned of the Civil War lawyers on both sides could not contend. Lawyers like Chase and Seward who had agitated for reform before the war retreated from their enthusiasm when the war's toll was counted. They had not withered into cynicism so much as returned their attention to ordinary legal business. Such matters lacked the drama of the war years, when so much seemed to depend on their contributions, but with peace, lawyers could do what no one else could—at least restate the importance of the rule of law. Black suitors in Southern courts did not autonomatically fail in their efforts. With the aid of white lawyers, and by admitting in court their dependence on white justice, black litigants won their suits more often then they lost. In courts and in political assemblages men paid homage to the return of law and order, and offered that, in the words of one Mississippi supreme court justice, the best friend of the black man was his lawyer. If the homage was sometimes only lip service, as the "Redemption" of white supremacy replaced the reform Reconstruction era, the influence of the lawyers had not waned. True legal equality had not followed the peace, but its power to elevate American constitutionalism did not disappear. No longer could secession become an escape from the ideal of equality, nor would slavery blight the land. The Civil War lawyers in peace did what the Civil War lawyers in war had yearned to do—knit the nation together in obedience to law.[5]

Mark Twain wrote that comparisons were odious, but they need not be malicious. And sometimes they are useful. Can the lawyer/politicians' performance in the Civil War tell us anything about the lawyer/politician in our system in time of crisis? There may be no more controverted a concept in history than "the lessons of history." History never repeats itself—context and people are always different. But similarities between past and present abound. There was nothing in our history to compare with the Civil War, or was there? Secessionist movements are a staple of modern politics. So is the persistence of "two Americas."

In the twenty-first century, the United States finds itself in perpetual war with "terrorists." The term is as slippery as it is ubiquitous. As the secessionists of 1861 saw the abolitionists, and the unionists of 1861 saw the secessionists, we see terrorism all around us. The temptation is to strike out with all the force we can muster against those who endanger our way of life. In the process, cherished civil liberties may be abridged. For some it is the price for freedom, though it takes freedom from all of us. Who is to constrain this visceral urge? What are the means by which it can be constrained?[6]

In the so-called war on terror, lawyers in the government have played controversial roles. Some aided and abetted practices that exceeded in illegality anything that the Lincoln and Davis administrations pursued. Others raised objections when civil rights of suspects and civilians were routinely sacrificed to an amorphous and veiled national security. Challenged by lawyers outside of government, some panicky and bigoted officials provided undeveloped and duplicitous explanations for torture, warrantless searches, and mass incarceration. Later, members of the Department of Justice defended themselves by saying that they simply provided zealous advocacy for policies that the executive branch adopted. They then returned to private practice, law school positions, and further government service.[7]

By contrast, one may argue that Lincoln, members of his cabinet, and Republicans in Congress stretched the bounds of the old Constitution to the breaking point. But they did this within the larger confines of legalism. Although the old Constitution restricted the role of the federal government and enlarged that of the states, nothing in the letter of the Constitution barred the shifting of those boundaries by legislation or amendment. In doing this, the Republicans trod carefully, never abandoning their commitment to the rule of law. Their view of law evolved with the felt necessities of the war. They refused to view the Constitution as a suicide pact. Instead, they read it in light of an event that had no precedent in national history. True, some of the actions Lincoln took precipitously and unilaterally were questionable even to his supporters. In particular, the imposition of courts martial in areas where the regular federal courts met and there was no imminent threat of domestic insurrection was unconstitutional, as was the wholesale suppression of Democratic newspaper coverage and editorial writing. When members of the executive branch, the Congress, and the judiciary do not perform their constitutional task of checking and balancing the power of the other branches, particularly in times of perceived national crisis; when the federal government's counsel ignore the boundaries of government action laid down in the Constitution, the last resort of the rule of law is the professionalism of the government lawyers. If lawyers in government regard themselves as servants of power beholden to their partisan employers, the Constitution is imperiled from within. When lawyers in government hold themselves bound to a higher standard, the Constitution is kept safe. And when lawyers glimpse in the law a way to a better world, they perform the highest duty of their profession.[8]

As I write this, an administration has come to power in our country that seems willing to do without legal counsel and at times shows strident indifference to legal precept, precedent, and procedure. The result is not, however, a decline in the value of public lawyering. Quite the contrary is true. The current state of play makes the roles of lawyers in and out of government, and lawyers on the bench, even more vital in protecting the new Constitution of hope and aspiration.

# NOTES

---

## Introduction

1. Peter Charles Hoffer, *A Nation of Laws: America's Imperfect Pursuit of Justice* (Lawrence: University Press of Kansas, 2008), 134–145; Phillip S. Paludan, "The American Civil War Considered as a Crisis in Law and Order," *American Historical Review* 77 (1972), 1013–1034; Stephen C. Neff, *Justice in Blue and Gray: A Legal History of the Civil War* (Cambridge, MA: Harvard University Press, 2010), 4. But see William H. Rehnquist, *All the Laws but One: Civil Liberties in Wartime* (New York: Knopf, 1998), 221 (in time of war, some civil liberties are curbed).

   An important note: it is assumed by many legal historians that the relationship between law and politics was discovered by Progressive jurists in the early twentieth century. This is not true. Every major lawyer/ politician in the antebellum and Civil War years knew (and worked in) the confluence of law and politics.

2. Census computation, Robert W. Fogel, Occupational Data from the 1860 United States Census. ICPSR09873-v1; Ann Arbor, MI: Inter-university Consortium for Political and Social Research [distributor], 1993, http:// doi.org/10.3886/ICPSR09873.v1

3. Tilden quoted in Russell McClinock, *Lincoln and the Decision for War, the Northern Response to Secession* (Chapel Hill: University of North Carolina Press, 2008), 35; Benjamin Robbins Curtis, *Executive Power* (Boston: Little, Brown, 1862); Louis P. Masur, *Lincoln's Hundred Days: The Emancipation Proclamation and the War for the Union* (Cambridge, MA: Harvard University Press, 2012), 118–121.

4. In Re Booth and Rycroft, 3 Wisc. 1 (1854) (Smith, J.) quoted in William E. Nelson, *The Fourteenth Amendment: From Political Principle to Judicial Doctrine* (Cambridge, MA: Harvard University Press, 1988), 38.

5. On the "dark war" behind the lines and among guerilla forces, and regular forces exceeding their commanders' instructions: Michael C .C. Adams, *Living Hell: The Dark Side of the Civil War* (Baltimore: Johns Hopkins University Press, 2014), 1; Daniel E. Sutherland's *Savage Conflict: The Decisive Role of the Guerrillas in the American Civil War* (Chapel Hill: University of North Carolina Press, 2009); and Mark Grimsley, *The Hard Hand of War: Union Military Policy toward Southern Civilians, 1861–1865* (New York: Cambridge University Press, 1996); but see Anne J. Bailey, "Henry McCulloch's Texans and the Defense of Arkansas, 1862," in Bailey and Daniel E. Sutherland, eds., *Civil War Arkansas* (Fayetteville: University of Arkansas Press, 2000), 35 (quoting Winston Churchill); Mark E. Neely, "Was the Civil War a Total War?" in Stig Foster and Jorg Nadler, eds., *On the Road to Total War: The American Civil War and the German Wars of Unification, 1861–1871* (Cambridge: Cambridge University Press, 1997), 30; Mark E. Neely, *The Civil War and the Limits of Destruction* (Cambridge, MA: Harvard University Press, 2007), 198–220; and D. H. Dilbeck, *A More Civil War: How the Union Waged a Just War* (Chapel Hill: University of North Carolina Press, 2016).

6. See, e.g., Harold M. Hyman and William M. Wiecek, *Equal Justice under Law: Constitutional Development 1835–1875* (New York: Harper, 1982), 20.

7. The concept of a critical "moment" derives from J. G. A. Pocock's *Machiavellian Moment* (Princeton, NJ: Princeton University Press, 1975), vii–viii, in which a republic faces a crisis or a series of closely related crisis threatening the very existence of the state. In such a moment, older ideas are put to the test, and the leaders of the state will either adapt or fail to adapt new ones.

8. Richard Posner, *Divergent Paths: The Academy and the Judiciary* (Cambridge, MA: Harvard University Press, 2016), x; Peter Charles Hoffer, Williamjames Hull Hoffer, and N. E. H. Hull, *The Federal Courts: An Essential History* (New York: Oxford University Press, 2016).

## Prologue

1. Alfred D. Chandler, *Scale and Scope: The Dynamics of Industrial Capitalism* (Cambridge, MA: Harvard University Press, 1990), 53; Daniel W. Stowell, introduction to *The Papers of Abraham Lincoln, Legal Documents, and Cases* (Charlottesville: University of Virginia Press, 2008), 1: xxxv; David Donald, *Lincoln's Herndon* (New York: Knopf, 1948), 38–39; *Herndon's Life of Lincoln*, ed. Paul M. Angle (New York: Fawcett, 1961), 169–171; John J. Duff, *A. Lincoln, Prairie Lawyer* (New York: Holt, Rinehart, and Winston, 1960), 35–50 (John Todd Stuart), 78–117 (Stephen

T. Logan and Herndon); Timothy H. Huebner, *Liberty and Union: The Civil War Era and American Constitutionalism* (Lawrence: University Press of Kansas, 2016), 101–102 (Lincoln's politics), 212–213 (Seward and Chase).

2.  David Hoffman, *A Course of Legal Study*, 2nd ed. (Baltimore: Neal, 1836), 2:758; M. H. Hoeflich, *Legal Publishing in Antebellum America* (New York: Cambridge University Press, 2010), 35–36; John G. Baker, "Indiana Judges: A Portrait of Judicial Evolution," in David J. Bodenhamer and Randall Shepard, eds., *A History of Indiana Law* (Athens: Ohio University Press, 2006), 306; Mark E. Steiner, *An Honest Calling: The Law Practice of Abraham Lincoln* (DeKalb: Northern Illinois University Press, 2006), 55.

3.  Joseph Story, "Discourse Produced on the Inauguration of the Author" (1829), in Perry Miller, ed., *The Legal Mind in America* (Garden City, NY: Anchor, 1961), 177; George Washington Harris, *Sut Lovingood: Tales Spun by a Nat'ral Born Drun'd Fool* (New York: Dick and Fitzgerald, 1867), 183; Emma Southworth, *Ishmael, or, In the Depths* ([1864]; New York: Federal Book Co, 1884), 472.

4.  Stowell, introduction, *Legal Documents*, 1: xxx; Alfred S. Konefsky, "The Legal Profession," in Michael Grossberg and Christopher Tomlins, eds., *The Cambridge History of Law in America* (New York: Cambridge University Press, 2008), 2:73; Duff, *Prairie Lawyer*, 43, 79.

5.  St. George Tucker quoted in E. Lee Shepard, "Breaking into the Profession: Establishing a Law Practice in Antebellum Virginia," *Journal of Southern History* 48 (1982), 393; Paul D. Carrington, "Teaching Law in the Antebellum Northwest," *University of Toledo Law Review* 23 (1991), 4; Harold Holzer, "Reassessing Lincoln's Legal Career," in Roger Billings and Frank Williams, eds., *Abraham Lincoln Esq.: The Legal Career of America's Greatest President* (Lexington: University Press of Kentucky, 2010), 15; story quoted in Norman W. Spaulding, "The Myth of Civic Republicanism: Interrogating the Ideology of Antebellum Legal Ethics," *Fordham Law Review* 71 (2003), 1424.

6.  See, e.g., Christopher Neff, "Those Cunning Spiders, the Lawyers: In Search of an Antebellum Legal Ethos," *Journal of the Legal Profession* 33 (2009), 326; Timothy S. Huebner, *The Southern Judicial Tradition: State Judges and Sectional Distinctiveness, 1790–1890* (Athens: University of Georgia Press, 1989), 133–134; Lieutenant General Jubal Anderson Early, *Autobiographical Sketch and Narrative of the War between the States* (Lynchburg, VA: n.p., 1912), 12; Thomas E. Schott, *Alexander H. Stephens of Georgia, A Biography* (Baton Rouge: Louisiana State University Press, 1988), 29.

7.  Allen C. Guelzo, *Lincoln and Douglas: The Debates that Defined America* (New York: Simon and Schuster, 2008), xiv; Louise L. Stevenson, *Lincoln in the Atlantic World* (New York: Cambridge University Press, 2015), 33,

112; Maurice G. Baxter, *Henry Clay the Lawyer* (Lexington: University Press of Kentucky, 2015), 15.

8.  S. T. Logan to John Nicolay, July 6, 1875, in Michael Burlingame, ed., *An Oral History of Abraham Lincoln: John G. Nicolay's Interviews and Essays* (Carbondale: Southern Illinois University Press, 1996), 37; Daniel W. Stowell, ed., *The Papers of Abraham Lincoln, Legal Documents and Cases* (Charlottesville: University of Virginia Press, 2008), 1:xxxix, xi; Lincoln to William H. Grigsby, August 3, 1858, in Stowell, *The Papers of Abraham Lincoln*, 10; Eric Foner, *The Fiery Trial: Abraham Lincoln and American Slavery* (New York: Norton, 2010), 33–62; Brian Dirck, *Lincoln the Lawyer* (Urbana: University of Illinois Press, 2007), 76–78.

9.  Reg Ankrom, *Stephen A. Douglas, The Political Apprenticeship* (Jefferson, NC: McFarland, 2015), 57, 189; Robert Walter Johannsen, *Stephen A. Douglas* (Urbana: University of Illinois Press, 1973), 88–89, 306–307. Lawyering for the railroads was the way to wealth for the lawyer/politicians. Samuel Tilden, for example, made millions from it during the decade before the war. Neither Lincoln nor Douglas did quite this well.

10. Fergus M. Bordewich, *America's Great Debate: Henry Clay, Stephen A. Douglas, and the Compromise that Preserved the Union* (New York: Simon and Schuster, 2013), 30. Text of the Ottawa debate from Rodney O. Davis and Douglas L. Wilson, eds., *The Lincoln-Douglas Debates* (Urbana: University of Illinois Press, 2008), 6–17 (Douglas), 17–34 (Lincoln), 35–41 (Douglas rejoinder). A convenient online source is Lincoln Home, National Park Service, "Lincoln Douglas Debates," http://www.nps.gov/liho/learn/historyculture/debates.htm. On the first debate, see Stephen Berry, *A House Dividing: The Lincoln-Douglas Debates of 1858* (New York: Oxford University Press, 2015), 1–24.

11. Alexis DeTocqueville, *Democracy in America*, trans. Henry Reeve (London: Saunders and Otley, 1838), 2, 109.

12. Dred Scott v. Sandford, 60 US 393, 403, 407 (1857) (Taney, C.J.); Herman Belz, *A New Birth of Freedom: The Republican Party and Freedman's Rights, 1861–1866* (New York: Fordham University Press, 2000), 38 (Montgomery Blair's views on race); Andrew W. Arpey, *The William Freeman Murder Trial: Insanity, Politics, and Race* (Syracuse, NY: Syracuse University Press, 2003), 144–145 (lawyers' views of race in antebellum New York murder case); Ariela J. Gross, *Double Character: Slavery and Mastery in the Southern Courtroom* (Princeton, NJ: Princeton University Press, 2000), 179–180 n. 50 (leading Southern lawyers regard slavery as positive good); but see Paul Finkelman, "Prelude to the Fourteenth Amendment: Black Legal Rights in the Antebellum North," *Rutgers Law Journal* 17 (1986), 417–418 (great variety in legal treatment of Northern free blacks).

13. Pheobe v. Jay, 1 Ill. 268 (1828) (slavery illegal in Illinois); Paul D. Escott, *What Shall We Do with the Negro?: Lincoln, White Racism, and Civil War America* (Charlottesville: University of Virginia Press, 2009), 94–118; Earl

Maltz, *Dred Scott and the Politics of Slavery* (Lawrence: University Press of Kansas, 2007), 101–154; Don E. Fehrenbacher, *The Dred Scott Case: Its Significance in American Law and Politics* (New York: Oxford University Press, 1978), 449–484; Nicole Etchison, *Bleeding Kansas: Contested Liberty in the Civil War Era* (Lawrence: University Press of Kansas, 2004), 139–189.

14. In actuality, the two men had been debating over slavery and race for four years. James Oakes, *The Scorpion's Sting: Antislavery and the Coming of the Civil War* (New York: Norton, 2014), 85–87; David Potter, *The Impending Crisis, 1848–1861*, completed and edited by Don E. Fehrenbacher (New York: Harper and Row, 1976), 340.

15. Oakes, *Scorpion's Sting*, 86–87; Peter Charles Hoffer, *For Ourselves and Our Posterity: The Preamble to the Constitution in American History* (New York: Oxford University Press, 2013), 69–82.

16. *Providence Journal*, February 29, 1860. End of slavery in the British Empire, in 1833–1838: P. J. Marshall, *The Cambridge Illustrated History of the British Empire* (Cambridge: Cambridge University Press, 2001), 44–45; end of slavery in the French Empire, 1848: Jeremy Black, *The Atlantic Slave Trade in World History* (New York: Routledge, 2015), 133; abolitionism in the United States: Manisha Sinha, *The Slave's Cause: A History of Abolition* (New Haven, CT: Yale University Press, 2016), 228–265, 461–499.

17. Lincoln, speech accepting the Republican Nomination for Senator, June 16, 1858, in Roy P. Basler, ed., *The Collected Works of Abraham Lincoln* (New Brunswick, NJ: Rutgers University Press, 1953), 2:461–469 ("House Divided Speech"); a convenient online source is http://www.abrahamlincolnonline.org/lincoln/speeches/house.htm; David Donald, *Lincoln* (New York: Simon and Schuster, 1995), 209 (reception at the time).

18. Daniel Farber, *Lincoln's Constitution* (Chicago: University of Chicago Press, 2003), 177 (quoting Lincoln), 178–179 (Lincoln on *Dred Scott*).

19. Davis and Wilson, *Lincoln-Douglas Debates*, 36.

## Chapter 1

1. See, e.g., James Oakes, *The Scorpion's Sting: Antislavery and the Coming of the Civil War* (New York: Norton, 2014), 38–39; Stephen A. Channing, *Crisis of Fear, Secession in South Carolina* (New York: Norton, 1974), 261–295; Michael P. Johnson, *Toward a Patriarchal Republic: The Secession of Georgia* (Baton Rouge: Louisiana State University Press, 1977), 17; Christopher J. Olson, *Political Culture and Secession in Mississippi: Masculinity, Honor, and the Antiparty Tradition, 1830–1860* (New York: Oxford University Press, 2002), 187–194.

2. John C. Calhoun, Speech to the Senate, March 4, 1850, *Congressional Globe*, 31st Cong. 1st sess., 454–455; William Freehling, *The Road*

*to Disunion 1: Secessionists at Bay, 1776–1854* (New York: Oxford University Press, 1990), 475–486, 522; Channing, *Crisis of Fear*, 149–150; Brockenborough quoted in Alfred L. Brophy, *University, Court, and Slave: Pro-Slavery Thought in Southern Colleges and Courts and the Coming of Civil War* (New York: Oxford University Press, 2016), 120.

3.  Thomas E. Schott, *Alexander H. Stephens of Georgia, a Biography* (Baton Rouge: Louisiana State University Press, 1988), 1–47.

4.  Alexander Stephens to J. Henly Smith, September 15, 1860, in Ulrich Bonnell Phillips, ed., *The Correspondence of Robert Toombs, Alexander H. Stephens, and Howell Cobb, Annual Report of the American Historical Association for the Year 1911*, vol. 2 (Washington, DC: American Historical Association, 1913), 496; Stephens to Smith, September 16, 1860, in Bonnell, *Correspondence*, 498–499.

5.  Schott, *Alexander Stephens of Georgia*, 304–311; Stephens, Speech to the Legislature, November 14, 1860, Milledgeville, Ga., in Henry Crawford, ed. *Alexander H. Stephens in Public and Private . . . With Letters and Speeches* (Philadelphia: National Publishing, 1866), 694-709; Stephens to Smith, November 21, 1860, in Phillips, *Correspondence*, 2:503.

6.  Lincoln to Stephens, in Roy P. Basler, ed., *The Collected Works of Abraham Lincoln* (New Brunswick, NJ: Rutgers University Press, 1953), 4:160; Stephens to Lincoln, in Schott, *Stephens*, 309–311.

7.  Craig M. Simpson, *A Good Southerner, The Life of Henry A. Wise of Virginia* (Chapel Hill: University of North Carolina Press, 1985), 9–11, 245–247.

8.  Francis Hopkins Heck, *Proud Kentuckian: John C. Breckinridge, 1821-1875* (Lexington: University of Kentucky Press, 1976), 101, 103, 105; Speech of John C. Breckinridge, September 5, 1860, *New York Times*, September 5, 1860, p. 1,

9.  Charles Colcock Jones Jr. to Charles Colcock Jones Sr., January 28, 1861, quoted in Robert Manson Myers, ed., *The Children of Pride: A True Story of Georgia and the Civil War* (New Haven, CT: Yale University Press, 1972), 648; T. R. R. Cobb, *An Inquiry into the Law of Negro Slavery in the United States of America* [1858] ed. Paul Finkelman (Athens: University of Georgia Press, 2009), 215; Brophy, *University, Court, and Slave*, 287–288; James M. McPherson, *Battle Cry of Freedom: The Civil War Era* (New York: Oxford University Press, 1988), 737.

10. The delegates supposedly represented the people of South Carolina, re-creating the ratification process that brought South Carolina into the federal union. Not every inhabitant of the state was permitted to cast a vote for the delegates, but limitations on the franchise in South Carolina were no more rigorous than in other states. The leaders of the movement assumed that the legality of the process rested on the consent of the governed, the same doctrine as underlay the American Revolution in 1776. Thus secession could be regarded as a second American Revolution

by its supporters. See, e.g., James M. McPherson, *Abraham Lincoln and the Second American Revolution* (New York: Oxford University Press, 1992), 27–28. Lincoln rejected this notion, arguing that secession was a counter-revolution.

11. Robert Barnwell Rhett, December 27, 1860, quoted in William C. Davis, ed., *A Fire-Eater Remembers: The Confederate Memoir of Robert Barnwell Rhett* (Columbia: University of South Carolina Press, 2000), 19; On Rhett in these weeks, William C. Davis, *Rhett: The Turbulent Life and Times of a Fire-Eater* (Columbia: University of South Carolina Press, 2001), 408–411. On Hutson: Lawrence Sanders Rowland, *The History of Beaufort County, South Carolina* (Columbia: University of South Carolina Press, 1996), 423–429; on Inglis: Thomas H. Robinson Jr., ed., *Resisting Sherman: A Confederate Surgeon's Journal and the Civil War in the Carolinas* (El Dorado Hill, CA: Savas Beatie, 2015), 44–46.

12. U. R. Brooks, *South Carolina Bench and Bar* (Columbia, SC: State Company, 1908), 87, 88, 93, 96, 104, 137; Thomas D. Morris, *Southern Slavery and the Law, 1619-1860* (Chapel Hill: University of North Carolina Press, 1996), 54.

13. "Declaration of the Immediate Causes Which Induce and Justify the Secession of South Carolina from the Federal Union," December 24, 1860, South Carolina Convention, *Journal of the Convention of the People of South Carolina, Together with the Ordinances . . . etc* (Columbia, SC, 1862), Appendix, 461–466; a convenient online version of which can be found at http://avalon.law.yale.edu/19th_century/csa_scarsec.asp.

14. [John C. Calhoun] Exposition and Protest, 1828, Robert E. Meriwether, ed., *Papers of John C. Calhoun* (Columbia: University of South Carolina Press, 1959—), 10:431–531; a convenient version is https://en.wikisource.org/wiki/South_Carolina_Exposition_and_Protest.

15. Jefferson and Madison, founders of the Republican Party, were protesting the Federalists' attempt to suppress Republican campaign efforts by criminalizing speech critical of the John Adams administration. Jefferson did use the term "interposition" to mean that states could step in between their citizens and the federal government when a federal act was unconstitutional. Madison did not go that far. Both men later recanted those views when they became leaders of the federal government. See Peter Charles Hoffer, *The Free Press Crisis of 1800: Thomas Cooper's Trial for Seditious Libel* (Lawrence: University Press of Kansas), 51–72.

16. On notions of Southern popular sovereignty in the secession era, see Stephanie McCurry, *Confederate Reckoning: Power and Politics in the Civil War South* (Cambridge, MA: Harvard University Press, 2010), 11–37; Roman J. Hoyos, "Peaceful Revolution and Popular Sovereignty: Reassessing the Constitutionality of Southern Secession" in Sally E. Hadden and Patricia Hagler Minter, eds., *Signposts: New*

*Directions in Southern Legal History* (Athens: University of Georgia Press, 2013), 241–264.

17.    Antonin Scalia and Bryan A. Garner, *Reading Law: The Interpretation of Texts* (St. Paul, MN: West, 2012), 16–28.

18.    Justice Henry Lewis Benning, dissenting in Cleland v. Waters (1855), quoted in Brophy, *University, Court, and Slave*, 219. But note that the majority opinion, crafted by Joseph Henry Lumpkin, upheld a will precisely because the rule of law must be maintained. Like Wardlaw, Lumpkin was a pro-slavery, pro-secession jurist who saw slavery as a positive good. Ibid., 289.

19.    Howell Cobb, "To The People of Georgia," December 6, 1860, in Phillips, *Correspondence*, 507; Cobb to James Buchanan, March 26, 1861, in Phillips, *Correspondence*, 555 (Cobb expected secession); William W. Freehling, *The Road to Disunion, II: Secessionists Triumphant, 1854–1861* (New York: Oxford University Press, 2008), 105–106.

20.    Anthony Gene Carey, *Parties, Slavery, and the Union in Antebellum Georgia* (Athens: University of Georgia Press, 2012), 227–230; John Hope Franklin, *The Militant South, 1800–1861* (Urbana: University of Illinois Press, 2002), 241–242; Jean Baker, *James Buchanan* (New York: Times Books, 2004), 121.

21.    James Buchanan, Message to Congress, December 3, 1860, in James D. Richardson, ed., *A Compilation of the Messages and Papers of the Presidents* (Washington, DC: Government Printing Office, 1899), 5:626–653.

22.    James Buchanan, Special Message to Congress, January 8, 1861, in Richardson, *Messages*, 5:655–659.

23.    William U. Hensel, "James Buchanan as a Lawyer: An Address before the Law School of the University of Pennsylvania on Wednesday, March 28, 1912," *University of Pennsylvania Law Review* (1912), 551, 552; Baker, *Buchanan*, 27.

24.    Mary Black Clayton, *Reminiscences of Jeremiah Sullivan Black* (St. Louis: Christian Publishing, 1887), 110, 168–169; William Marvel, *Lincoln's Autocrat: The Life of Edwin Stanton* (Chapel Hill: University of North Carolina Press, 2015), xiv, 47–48; Joseph Holt, *Letters of the Honorable Joseph Holt . . . On the Present Situation* (Philadelphia: Martien, 1861), 8, 9.

25.    Baker, *Buchanan*, 135–136.

26.    Leonard Richards, *Who Freed the Slaves? The Fight over the Thirteenth Amendment* (Chicago: University of Chicago Press, 2015), 17, 34–35; Peace Conference proposed amendment, February 27, 1861, in Paul L. Ford, ed., *The Federalist* (New York: Holt, 1898), 719.

27.    J. Holt reply to Hayne, February 6, 1861, in John Bassett Moore, ed., *The Works of James Buchanan* (Philadelphia: Lippincott, 1910), 11:136; Buchanan, Memorandum, February 8, 1861, in Moore, *Works of James Buchanan*, 141.

28. James Buchanan, *Mr. Buchanan's Administration on the Eve of the Rebellion* (New York: Appleton, 1866), 153–154.

29. Buchanan blamed Lincoln for the coming of the war, and so do many historians; see, e.g., George Ticknor Curtis, *The Life of James Buchanan* (New York: Harper, 1883), 2:418–430; Claude G. Bowers, *The Tragic Era* (New York: Houghton Mifflin, 1929), 8; Harold Holzer, "The Silent President-Elect: Abraham Lincoln, the Orator Who Would Not Speak," in Harold Holzer, Thomas Horrocks, and Frank J. Williams, eds., *The Living Lincoln* (Carbondale: Southern Illinois University Press, 2010), 42; Sean Wilentz, "Democracy at Gettysburg," in Sean Conant, ed., *The Gettysburg Address: Perspectives on Lincoln's Greatest Speech* (New York: Oxford University Press, 2015), 61. But Buchanan's finger wagging was more than a little self-serving, for when Lincoln did order the resupply of Fort Sumter, Buchanan told Stanton, his former secretary of war (and soon to be Lincoln's), that the Republicans had "delayed too long and talked too much." Buchanan to Stanton, April 9, 1861, quoted in Kenneth M. Stampp, *And the War Came: The North and the Secession Crisis, 1860–1861* (Chicago: University of Chicago Press, 1950), 288.

30. Whatever view one takes of the correctness of Lincoln's constitutional interpretation, it is crystal clear that the address was riven with legalisms. It was, in fact, one of the foremost constitutional exegeses of its day. "Duty": Michael Stokes Paulsen, "The Civil War as Constitutional Interpretation," *University of Chicago Law Review* 71 (2004), 706. Harold Holzer, *Lincoln President-Elect: Abraham Lincoln and the Great Secession Winter, 1860–1861* (New York: Simon and Schuster, 2008), 263–266, describes Lincoln's search for a little peace and quiet to write the Inaugural Address.

31. Lincoln, "Address at Cooper Institute," February 27, 1860, in Basler, *Collected Works*, 3:523. On the address in context, see Harold Holzer, *Lincoln at Cooper Union: The Speech that Made Abraham Lincoln President* (New York: Simon and Schuster, 2004), 249–284.

32. Lincoln, Cooper Institute, in Basler, *Collected Works*, 3:530.

33. Lincoln, Cooper Institute, in Basler, *Collected Works*, 3:527.

34. Lincoln, Cooper Institute, in Basler, *Collected Works*, 3:543; Eric Foner, *The Fiery Trial: Abraham Lincoln and American Slavery* (New York: Norton, 2010), 136–137.

35. "Resolutions Drawn Up for Republican Members of the Committee of Thirteen," December 20, 1860, enclosed in Abraham Lincoln to Lyman Trumbull, December 21, 1860, in Basler, *Collected Works*, 4:156–157, 158; Michael Burlingame, *Abraham Lincoln: A Life* (Baltimore: Johns Hopkins University Press, 2013), 1:714–715; Lincoln, "First Inaugural Address, Final Version," March 4, 1861, in Basler, *Collected Works*, 4:262–271, for which a convenient online source is http://avalon.law.yale.edu/19th_century/

lincoln1.asp. The reference to a lawless invasion surely meant John Brown's raid at Harpers Ferry, but it was federal territory, not Virginia's.

36.    Lincoln, "First Inaugural Address, in Basler, *Collected Works*, 4:264; Charles Hobson, *The Great Chief Justice: John Marshall and the Rule of Law* (Lawrence: University Press of Kansas, 1996) 26; Peter Charles Hoffer, *Rutgers v. Waddington: Alexander Hamilton, the End of the War for Independence, and the Origins of Judicial Review* (Lawrence: University Press of Kansas, 2016), 54, 63, 68. The law of nations was a basic subject for any student of law in America, for the country had originated in the colonies of a vast empire. See, e.g., Mark W. Janis, "North America: American Exceptionalism in International Law," in Bardo Fassbender and Anne Peters, eds., *The Oxford Handbook of International Law* (Oxford: Oxford University Press, 2012), 526–542.

37.    "First Inaugural Address," in Basler, *Collected Works*, 4:264.

38.    "First Inaugural Address," in Basler, *Collected Works*, 4:265. See, on this, Akhil Reed Amar, *America's Constitution* (New York: Basic Books, 2015), 6.

39.    "First Inaugural Address," in Basler, *Collected Works*, 4:265.

40.    "First Inaugural Address," in Basler, *Collected Works*, 4:266.

41.    "First Inaugural Address," in Basler, *Collected Works*, 4:266; Lacey K. Ford, *Deliver Us from Evil: The Slavery Question in the Old South* (New York: Oxford University Press, 2009), 493–495 (anti-abolitionist post office raids).

42.    "First Inaugural Address," in Basler, *Collected Works*, 4:266–267, 271.

43.    The observer was newspaper man William Henry Hulbert and the account was "The Diary of a Public Man." The lines quoted appear in the appendix to Daniel W. Crofts, ed., *A Secession Crisis Enigma: William Henry Hulbert and "The Diary of a Public Man"* (Baton Rouge: Louisiana State University Press, 2010), 255. On abolitionist criticism, Foner, *Fiery Trial*, 160; on Seward's concerns, Doris Kearns Goodwin, *Team of Rivals: The Political Genius of Abraham Lincoln* (New York: Simon and Schuster, 2005), 324; on sectional reasons for criticism, Goodwin, *Team of Rivals*, 329–331; on the theory that Lincoln would not compromise on slavery: Mark Tooley, *The Peace that Almost Was* (Nashville, TN: Thomas Nelson, 2015), xv; "Failure": James Oakes, *Freedom National: The Destruction of Slavery in the United States, 1861–1865* (New York: Norton, 2013), 78.

44.    See, e.g., Walter Edgar, *South Carolina: A History* (Columbia: University of South Carolina Press, 1988), 355, and the notes in Waldo W. Braden, "The First Inaugural Address, a Study in Strategy and Persuasion," in Waldo W. Braden, *Abraham Lincoln, Public Speaker* (Baton Rouge: Louisiana State University Press, 1993), 67–80. Could states secede as states when their very existence was defined by the federal Constitution? The answer, to the secessionists, was "yes" because states

had never lost their sovereignty when they entered into the federal union. They were sovereign prior to their ratification of the federal Constitution and that Constitution accepted their sovereignty. If the Union was perpetual, however, there were certain acts a state could not legally perform, and dissolving the Union was certainly one of these. The leaders of the Confederacy no sooner gathered in Montgomery than they created a provisional government and named a committee to write a constitution for the Confederate States of America. It was to be sent to the various states that had passed ordinances of secession for ratification. The provisional government also named Davis and Stephens as president and vice president. In short, even before there was a Confederate States of America, the secessionists were acting as though their proceedings were legal.

## Chapter 2

1. Jefferson Davis, Message to the [Confederate] Congress, April 29, 1861, James D. Richardson, ed., *A Compilation of the Papers and Messages of the Confederacy* (Nashville: US Publishing Company, 1904), 1:63–82; a convenient source for this online is http://avalon.law.yale.edu/19th_century/csa_mo42961.asp.

2. Gideon Welles, Diary Entry, March 30, 1864, in William E. Gienapp and Erica L. Gienapp, eds., *The Civil War Diary of Gideon Welles* (Urbana: University of Illinois Press, 2014), 382. Welles referred to the War of 1812, which entailed a British invasion of the United States, but omitted the Mexican American war of 1846–1848, which did not involve an invasion of US territory.

3. "Law Office Cabinet": Daniel W. Stowell, "Abraham Lincoln: Lawyer, Leader, President," in Charles M. Hubbard, ed., *Lincoln, the Law, and Presidential Leadership* (Carbondale: Southern Illinois University Press, 2015), 24; Speed quoted in Victor B. Howard, *Black Liberation in Kentucky, Emancipation and Freedom, 1862–1884* (Lexington: University of Kentucky Press, 2015), 88.

4. Lincoln quoted in Doris Kearns Goodwin, *Team of Rivals: The Political Genius of Abraham Lincoln* (New York: Simon and Schuster, 2005), 319; in Don E. Fehrenbacher and Virginia Fehrenbacher, eds., *Recollected Words of Abraham Lincoln* (Palo Alto, CA: Stanford University Press, 1996), 243; Ronald C. White Jr., *A. Lincoln: A Biography* (New York: Random House, 2009), 355 (Cameron choice). Franklin Pierce and James Buchanan both turned to lawyers in their cabinets (the exception being Jefferson Davis in Pierce's cabinet), as both Pierce and Buchanan were lawyers themselves. Lawyers were perhaps more comfortable with other lawyers as advisors.

5. Goodwin, *Team of Rivals*, 62, 65, 69, 85, 86, 112, 117; Frederick J. Blue, *Salmon P. Chase, a Life in Politics* (Kent, OH: Kent State University Press, 1987), 10, 42, 244; William Frederick Seward, *Autobiography of*

*William Seward . . . with a Memoir of His Life* (New York: Appleton, 1877), 477–478; "good at it": Walter Stahr, *Seward: Lincoln's Indispensable Man* (New York: Simon and Schuster, 2013), 545; "slender": John Niven, *Salmon P. Chase: A Biography* (New York: Oxford University Press, 1995), 104, 283; Arvin R. Cain, *Lincoln's Attorney General: Edward Bates of Missouri* (Columbia: University of Missouri Press, 1965), 90–91; "personally unexceptionable": Edward Bates, Diary Entry, May 19, 1860, in Howard K. Beale, ed., *Diary of Edward Bates, 1859–1866* (Washington DC: American Historical Association, 1930), 131.

6. Melvin A. Eisenberg, *The Nature of the Common Law* (Cambridge, MA: Harvard University Press, 1991), 99; Chester G. Hearn, *Lincoln, the Cabinet, and the Generals* (Baton Rouge: Louisiana State University Press, 2010), ix; Goodwin, *Team of Rivals*, 148, 412, 668.

7. Goodwin, *Team of Rivals*, 334–344.

8. Seward to Lincoln, March 15, 1861; Chase to Lincoln, March 16, 1861, Lincoln Papers, Library of Congress.

9. Seward to Lincoln, April 1, 1861, in Roy P. Basler, ed., *The Collected Works of Abraham Lincoln* (New Brunswick, NJ: Rutgers University Press, 1953), 4:317–318.

10. Stephen C. Neff, *Justice in Blue and Gray: A Legal History of the Civil War* (Cambridge, MA: Harvard University Press, 2010), 40–44. John C. Fremont, military governor of Missouri at the start of the war, declared martial law and under it freed the slaves. Lincoln countermanded both orders and removed Fremont when he refused to rescind the emancipation order. In 1864, because of the almost continuous operation of Confederate marauders, martial law was declared over the entire state of Kentucky. Martial law was sometimes declared in localities when draft resistance broke out. There as in southern Illinois, Ohio, and Indiana, state courts did little to restrain the imposition of martial law by Union commanders.

11. Abraham Lincoln to William H. Seward, April 1, 1861, in Basler, *Collected Works*, 4: 318.

12. On the discussions in the cabinet, see Stahr, *Seward*, 317–318; Charles Francis Adams Sr. to William Henry Seward, January 17, 1862, Enclosure in Message of the President to Congress, US Department of State, *Foreign Relations of the United States, Correspondence* (Washington, DC: Government Printing Office, 1862), 14: "I need not add my testimony to the general admiration of the skillful manner in which the various difficulties attending this unfortunate business have been met or avoided." But see Charles Francis Adams Jr., *The Trent Affair, An Historical Retrospect* (Boston, 1912), 42: "Of the elaborate, and in many respects memorable, dispatch addressed by Secretary Seward to Lord Lyons," Adams declined to elaborate. On Bigelow, see Don H. Doyle, *The Cause of All Nations: An International History of the American Civil War* (New York: Basic Books, 2014), 74–86.

13. See, e.g., George F. Kennan, *American Diplomacy, 1900–1950*, 60th expanded edition ([1950]; Chicago: University of Chicago Press, 2012), 107. Kennan was referring to Woodrow Wilson but could just as easily have applied the aphorism to Seward.

14. A forthcoming study of the Revolutionary lawyers by the present author will conclude with a chapter on the lawyers and lawyering in Washington's cabinet.

15. Robert Aitkin and Marilyn Aitkin, *Law Makers, Law Breakers, and Uncommon Trials* (Washington, DC: American Bar Association, 2007), 89; Robert Douthat Meade, *Judah P. Benjamin, Confederate Statesman* (New York: Oxford University Press, 1943), 44, 156.

16. Mark Scroggins, *Robert Toombs, the Civil Wars of a United States Senator* (Jefferson, NC: McFarland, 2011), 13, 14, 15, 19, 198; Pleasant A. Stovall, *Robert Toombs: Statesman, Speaker, Soldier, Sage* (New York: Cassel, 1892), 15–28; William C. Davis, *The Union that Shaped the Confederacy: Robert Toombs and Alexander H. Stephens* (Lawrence: University Press of Kansas, 2001), 109, 128, 131–139.

17. Doyle, *Cause of All Nations*, 187; Howard Jones, *Blue and Gray Diplomacy: A History of Union and Confederate Foreign Relations* (Chapel Hill: University of North Carolina Press, 2010), 19–20; Charles M. Hubbard, *The Burden of Confederate Diplomacy* (Knoxville: University of Tennessee Press, 2000), 70.

18. Timothy Huebner, *Southern Judicial Tradition: State Judges and Sectional Distinctiveness, 1790–1890* (Athens: University of Georgia Press, 1999), 76–77; T. R. R. Cobb, *An Inquiry into the Law of Negro Slavery in the United States of America* (Philadelphia: Johnson, 1858), 128.

19. T. R. R. Cobb, Speech to the Georgia State Legislature, November 13, 1860, reprinted in William W. Freehling and Craig M. Simpson, *Secession Debated: Georgia's Showdown in 1860* (New York: Oxford University Press, 1992), 5, 6, 7, 8. Cobb on the Confederate constitution quoted in William B. McCash, *Thomas R. R. Cobb: The Making of a Southern Unionist, 1823–1862* (Macon, GA: Mercer University Press, 1983), 218. On honor as an alternative to legalism, see, e.g., Bertram Wyatt-Brown, *Southern Honor: Ethics and Behavior in the Old South*, 25th anniversary ed. (New York: Oxford University Press, 2007), vii and after; Ariela J. Gross, *Double Character: Slavery and Mastery in the Antebellum Southern Courtroom* (Princeton, NJ: Princeton University Press, 2000), 47 and after.

20. Davis, *Union*, 126–128, 151.

21. "Thus far in a most remarkable way events have been so tempered and restrained, as to avoid bloodshed. Can this be always?" Charles Sumner to the Duchess of Argyll, March 19, 1861, in Beverly Wilson Palmer, ed., *The Selected Letters of Charles Sumner* (Boston: Northeastern University Press, 1990), 2:61; "desperate": Russell McClintock, *Lincoln and the Decision for War: The Northern Response to Secession* (Chapel Hill: University of North Carolina Press, 2008), 238.

22.    Alexander H. Stephens, Speech at Savannah, March 21, 1861, in *Alexander H. Stephens in Public and Private: With Letters and Speeches before, during and since the War*, ed. Henry Cleveland (Philadelphia: National Publishing Co., 1866), 717–729; Thomas E. Schott, *Alexander H. Stephens of Georgia, a Biography* (Baton Rouge: Louisiana State University Press, 1988), 335–336; Davis, *Union*, 112–113, 128.

23.    William J. Cooper Jr., *Jefferson Davis and the Civil War Era* (Baton Rouge: Louisiana State University Press, 2013), 59–60. Indeed, it is by his absence and silence that one knows him in these days. See, e.g., William J. Cooper Jr., *Jefferson Davis, American* (New York: Knopf, 2000), 359–363.

24.    Seddon quoted in James McPherson, *Embattled Rebel: Jefferson Davis as Commander in Chief* (New York: Penguin), 115.

25.    Goodwin, *Team of Rivals*, 526; William C. Davis, *Jefferson Davis: The Man and His Hour* (Baton Rouge: Louisiana State University Press, 1966), 264.

26.    Anne-Marie Taylor, *Young Charles Sumner and the Legacy of the American Enlightenment, 1811–1851* (Amherst: University of Massachusetts Press, 2001), 202–203; Sumner, "Equal Suffrage at Once by Act of Congress" April 20, 1867, in *Charles Sumner: His Complete Works* (Boston: Lee and Shepard, 1900), 179; Jon L. Myers, *Henry Wilson and the Era of Reconstruction* (Lanham, MD: University Press of America, 2009), 24–25; James Oakes, *Freedom National: The Destruction of Slavery in the United States, 1861–1865* (New York: Norton, 2013), 188–189, 228–229, 434.

27.    Wilfred B. Yearns, *The Confederate Congress* (Athens: University of Georgia Press, 2010), vii; E. Merton Coulter, *The Confederate States of America, 1861–1865* (Baton Rouge: Louisiana State University Press, 1950), 134; Jon L. Waklyn, *Confederates against the Confederacy* (Westport, CT: Praeger, 2002), 54.

28.    The old epithet that the Confederacy "died of states rights" may be a little overdone, but it has substantial truth. It was a "foundational stone" of the Confederacy, anchored in the Confederate constitution, and strongly supported by the individual Confederate state governments. Jefferson Davis tried to subordinate it to national defense issues but was only partially successful. William J. Cooper Jr., *Jefferson Davis and the Civil War Era* (Baton Rouge: Louisiana State University Press, 2013), 36–37; Paul D. Escott, *After Secession, Jefferson Davis and the Failure of Confederate Nationalism* (Baton Rouge: Louisiana State University Press, 1993), 92–93.

29.    Henry W. Bellows quoted in George M. Frederickson, *The Inner Civil War: Northern Intellectuals and the Crisis of the Union* (New York: Harper, 1965), 54, 101; Dwight Lowell Dumond, *Antislavery Origins of the Civil War in the United States* (Ann Arbor: University of Michigan Press, 1939), 130; Stephen A. Douglas, Public Statement [memo of visit with Lincoln], April 14, 1861, Robert W. Johannsen, ed., *The Letters of Stephen A. Douglas* (Urbana: University of Illinois Press, 1961), 509–510.

30. Laura F. Edwards, *A Legal History of the Civil War and Reconstruction* (New York: Cambridge University Press, 2015), 55; Emory M. Thomas, *The Confederate Nation, 1861–1865* (New York: Harper, 1979), 138.

31. Here I follow Williamjames Hull Hoffer, *The Caning of Charles Sumner: Honor, Idealism, and the Origins of the Civil War* (Baltimore: Johns Hopkins University Press, 2010), 27–31, 87–90, 130, and Wyatt-Brown, *Southern Honor*, 34–35, but I want to stress that the argument in this paragraph is highly speculative.

## Chapter 3

1. The story is exceptionally well told in Brian McGinty, *The Body of John Merryman: Abraham Lincoln and the Suspension of Habeas Corpus* (Cambridge, MA: Harvard University Press, 2011), *passim*, but the literature on the case is immense. See the notes in Seth Tillman, "Ex Parte Merryman, Myth History, and Scholarship," *Military Law Review* 223 (2015), 941 n.1, and 942, n.2, as well as his discussion on pages 942–954 (considerable confusion as to the facts of the case in later scholarship on it).

2. See, generally, William C. Harris, *Lincoln and the Border States: Preserving the Union* (Lawrence: University of Press of Kansas, 2011), 42–79.

3. Laura F. Edwards, *A Legal History of the Civil War and Reconstruction* (New York: Cambridge University Press, 2015), 20–21.

4. Abraham Lincoln to Winfield Scott, April 25 and April 27, 1861, in Roy P. Basler, ed., *The Collected Works of Abraham Lincoln* (New Brunswick, NJ: Rutgers University Press, 1953), 4:344, 347.

5. McGinty, *Body of Merryman*, 28–29, 76.

6. McGinty, *Body of Merryman*, 79.

7. Ex Parte Merryman, 17 F. Cas. 144, 147, 148 (C.C.D. Md. 1861) (No. 9487) (Taney, J.).

8. 17 F. Cas. at 149.

9. U.S. v. Rogers 45 U.S. 567 (1846); R. Kent Newmyer, *John Marshall and the Heroic Age of the Supreme Court* (Baton Rouge: Louisiana State University Press, 2007), 376; for the rulings, see, e.g., McCulloch v. Maryland 17 U.S. 316 (1819) (establishing the constitutionality of the Bank). On Taney as politician in Merryman: James F. Simon, *Lincoln and Chief Justice Taney: Slavery, Secession and the President's War Powers* (New York: Simon and Schuster, 2007), 272.

10. 17. F. Cas. at 152; Simon, *Lincoln and Taney*, 42 (Taney concurrence in Prigg v. Pennsylvania [1842]), 44 (Taney concurrence in Passenger Cases [1849]), but Taney could reject states' rights when slavery had to be protected; see, e.g., Bernard C. Steiner, *Life of Roger Brooke Taney, Chief Justice of the United States* (Baltimore, MD: Williams and Wilkins, 1922), 428 (rejecting state personal freedom laws).

11. 17 F. Cas. at 152.

12.  17 F. Cas. at 152.

13.  17 F. Cas. at 152.

14.  17 F. Cas. at 152, 152–153.

15.  Abraham Lincoln, Special Message to Congress, July 4, 1861, in Basler, *Collected Works*, 4:429.

16.  Sometimes called inherent or implied powers, the residual powers doctrine is usually associated with presidential action in the absence of or before congressional action. See, e.g., Saikrishna Bangalore Prakash, "Taxonomy of Presidential Powers," *Boston University Law Review* 88 (2008), 335.

17.  Special Message, in Basler, *Collected Works*, 4:430.

18.  Special Message, in Basler, *Collected Works*, 4:430.

19.  Special Message, in Basler, *Collected Works*, 4:430. Lincoln edged close to the unacceptable stance that the civilian power (Congress and the courts) had to bow to the commander in chief—in effect, that civilian government no longer had control over the nation's armed forces. The confederacy edged even closer to that precipice. See Paul D. Escott, *Military Necessity: Civil-Military Relations in the Confederacy* (Westport, CT: Praeger, 2006), 177–178.

20.  John Fabian Witt, *Lincoln's Code: The Laws of War in American History* (New York: Free Press, 2012), 198–199, 208, 237; Anthony J. Bellia Jr. and Bradford R. Clark, "The Law of Nations as Constitutional Law," *Virginia Law Review* 98 (2012), 729–838; and David M. Golove and Daniel Hulsebosch, "A Civilized Nation: The Early American Constitution, the Law of Nations, and the Pursuit of International Recognition," *New York University Law Review* 85 (2010), 932–1066.

21.  Marvin R. Cain, *Lincoln's Attorney General: Edward Bates of Missouri* (Columbia: University of Missouri Press, 1965), 90–146.

22.  Edward Bates, Ex Parte Merriman, in *Official Opinions of the Attorneys General of the United States*, ed. J. Hubley Ashton (Washington, DC: W.H. & O.H. Morrison, 1868), 10: 81; political question doctrine: Luther v. Borden, 48 U.S. 1 (1849).

23.  Whiskey Rebellion: President George Washington, "Proclamation" August 11, 1794, in James D. Richardson, ed., *A Compilation of the Messages and Papers of the Presidents* (Washington, DC: Government Printing Office, 1899), 1: 161; May 1795 Criminal Case Files, C.C.D.Pa. National Archives and Records Administration [NARA] Philadelphia; Thomas Slaughter, *The Whiskey Rebellion: Frontier Epilogue to the American Revolution* (New York: Oxford University Press, 1988); Burr trial: Peter Charles Hoffer, *The Treason Trials of Aaron Burr* (Lawrence: University Press of Kansas, 2008), 146–171; presidential provision of documentary evidence, U.S. v. Nixon, 418 U.S. 683 (1974); presidential testimony in civil case: Clinton v. Jones, 520 U.S. 681 (1997).

24. McGinty, *Body of Merryman*, 170–171; Mark Neely, *The Fate of Liberty: Abraham Lincoln and Civil Liberties* (New York: Oxford University Press, 1991), 10, 56; Harold M. Hyman and William M. Wiecek, *Equal Justice under Law: Constitutional Development 1835–1875* (New York: Harper, 1982), 234.

25. Potter resolution, July 8, 1861, 37th Cong. 1st sess., *Congressional Globe*, p. 26; Charles W. Twinning, "John Fox Potter," in John T. Hubbell and James W. Geary, eds., *Biographical Dictionary of Northern Leaders during the Civil War* (Westport, CT: Greenwood, 1995), 423.

26. Harold Holzer, *Lincoln and the Power of the Press, The War for Public Opinion* (New York: Simon and Schuster, 2014), 336–337, 435; Ian C. Friedman, *Freedom of Speech and the Press* (New York: Facts on File, 2005), 31; Douglas M. Fraleigh and Joseph S. Tuman, *Freedom of Expression in the Marketplace of Ideas* (Thousand Oaks, CA: Sage, 2013), 48.

27. See, e.g., Jonathan Lurie, *The Chase Court: Justices, Rulings, and Legacy* (Santa Barbara, CA: ABC-CLIO, 2004), 55–58; Neely, *Fate of Liberty*, 179–184.

28. Oakes, *Freedom National*, 113–114.

29. Ex Parte Vallandingham, 28 F. Cas. 874, 920 (1863) (Leavitt J.); Christopher Phillips, *Missouri's Confederate: Claiborne Fox Jackson and the Creation of Southern Identity in the Border West* (Columbia: University of Missouri Press, 2000), 20–273; Ann Blackman, *Wild Rose: The True Story of a Civil War Spy* (New York: Random House, 2006), 222.

30. Ex parte Vallandingham, 68 U.S.243, 251 (1864) (Wayne, J.); Frank L. Klement, *The Limits of Dissent: Clement L. Vallandingham and the Civil War* (Lexington: University Press of Kentucky, 2015), 163–171.

31. I. Winslow Ayer, *The Great North-Western Conspiracy* (Chicago: Rounds and James, 1865), iii; iv; James Ford Rhodes, *History of the United States* (New York: Macmillan, 1904), 5:317–329.

32. Ex parte Milligan, 71 U.S. 2, 108 (1866) (Davis, J.); Jonathan Lurie, *The Chase Court: Justices, Rulings, and Legacy* (Santa Barbara, CA: ABC-CLIO, 2004), 55–58; Witt, *Lincoln's Code*, 309–313.

33. See, e.g., Neely, *The Fate of Liberty*, 123–124; Benjamin R. Curtis, *Executive Power* (Boston: Little, Brown, 1862), 11–12.

## Chapter 4

1. Cobb quoted in William Freehling, *The Road to Disunion: Secessionists at Bay, 1776–1854* (New York: Oxford University Press, 1990), 2:440; James M. Smyth to Howell Cobb, December 17, 1862, in Ulrich Bonnell Phillips, ed., *The Correspondence of Robert Toombs, Alexander H. Stephens, and Howell Cobb, Annual Report of the American Historical Association for the Year 1911*, vol. 2 (Washington, DC, American Historical Association, 1913), 2:609; Lincoln quoted in Michael Burlingame, *The Inner World*

*of Abraham Lincoln* (Urbana: University of Illinois Press, 1997), 105; John Sherman to William T. Sherman, May 6, 1863, in Rachel Sherman Thorndike, ed., *The Sherman Letters* (New York: Scribners, 1894), 205.

2.    Salmon Chase, journal entry, December 11, 1861, in John Niven, ed., *Salmon P. Chase Papers* Volume 1: *Journals, 1829–1872* (Kent, OH: Kent State University Press, 1993), 315.

3.    Modern law is clear: "Whoever incites, sets on foot, assists, or engages in any rebellion or insurrection against the authority of the United States or the laws thereof, or gives aid or comfort thereto, shall be fined under this title or imprisoned not more than ten years, or both; and shall be incapable of holding any office under the United States." June 25, 1948, ch. 645, 62 Stat. 808; Pub. L. 103–322, title XXXIII, § 330016(1)(L), Sept. 13, 1994, 108 Stat. 2147. But today as in 1861, the question remains when does opposition to government policies by word or deed amount to rebellion? Great discretion is left to US attorneys to prosecute such acts, and sometimes that discretion reflects the political views of the administration that appointed the US attorneys. Precedents for both civil disobedience and insurrection are abundant in American history.

4.    Text adapted from Peter Charles Hoffer, Williamjames Hull Hoffer, and N. E. H. Hull, *The Federal Courts: An Essential History* (New York: Oxford University Press, 2016), 159–161.

5.    A. F. Warburton, *Trial of the officers and crew of the privateer Savannah, on the charge of piracy, in the United States Circuit Court for the Southern District of New York, Hon. Judges Nelson and Shipman, presiding.* (Washington, DC: Government Printing Office, 1862), and Mark A. Weitz, *The Confederacy on Trial* (Lawrence: University Press of Kansas, 2005), are the sources for the two cases. *Savannah* case: US v. Baker et al., 24 F. Cas. 962 (C.C. S.D. NY, 1861); *Enchantress* case: US v. Smith, 27 F. Cas. 1134 (C.C.E. D. Pa 1861).

6.    Weitz, *Confederacy on Trial*, 87–88.

7.    Stacy Pratt McDermott, *The Jury in Lincoln's America* (Athens: Ohio University Press, 2013), 49–50; Robert Ferguson, *The Trial in American Life* (Chicago: University of Chicago Press, 2007), 54; Trial of David E. Herold, 1865, in John D. Lawson, *American State Trials* (St. Louis: Thomas Law Book Co., 1917), 8: 113 (citing article 6 of General Order 100).

8.    Lonnie R. Speer, *Portals to Hell: Military Prisons of the Civil War* (Lincoln: University of Nebraska Press, 2005), 97–105.

9.    Weitz, *Confederacy on Trial*, 195.

10.    Peter Charles Hoffer, Williamjames Hull Hoffer, and N. E. H. Hull, *The Supreme Court: An Essential History* (Lawrence, KS: University Press of Kansas, 2007), 87.

11.    William J. Cooper, *We Have the War upon Us: The Onset of the Civil War, November 1860–April 1861* (New York: Knopf, 2013), 236; William

A. Blair, *With Malice toward Some: Treason and Loyalty in the Civil War Era* (Chapel Hill: University of North Carolina Press, 2014), 75; Hoffer, Hoffer, and Hull, *Supreme Court*, 86.

12. The Brig Amy Warwick, 67 US 635 (1863).

13. Abraham Lincoln, Proclamation of a Blockade" April 19, 1861, in Roy P. Basler, ed., *The Collected Works of Abraham Lincoln* (New Brunswick, NJ: Rutgers University Press, 1953), 4:338–339.

14. Basler, *Collected Works*, 4:339. As William Evarts argued for the government in the subsequent *Prize Cases*, "War is, emphatically, a question of actualities." Evarts quoted in Bernard Schwartz, *A History of the Supreme Court* (New York: Oxford University Press, 1993), 131. This was Lincoln's thinking as well, but phrased as Evarts had, it conceded the point in dispute—the struggle against secession was a war, not an effort to suppress domestic insurrection.

15. Jeffrey L. Amestoy, *Slavish Shore: The Odyssey of Richard Henry Dana* (Cambridge, MA: Harvard University Press, 2015), 237–252.

16. Clinton Rossiter, *Parties and Politics in America* (Ithaca, NY: Cornell University Press, 1964), 39; Lee Epstein, William M. Landes, and Richard A. Posner, *The Behavior of Federal Judges: A Theoretical and Empirical Study of Rational Choice* (Cambridge, MA: Harvard University Press, 2013) (ideology and partisan identification important, though less so in the lower courts); Andres Sawicki, David Schkade, Cass Sunstein, and Lisa M. Ellman, *Are Judges Political? An Empirical Analysis of the Federal Judiciary* (Washington, DC: Brookings Institution, 2006) (on controversial political issues, federal appeals court judges tend to divide along partisan lines).

17. This and the subsequent paragraphs on Lincoln's Court from Hoffer, Hoffer, and Hull, *The Supreme Court*, 103–106.

18. Michael A. Ross, *Justice of Shattered Dreams: Samuel Freeman Miller and the Supreme Court during the Civil War Era* (Baton Rouge: Louisiana State University Press, 2003), 3, 184.

19. Elizur Southworth, *A Memorial Address on the Life and Character of David Davis* (Litchfield, IL: n.p. 1887), 3.

20. David Mayer Silver, *Lincoln's Supreme Court* (Urbana: University of Illinois Press, 1956), 34; A. E. Keir Nash, "John Catron," in Melvin Urofsky, ed., *The Supreme Court Justices: A Biographical Dictionary* (New York: Routledge, 1994), 98–99; Catron quoted in Timothy S. Huebner, *The Southern Judicial Tradition: State Judges and Sectional Distinctiveness, 1790–1890* (Athens: University of Georgia Press, 1999), 61; Erwin C. Surrency, "Nathan Clifford," in Kermit L. Hall et al., eds., *The Oxford Companion to the Supreme Court of the United States* (New York: Oxford University Press, 1992), 161.

21. U. S. v. William Smith, 27 F. Cas. 1134, 1145 (Grier, J.).

22.  Federal Judicial Center, History of the Federal Courts, "Admiralty
     and Maritime Jurisdiction in the Federal Courts," http://www.fjc.gov/
     history/home.nsf/page/jurisdiction_admiralty.html; Stewart L. Bernarth,
     *Squall across the Atlantic: American Civil War Prize Cases and Diplomacy*
     (Berkeley: University of California Press, 1970), 18–33; Federal Judicial
     Center, Biographical Directory of Federal Judges, http://www.fjc.gov/
     history/home.nsf/page/judges.html.
23.  Here and after, quotations from The Prize Cases, 67 US 635 (1863).
24.  Jeffrey L. Amestoy, "The Supreme Court Argument that Saved the
     Union: Richard Henry Dana Jr. and the *Prize Cases*," *Journal of Supreme
     Court History* 35 (2010), 10–24. The debate goes on: Stuart W. Bernath,
     "British Neutrality and the Civil War *Prize Cases*," *Civil War History* 15
     (1969), 320–331; Thomas E. Lee, "The Civil War in US Foreign Relations
     Law: A Dress Rehearsal for Modern Transformations," *St. Louis University
     Law Review* 53 (2008), 53–71; Stephen L. Vladek, "Re-Rethinking the
     *Prize Cases*: Some Remarks in Response to Professor Lee," *St. Louis
     University Law Review* 53 (2008), 85–91.
25.  The Brig Amy Warwick, 1 F. Cas. 799, 803 (D. Mass) (Sprague J.) (1862).
     Dana oral argument, in The Brig Amy Warwick, 67 US 635 (1863),
     p. 27. No page numbers are given in Black's report for the counsels' oral
     argument. West, however, assigned internal numbers.
26.  Dana oral argument, 67 US at 27; James Madison, "Special Message
     to Congress on the Foreign Policy Crisis—War Message, June 1, 1812,
     Gaillard Hunt, ed., *The Writings of James Madison* (New York: Putnam,
     1908), 8:192–200; online version at http://millercenter.org/president/
     madison/speeches/speech-3614; Don Hickey, "Belligerent Rights at
     Sea" in Spencer C. Tucker, ed., *Encyclopedia of the War of 1812* (Santa
     Barbara: ABC-CLIO, 2012), 55–56.
27.  Hickey, "Belligerent Rights at Sea," 55–56. 67 US at 31.
28.  Hickey, "Belligerent Rights at Sea," 28. Written briefs were required after
     1821 by rule of the Supreme Court, Rule of pleading xxx, in February
     Term, 1821. 67 US at 35.
29.  Hickey, "Belligerent Rights at Sea," 28–30.
30.  Hickey, "Belligerent Rights at Sea," 30. Daniel W. Hamilton, *The Limits
     of Sovereignty: Property Confiscation in the Union and the Confederacy
     during the Civil War* (Chicago: University of Chicago Press, 2007), 19–21.
31.  Hamilton, *Limits of Sovereignty*, 31. 67 US at 29–30.
32.  67 US 35. See, e.g., John Syrett, *The Civil War Confiscation Acts: Failing to
     Reconstruct the South* (New York: Fordham University Press, 2005), 25–26
     and after.
33.  67 US at 36. "Enemy property" is a broader concept than "contraband."
     Contraband is property that furthers the enemy's ability to prosecute
     its military efforts. Slaves were confiscated as contraband because their
     labor could, conceivably, enhance the Confederacy ability to wage war.

Sequestration by a government was another form of seizure that did not necessarily involve contraband. It simply meant government taking for a legal purpose. Thus the Confederate government in Richmond took slaves from their owners to build fortifications.

34. 67 US at 44, 46, 28.

35. Carlisle oral argument, 67 US at 9; James F. Simon, *Lincoln and Chief Justice Taney: Slavery, Secession and the President's War Powers* (New York: Simon and Schuster, 2007), 222.

36. 67 US at 10.

37. 67 US at 11.

38. *Statutes at Large of the Provincial Government of the Confederate States of America* . . . (Richmond, VA: R. M. Smith, 1864), 100.

39. 67 US at 11. But not if the courts upheld the condemnations: see, e.g., Ludwell H. Johnson III, "Abraham Lincoln and the Development of President War-Making Powers: Prize Cases (1863) Revisited," *Civil War History* 35 (1989), 215.

40. 67 US at 13. "Municipal" here was a term of art. It did not refer to city jurisdictions but meant the internal affairs of a state.

41. 67 US at 13, 17.

42. 67 US at 13, 19.

43. 67 US at 13, 20. Antebellum Supreme Court oratory: Craig R. Smith, *Daniel Webster and the Oratory of Civil Religion* (Columbia: University of Missouri Press, 2005), 48; Joseph Whelan, *Mr. Adams' Last Crusade: John Quincy Adams Extraordinary Post-Presidential Life in Congress* (New York: PublicAffairs, 2009), 183.

44. 67 US at 23, 24.

45. See, e.g., Mark Tushnet, "Defending the Indeterminacy Thesis," *Quinnipiac Law Review* 16 (1996), 341–344; David M. Trubek, "Where the Action Is: Critical Legal Studies and Empiricism," *Stanford Law Review* 36 (1984), 578–579.

46. 67 US at 666 (Grier, J.). Grier's opinion has been described as "not a model of clarity" (G. Edward White, *The Law in America*, Volume 1: *From the Colonial Years through the Civil War* [New York: Oxford University Press, 2012], 438), though the decision was clear enough.

47. 67 US at 667.

48. 67 US at 669.

49. 67 US at 670.

50. 67 US at 671, 673.

51. 67 US at 685 (Nelson, J.).

52. 67 US at 685 (Nelson, J.); Maryland Insurance Co. v. Woods, 10 US 29, 49 (1810) (Marshall, C.J.).

53. 67 US at 686, 687, 690. Nelson aimed his fire directly at Lincoln. Peter Irons, *War Powers: How the Imperial Presidency Hijacked the Constitution* (New York: Macmillan, 2006), 74–75. After the Vietnam War, Congress

attempted to limit presidential powers along the lines that Justice Nelson foresaw. See, e.g., War Powers Act of 1973, 50 U.S.C. 1541, requiring the president to notify Congress within forty-eight hours of committing US armed forces to combat, and denies the president the authority to engage in warfare without a declaration of Congress, existence of a national security emergency, or under a statute of Congress. The act was "supposed to restrain" the president. Arthur M. Schlesinger, *The Imperial Presidency*, rev. ed. (New York: Houghton Mifflin, 2004), 423. The limitations of presidential authority to declare war have become even more controversial in an era of drone strikes, electronic surveillance, and other modern technologies.

54. 67 US at 690. For a survey of the origins of modern originalism, see Stephen G. Calabresi, ed., *Originalism: A Quarter Century of Debate* (Washington, DC: Regnery, 2007), 1–42, and Frank Cross, *The Failed Promise of Originalism* (Palo Alto, CA: Stanford University Press, 2013), 1–22.

55. 67 US at 693, 694.

56. 67 US at 698.

57. Stephen C. Neff, *War and the Law of Nations, A General History* (Cambridge: Cambridge University Press, 2005), 190–210.

58. John F. Marszalek, *Commander of All Lincoln's Armies: A Life of General Henry F. Halleck* (Cambridge, MA: Harvard University Press, 2004), 90–93, 134–135.

59. William Marvel, *Lincoln's Autocrat: The Life of Edwin Stanton* (Chapel Hill: University of North Carolina Press, 2015), 286; Marszalek, *Halleck*, 168, 176–178; James G. Garner, "Order 100 Revisited," *Military Law Review* 27 (1965), 5.

60. Francis Lieber's great tract on hermeneutics was his *Legal and Political Hermeneutics, or Principles of Interpretation and Construction in Law and Politics*, enlarged ed. (Boston: Little and Brown, 1839), quotations at 39, 40, 48, 52, 56, 57, 59.

61. Emmerich de Vattel, *The Law of Nations* ([1757]; New Edition, London: Robinson, 1797), 421–428.

62. John Fabian Witt, *Lincoln's Code: The Laws of War in American History* (New York: Free Press, 2012), 170–285.

63. *Instructions for the Government of Armies of the United States in the Field, Prepared by Francis Lieber* [Order 100, 1863] (Washington, DC: Government Printing Office, 1894), 18.

64. Jefferson Davis, General Orders 111, *The War of the Rebellion*, 128 vols. (Washington, DC: US War Department, 1888–1901), ser. 2, 5: 795–797.

65. *Government of Armies*, 12–14.

66. *Government of Armies*, 15. Was slavery forbidden by natural law? Enslaving a free person on the high seas was a federal offense. Piracy Act of 1823, 3 Stats. 721, sections 4 and 5; but persons already legally enslaved were

not freed by force of law on the high seas—see, e.g., The Antelope, 23 US 63, 115 (1825) (Marshall C. J.): "However abhorrent this traffic may be to a mind whose original feelings are not blunted by familiarity with the practice, it has been sanctioned in modern times by the laws of all nations who possess distant colonies, each of whom has engaged in it as a common commercial business which no other could rightfully interrupt. It has claimed all the sanction which could be derived from long usage and general acquiescence. That trade could not be considered as contrary to the law of nations which was authorized and protected by the laws of all commercial nations, the right to carry on which was claimed by each and allowed by each."

67. *Government of Armies*, 15–16.

68. Witt, *Lincoln's Code*, 193.

69. Stephen C. Neff, *Justice in Blue and Gray: A Legal History of the Civil War* (Cambridge, MA: Harvard University Press, 2010), 57–58, 61; Elizabeth D. Leonard, *Lincoln's Forgotten Ally: Advocate General Joseph Holt of Kentucky* (Chapel Hill: University of North Carolina Press, 2011), 23, 109, 114, 162.

70. Leonard, *Holt*, 163–164; Neff, *Justice in Blue and Gray*, 63–68.

71. Neff, *Justice in Blue and Gray*, 84; Joanne Chiles Eakin and Annette Curtis, *The Little Gods: Union Provost Marshals in Missouri, 1861–1865* (Independence, MO: Two Trails, 2002), 8–9; Jeremy Neely, *The Border between Them: Violence and Reconciliation on the Kansas Missouri Line* (Columbia: University of Missouri Press, 2007), 116–117, 121; C.C. E.D. Mo. Law and Equity Index, 1860–1865, National Archives and Records Administration, Kansas City, MO; US v. John Rucker, Joseph Richards, and 24 others, grand jury indictments in case file No. 49, September 1862, DC W. D. Mo. Criminal Case Files, volume 2, Kansas City, National Archives and Records Administration (hereafter, NARA).

72. William T. Sherman to John Sherman, August 26, 1862, in Thorndike, *Sherman Letters*, 160; William T. Sherman to James M. Calhoun, September 12, 1864, in *Sherman's Civil War: Selected Correspondence of William T. Sherman, 1860–1865*, eds. Jean V. Berlin and Brooks D. Simpson (Chapel Hill: University of North Carolina Press, 1999), 707–709; Robert L. O'Connell, *Fierce Patriot: The Tangled Lives of William Tecumseh Sherman* (New York: Random House, 2014), 108; Charles Royster, *The Destructive War: William Tecumseh Sherman, Stonewall Jackson, and the Americans* (New York: Knopf, 1991), 117; Witt, *Lincoln's Code*, 280–281.

73. Adam Rothman, *Beyond Freedom's Reach: A Kidnaping in the Twilight of Slavery* (Cambridge, MA: Harvard University Press, 2015), 149–150; James G. Hollingsworth Jr., *Pretense of Glory: The Life of Nathaniel P. Banks* (Baton Rouge: University of Louisiana State Press, 1998), 223.

## Chapter 5

1.  See, e.g., Harold M. Hyman, "Introduction," to Hyman, ed., *The Radical Republicans and Reconstruction* (Indianapolis: Bobbs Merrill, 1967), lxvii; Harold M. Hyman and William M. Wiecek, *Equal Justice under Law: Constitutional Development 1835–1875* (New York: Harper, 1982), 246, 253; Eric Foner, *The Fiery Trial: Abraham Lincoln and American Slavery* (New York: Norton, 2010), 175; David Herbert Donald, *Charles Sumner and the Rights of Man* (New York: Knopf, 1970), 16–17; Wendell Phillips, "The War for the Union, December 1861," in Louis Filler, ed., *Wendell Phillips on Civil Rights and Freedom* (New York: Hill and Wang, 1965), 151.

2.  Benjamin F. Butler, *Autobiography and Personal Reminiscences* (Boston: A. M. Thayer, 1892), 129, 263; Louise L. Stevenson, *Lincoln in the Atlantic World* (New York: Cambridge University Press, 2015), 173–174; James Oakes, *Freedom National: The Destruction of Slavery in the United States, 1861–1865* (New York: Norton, 2013), 91–98; Herbert C. Covey and Dwight Eisnach, *How the Slaves Saw the Civil War* (Santa Barbara, CA: Praeger, 2014), 60–62.

3.  Salmon P. Chase, Journal Entry, August 3, 1862, in John Niven, ed., *Salmon P. Chase Papers,* Volume 1: *Journals, 1829–1872* (Kent, OH: Kent State University Press, 1993), 357–358.

4.  Foner, *Fiery Trial,* 175–218. On the abolitionists' case for the unconstitutionality of slavery, see, e.g., Lysander Spooner, *The Unconstitutionality of Slavery* (Boston: n.p. 1845), 105–106; Joel Tiffany, *A Treatise on the Unconstitutionality of Slavery* (Cleveland, n.p. 1849), 7.

5.  Adam Rothman, *Beyond Freedom's Reach: A Kidnaping in the Twilight of Slavery* (Cambridge, MA: Harvard University Press, 2015), 105, 106; "Emancipation in Louisiana," *New York Times,* February 2, 1863, p.1. The others included Grosvenor Lowery and Charles Kirkland, New York attorneys, who insisted that Curtis had misunderstood the military nature of the proclamation. Louis P. Masur, *Lincoln's Hundred Days: The Emancipation Proclamation and the War for the Union* (Cambridge, MA: Harvard University Press, 2012), 121–122.

6.  Foner, *Fiery Trial,* 210; David Donald, *Lincoln* (New York: Simon and Schuster, 1995), 308, 364; Oakes, *Freedom National,* 252–255.

7.  Foner, *Fiery Trial,* 213.

8.  Joel Parker, *Constitutional Law, with Reference to the Present Condition of the United States* (Cambridge MA: Printers to the College, 1862), 20, 22.

9.  *Memoir of the Hon. William Whiting* (Boston, 1874), 14; William Whiting, *The War Powers of the President . . . In Relation to Rebellion, Treason, and Slavery* (Boston: Shorey, 1862), 6, 10, 12, 19, 21, 30, 66, 67, 68, 70.

10. Masur, *Lincoln's Hundred Days,* 244; Foner, *Fiery Trial,* 216–217; Doris Kearns Goodwin, *Team of Rivals: The Political Genius of Abraham Lincoln* (New York: Simon and Schuster, 2005), 459–472.

11.    Oakes, *Freedom National*, 309–310, 346; Don H. Doyle, *The Cause of All Nations: An International History of the American Civil War* (New York: Basic Books, 2014), 242.

12.    Harold Holzer, *Emancipating Lincoln: The Proclamation in Text, Context, and Memory* (Cambridge, MA: Harvard University Press, 2012), 17–19, 29, 30; Oakes, *Freedom National*, 313–317.

13.    An Act to Suppress insurrection . . . and for other purposes, 12 Stat. 589, July 17, 1862; Henry L. Chambers Jr., "Lincoln, the Emancipation Proclamation, and Executive Power," *Maryland Law Review* 73 (2013), 107–110.

14.    Lincoln, "Preliminary Emancipation Proclamation" September 22, 1862, in Roy P. Basler, ed., *The Collected Works of Abraham Lincoln* (New Brunswick, NJ: Rutgers University Press, 1953), 5:433–434. Manisha Sinha, *The Slave's Cause: A History of Abolitionism* (New Haven, CT: Yale University Press, 2016), 579, argues that by this time the Republicans, Lincoln included, had abandoned any support for forced emigration. Any reference to it, thus, was a bone tossed to the loyal Democrats.

15.    Abraham Lincoln, Preliminary Emancipation Proclamation, in Basler, *Collected Works*, 5:434.

16.    Compare, e.g., Jeremy Popkin, *A Concise History of the Haitian Revolution* (New York: Wiley, 2111), 4 and after with Eric Foner, *Nothing but Freedom: Emancipation and Its Legacy* (Baton Rouge: Louisiana State University Press, 1983), 46–47.

17.    Basler, *Collected Works*, 5, 433; Foner, *Fiery Trial*, 231.

18.    Foner, *Fiery Trial*, 224, 235, 240.

19.    Editorial, *Providence Journal*, September 24, 1862; James Oakes, *The Scorpion's Sting: Antislavery and the Coming of the Civil War* (New York: Norton, 2014), 57–58; James G. Randall, *Constitutional Problems under Lincoln* (New York: Appleton, 1926), 29–32; Peter Charles Hoffer, Williamjames Hull Hoffer, and N. E. H. Hull, *The Federal Courts: An Essential History* (New York: Oxford University Press, 2016), 1, 24–25; Foner, *Fiery Trial*, 219–220; Sanford Levinson, "Was the Emancipation Proclamation Constitutional? Do We/Should We Care What the Answer Is? *University of Illinois Law Review* 2001 (2001), 1140. Controversy over the question of the legitimacy of a president's wartime powers continued after Lincoln had gone to his reward and the war was long over. During World War I, Woodrow Wilson, a Southern Democrat, far exceeded Lincoln's use of wartime powers. Writing in 1926, with the benefit of hindsight that the gruesome spectacle of World War I provided, Civil War scholar James G. Randall asked whether "constitutional government" could be "maintained" in the midst of a civil war—in particular, whether Lincoln overstepped the bounds of his constitutional duties with the proclamations. Randall had little interest in the "technicalities" and "cases" of law, though his subject was a legal

one, and preferred to look at "principles." How these might be abstracted from the way that lawyers like Lincoln tackled problems is not clear, and not really apposite for the purposes of this book. Lincoln did not ignore technicalities or cases. Randall's student, David Donald, regarded the Proclamation as pure politics. David Rabban, *Free Speech in the Forgotten Years, 1870–1920* (New York: Cambridge University Press, 1997); 248–298; John Milton Cooper, *Woodrow Wilson, a Biography* (New York: Random House, 2111), 432–433; Richard Striner, *Woodrow Wilson and World War I: A Burden too Great to Bear* (Lanham, MD: Rowman and Littlefield, 2014), 126–127; Randall, *Constitutional Problems*, vii, 5, 14, 21. Richard Hofstadter's first book, *The American Political Tradition* (1948), regarded the Proclamation's text as little more than a "bill of lading" hardly matching the grandeur of the first inaugural address. Hofstadter's Lincoln was anything but a lawyer with a lawyer's concern for precision, "frankly conservative," always political, for whom "the Negro was secondary," and who wrote the Proclamation "in an unhappy frame of mind." Even those who recognized the long intellectual road that Lincoln had traveled to reach emancipation noted that he spent the fall of 1862 qualifying and downplaying the revolutionary aspects of the proclamation. Eric Foner, for example, gave as much space to Lincoln's December 1862 message to Congress, hinting that colonization of the newly freed men and women was still his desire. David Donald, *Lincoln Reconsidered: Essays on the Civil War Era* (New York: Knopf, 1956), vii, 69–70; Richard Hofstadter, *The American Political Tradition and the Men Who Made It* (New York: Knopf, 1948), 110, 125, 131, 132; Foner, *Fiery Trial*, 236–237.

20. Paul Finkelman, "Lincoln, Emancipation, and the Limits of Constitutional Change," *Supreme Court Review* 2008: 352, 354, 359, 362,369, 377, recognizes that these contemporary and later criticisms of Lincoln's language miss the mark—he had to write as he did precisely because the Emancipation Proclamation was a legal document.

21. Edward Bates, *Opinion of Attorney General Edward Bates on Citizenship* (Washington: Government Printing Office, 1862), 1–9, 13, 14.

22. Austin Allen, *Origins of the Dred Scott Case: Jacksonian Jurisprudence and the Supreme Court, 1837–1857* (Athens: University of Georgia Press, 2006), 203–207; Stuart Streichler, *Justice Curtis in the Civil War Era: At the Crossroads of American Constitutionalism* (Charlottesville: University of Virginia Press, 2005), 151–156; B. R. (Benjamin Robbins) Curtis, *Executive Power* (Boston: Little, Brown, 1862), 11–12.

23. Curtis, *Executive Power*, 11, 12, 14, 15, 16, 17, 22, 26, 28, 33.

24. Lincoln, "Proclamation of Amnesty and Reconstruction," December 8, 1863, in Basler, *Collected Works*, 7: 53–54; Don H. Doyle, *The Cause of All Nations: An International History of the American Civil War* (New York: Basic Books, 2015), 244–245.

25. Jefferson Davis, General Orders III, December 24, 1862, *War of the Rebellion*, ser. 2. 5:795.

26. John Seddon to Robert Ould, June 24, 1863, *War of the Rebellion*, ser. 2, 6:41–47.

27. Emory M. Thomas, *The Confederate Nation: 1861–1865* (New York: Harper, 1979), 261–264; Stephanie McCurry, *Confederate Reckoning* (Cambridge, MA: Harvard University Press, 2010), 327–330; Robert F. Durden, *The Gray and the Black: The Confederate Debate on Emancipation* (Baton Rouge: Louisiana State University Press, 1972), 110, 291–296.

28. Muriel Phillips Goslyn, ed., *A Meteor Shining Brightly: Essays on the Life and Career of Major General Patrick R. Cleburne* (Macon, GA: Mercer University Press, 2000), 26, 29, 31; Carl J. Barger, *Cleburne County and Its People* (Bloomington, IN: Authorhouse, 2008), 1: 14.

29. General Cleburne's Memorial, [January 24] 1864; http://web.utk.edu/ ~mfitzge1/docs/374/GCM1864.pdf.

30. Augusta County: Edward L. Ayers, *In the Presence of Mine Enemies: The Civil War in the Heart of America, 1859–1863* (New York: Norton, 2003), 18; Samuel H. Williamson and Louis P. Cain, "Measuring Slavery in 2011 Dollars," https://www.measuringworth.com/slavery.php; Robert William Fogel and Stanley L. Engerman, *Time on the Cross: The Economics of American Negro Slavery* (Boston: Little, Brown, 1974), 93–94; James L. Huston, *Calculating the Value of the Union: Slavery, Property Rights, and the Economic Origins of the Civil War* (Chapel Hill: University of North Carolina Press, 2003), 24.

31. Christopher Michael Shepard, *The Civil War Income Tax and the Republican Party, 1861–1872* (New York: Algora, 2010), 33 and after; Sheldon D. Pollack, "The First National Income Tax, 1861–1872," *Tax Lawyer* 67 (2012), 8, 14–16.

32. Eric Foner, *Reconstruction: America's Unfinished Revolution, 1863–1877* (New York: Harper, 1988), 35–36; Lincoln, "Proclamation of Amnesty and Reconstruction," December 8, 1863, in Basler, *Collected Works*, 7: 54; Hans Trefousse, "Amnesty Proclamations" in Richard Zucrek, ed., *Reconstruction: A Historical Encyclopedia of the American Mosaic* (Santa Barbara, CA: ABC-CLIO, 2015), 19–20.

33. Louis Mazur, *Lincoln's Last Speech: Wartime Reconstruction and the Crisis of Reunion* (New York: Oxford University Press, 2015), 8.

34. See the discussion of Ex Parte Martin (1793) in Maeva Marcus et al., *Documentary History of the Supreme Court of the United States, 1789–1800* (New York: Columbia University Press, 1998), 6: 199–206.

## Chapter 6

1. Leonard Richards, *Who Freed the Slaves? The Fight over the Thirteenth Amendment* (Chicago: University of Chicago Press, 2015), 29 and after, is

a very effective brief for the crucial role of Ashley in the ending of slavery; see also Robert F. Horowitz, *The Great Impeacher: A Political Biography of James M. Ashley* (New York: Columbia University Press, 1973), 92–95. On Hale and the other proponents of further congressional action, see James Oakes, *Freedom National: The Destruction of Slavery in the United States, 1861–1865* (New York: Norton, 2013), 431–440, and Richard H. Sewell, *John P. Hale and the Politics of Abolition* (Cambridge, MA: Harvard University Press, 1965), 211–212.

2. Richards, *Who Freed the Slaves?* 132–133 (battle within the Republican Party); 154–185 (Democrats versus Republicans); 118–119, 186–187, 193–194 (lining up votes).

3. Richards, *Who Freed the Slaves?* 204–213; Eric Foner, *The Fiery Trial: Abraham Lincoln and American Slavery* (New York: Norton, 2010), 258–261.

4. Michael Vorenberg, *Final Freedom: The Civil War, the Abolition of Slavery, and the Thirteenth Amendment* (New York: Cambridge University Press, 2001), 91–92.

5. See Peter Charles Hoffer, *John Quincy Adams and the Gag Rule, 1835–1850* (Baltimore: Johns Hopkins University Press, 2017).

6. James F. Wilson, *A Free Constitution, Speech . . . Delivered in the House of Representatives March 19, 1864* (Washington DC: W. H. Moore, 1864), 1–7, 9. On the idea that the Preamble to the federal Constitution should be read as self-enabling, see Peter Charles Hoffer, *For Ourselves and Our Posterity: The Preamble to the Constitution in American History* (New York: Oxford University Press, 2013), 150–152.

7. Carl Sandburg, *Abraham Lincoln: The War Years* (New York: Harcourt, 1939), 2: 558; Richards, *Who Freed the Slaves?*, 44.

8. Vorenberg, *Final Freedom*, 97–98; Patricia Ann Reid, "Between Slavery and Freedom" (PhD dissertation, University of Iowa, 2006), 123–124; Norman B. Ferris, "Reverdy Johnson," in John R. Vile, ed., *Great American Lawyers, An Encyclopedia* (Santa Barbara, CA: ABC-CLIO, 2001), 1:409–410.

9. George Ticknor Curtis quoted in Bernard Christian Steiner, *Life of Reverdy Johnson* (Baltimore: Norman, Remington, 1914), 38; Reverdy Johnson, *Speech . . . in Support of the Resolution to Amend the Constitution So as to Abolish Slavery*, April 5, 1864 (Washington, DC: n.p., 1864), 1.

10. Johnson, *Speech*, 3, 4, 5.

11. Johnson, *Speech*, 12.

12. Johnson, *Speech*, 17. Hoffer, *Ourselves and Our Posterity*, 112–127, argues that Madison, in his last years, and Joseph Story, in his Commentaries on the Constitution, both drained the Preamble of its puissance because they were afraid that federal laws or court decisions enabling the "Blessings of Liberty Clause" would lead to secession. Their fears were well grounded, as secessionists were afraid that the Lincoln administration would interfere with slave owners' rights.

13. Johnson, *Speech*, 18–19.

14. Vorenberg, *Final Freedom*, 97; Lowell H. Harrison, *The Civil War in Kentucky* (Lexington: University Press of Kentucky, 1987), 114.

15. Vorenberg, *Final Freedom*, 134–135; Mark Tushnet, "Constitution Making: An Introduction," *Texas Law Review* 91 (2013), 2007 (possibility of unconstitutional amendments); Akhil Amar, "Philadelphia Revisited," *University of Chicago Law Review* 55 (1988), 1054 (Article V inconclusive).

16. There is a debate over this question among jurists, scholars, and judges. See, e.g., Kenneth R. Thomas, *Federalism, State Sovereignty, and the Constitution* (Washington, DC: Congressional Research Service, 2008), 10–12 (amendment led to a huge shift from state to federal power); William E. Nelson, *The Fourteenth Amendment, from Political Principle to Judicial Doctrine* (Cambridge, MA: Harvard University Press, 1988), 120–122 (most Republicans did not see a huge shift from state to federal power).

17. Vorenberg, *Final Freedom*, 106. Enforcement clause and enumerated powers: Timothy S. Huebner, *Liberty and Union: The Civil War Era and American Constitutionalism* (Lawrence: University Press of Kansas, 2016), 329.

18. Garrett Davis, Speech to Senate, March 30, 1864, *Congressional Globe*, 38th Cong, 1st sess., pp. 104, 105; Vorenberg, *Final Freedom*, 98–100, 112.

19. Vorenberg, *Final Freedom*, 100–113.

20. See, e.g., Michael F. Conlin, "The Dangerous *Isms* and the Fanatical *Ists*," *Journal of the Civil War Era* 4 (2004), 206–208; the stance has a staying power stretching from advocates of the "lost cause" through the "Agrarian" movement of the 1920s and 1930s, to the Memorialists in Congress who opposed *Brown v. Board of Education* as a dangerous constitutional innovation, to modern conservatives who advocate the "new federalism." Of course the argument is not exactly the same in all these movements, but they share the same reverence for tradition, states' rights, and a fidelity to what they conceive as the intent of the framers.

21. Bernard Bailyn, *The Ideological Origins of the American Revolution*, enlarged ed. (Cambridge, MA: Harvard University Press, 1992), 95, 232.

22. Goodwin, *Team of Rivals: The Political Genius of Abraham Lincoln* (New York: Simon and Schuster, 2005), 686–690; Foner, *Fiery Trial*, 311–314; David E. Long, *The Jewel of Liberty: Abraham Lincoln's Re-election and the End of Slavery* (Mechanicsburg, PA: Stackpole, 1994), 153–178.

23. Lincoln, "Fourth Message to Congress," December 6, 1864, in Roy P. Basler, ed., *The Collected Works of Abraham Lincoln* (New Brunswick, NJ: Rutgers University Press, 1953), 8:149.

24. Basler, *Collected Works*, 8:149.

25. Basler, *Collected Works*, 8:149.

26. Abraham Lincoln to the Senate, December 6, 1864, in J. W. Schuckers, *The Life and Public Services of Salmon Portland Chase* (New York: Appleton, 1874), 514; Vorenberg, *Final Freedom*, 176–179.

27. Vorenberg, *Final Freedom*, 130, 131, 134, 135, 180–187; Paul D. Escott, *Lincoln's Dilemma: Blair, Sumner, and the Republican Struggle over Racism and Equality in the Civil War Era* (Charlottesville: University of Virginia Press, 2014), 182–183; Long, *Jewel of Liberty*, 153–177.

28. Lincoln, "Second Inaugural Address," March 4, 1865, in Basler, *Collected Works*, 8:333.

29. Lincoln, "Second Inaugural Address," 8:33; Foner, *Fiery Trial*, 325; Goodwin, *Team of Rivals*, 695, 698, 700.

30. David Donald, *Lincoln* (New York: Simon and Schuster, 1995), 567–569.

31. Michael Vorenberg, "Citizenship and the Thirteenth Amendment: Understanding the Deafening Silence," in Alexander Tsesis, ed., *The Promise of Liberty: The History and Contemporary Relevance of the Thirteenth Amendment* (New York: Columbia University Press, 2010), 58–77. Hesitantly: Earl M. Maltz; *Civil Rights, the Constitution, and Congress, 1863–1869* (Lawrence: University Press of Kansas, 1990), 12, 72–75; not quite so hesitantly, Robert J. Kaczorowski, *The Nationalization of Civil Rights: Constitutional Theory and Practice in a Racist Society, 1866–1883* (New York: Garland, 1987), 65–66.

32. Gideon Welles, August 13, diary entry, August 13, 1863, William E. Gienapp and Erica L. Gienapp, eds., *The Civil War Diary of Gideon Welles* (Urbana: University of Illinois Press, 2014), 274; Welles, diary entry, January 31, 1865, Gienapp and Gienapp, *Civil War Diary of Gideon Welles*, 582; Bruce Ackerman, *We the People*, Volume 1: *Foundations* (Cambridge, MA: Harvard University Press, 1991), 45–46; Bruce Ackerman, *We The People*, Volume 3: *The Civil Rights Revolution* (Cambridge, MA: Harvard University Press, 2014), 4; Vallandingham to George W. Morgan, December 11, 1866, quoted in Vorenberg, *Final Freedom*, 238; Philip S. Paludan, "Law and the Failure of Reconstruction: The Case of Thomas Cooley" [1972], reprinted in Wythe Holt, ed., *Essays in Nineteenth-Century American Legal History* (Westport, CT: Greenwood, 1976). 569.

## Epilogue

1. Reid Mitchell, *Civil War Soldiers, Their Expectations and Their Experiences* (New York: Simon and Schuster, 1988), 208–209; Drew Gilpin Faust, *This Republic of Suffering: Death and the American Civil War* (New York: Knopf, 2008), 5, 59; Edward L. Ayers, *In the Presence of Mine Enemies: The Civil War in the Heart of America, 1859–1863* (New York: Norton, 2003), 54–55, 304–305; William T. Sherman to John Sherman, August 3, 1863, in Rachel Sherman Thorndike, ed., *The Sherman Letters* (New York: Scribners, 1894), 211; Scott Reynolds Nelson and Carol Sheriff, *A People at War: Soldiers and Civilians in America's Civil*

*war, 1854–1877* (New York: Oxford University Press, 2008), 295–296; George H. Murphy Diary entry, March 6, 1865, University of Notre Dame Special Collections.

2. Woodhull to Rear Admiral Dupont, *War of the Rebellion, Official Records . . . Union and Confederate Navies,* Series I, v. 13: 467; Thomas E. Pope, *The Weary Boys: Colonel J. Warren Kiefer and the 110th Ohio Volunteer Infantry* (Kent, OH: Kent State University Press, 2002), 2–3, 112–113; Edward Mortimer Haynes, *History of the Tenth Regiment, Vt. Vols.* (Rutland, VT: Tuttle, 1894), 160–162; William S. Morris, L. D. Hartwell Jr., and J. D. Kuykendall, *History of the 31st Illinois* (Robinson, IL: Keller Printing, 1902), xx.

3. Arthur T. Downey, *Civil War Lawyers, Constitutional Questions, Courtroom Dramas, and the Men behind Them* (Chicago: American Bar Association, 2010), 295–327; William D. Driscoll, *Benjamin F. Butler, Lawyer and Regency Chief* (New York: Garland, 1965).

4. Frank J. Williams, "Edward Bates," in John R. Vile, ed., *Great American Lawyers, An Encyclopedia* (Santa Barbara, CA: ABC-CLIO, 2001), 1: 36; John Niven, *Gideon Welles, Lincoln's Secretary of the Navy* (New York: Oxford University Press, 1973), 566–580; Williamjames Hull Hoffer, "William Evarts," in Roger K. Newman, ed., *Yale Biographical Dictionary of American Law* (New Haven, CT: Yale University Press, 2009), 190; Doris Kearns Goodwin, *Team of Rivals: The Political Genius of Abraham Lincoln* (New York: Simon and Schuster, 2005), 752–753; Elizabeth D. Leonard, *Lincoln's Forgotten Ally: Advocate General Joseph Holt of Kentucky* (Chapel Hill: University of North Carolina Press, 2011), 292–293.

5. William Marvel, *Lincoln's Autocrat: The Life of Edwin Stanton* (Chapel Hill: University of North Carolina Press, 2015), 451–469; John Niven, *Salmon P. Chase: A Biography* (New York: Oxford University Press, 1995), 461.

6. Thomas E. Schott, *Alexander H. Stephens of Georgia, a Biography* (Baton Rouge: Louisiana State University Press, 1988), 451–458; Mark Scroggins, *Robert Toombs, the Civil Wars of a United States Senator* (Jefferson, NC: McFarland, 2011), 165; Cynthia Nicolette, *Secession on Trial, The Treason Prosecution of Jefferson Davis* (New York: Cambridge University Press, 2017), 26-30, 64, 77; Eli N. Evans, *Judah P. Benjamin, The Jewish Confederate* (New York: Free Press, 1988), 399; T. Frederick Davis, *History of Jacksonville, Florida, and Vicinity* (Jacksonville: Florida Historical Society, 1925), 91, 138, 149. .

7. Charles Elliott, "Joseph Horace Lewis," in Bruce S. Allardice and Lawrence Lee Hewitt, eds., *Kentuckians in Gray: Confederate Generals and Field Officers of the Blue Grass State* (Lexington: University Press of Kentucky, 2015), 178; Asa Biggs, *Autobiography of Asa Biggs,* ed. R. D. W. Connor (Raleigh: North Carolina Historical Society, 1915), 24, 26, 29;

Nicoletti, *Secession on Trial*, 101-103; Alexander Stephens, *A Constitutional View of the Late War Between the States* (Philadelphia: National Publishing Co, 1868), 1: 412, 414, 416; Albert Taylor Bledsoe, *Is Davis a Traitor, Or Is Secession a Constitutional Right?* (Baltimore: printed for the author, 1866), v, 1, 235, 250, 253. 74-86.

8. Docket books for the Northern District of Georgia, 1865–1866, NARA , Atlanta (Morrow), Georgia; Howell Cobb to his wife, December 7, 1865, in Ulrich Bonnell Phillips, ed., *The Correspondence of Robert Toombs, Alexander H. Stephens, and Howell Cobb, Annual Report of the American Historical Association for the Year 1911*, vol. 2 (Washington, DC, American Historical Association, 1913), 672; Stephens to J. Barrett Cohen, July 4, 1866, Phillips, *Correspondence*, 681.

9. Material here and hereafter from Peter Charles Hoffer, Williamjames Hull Hoffer, and N. E. H. Hull, *The Federal Courts: An Essential History* (New York: Oxford University Press, 2016), 170–184.

10. Michael Vorenberg, *Final Freedom: The Civil War, the Abolition of Slavery, and the Thirteenth Amendment* (New York: Cambridge University Press, 2001), 132–133; "An Act to protect all Persons in the United States in their Civil Rights, and furnish the Means of their Vindication," 14 Stat. 27–30; Laura F. Edwards, *A Legal History of the Civil War and Reconstruction* (New York: Cambridge University Press, 2015), 101–103; Local Prejudice Act of 1867, Ch. 196, 14 Stats 558; "Northern Claims in Southern Courts," *New York Times*, January 7, 1866, p. 4.

11. Habeas Corpus Act of 1867, ch. 28, 14 Stat. 385; Lewis Mayers, "The Habeas Corpus Act of 1867," *University of Chicago Law Review* 33 (1965), 39–40; J. Clay Smith Jr., "In Freedom's Birthplace: The Making of George Lewis Ruffin, the First Black Law Graduate of Harvard University," *Howard Law Review* 39 (1995), 218–229; William M. Wiecek, "The Reconstruction of Federal Judicial Power," in Lawrence M. Friedman and Harry N. Scheiber, eds., *American Law and the Constitutional Order: Historical Perspectives* (Cambridge, MA: Harvard University Press, 1988), 240.

12. See, e.g., Bruce Ackerman, *We the People*, Volume 2: *Transformations* (Cambridge, MA: Harvard University Press, 2000), 121 (claiming that the Fourteenth Amendment was the centerpiece of a new and revolutionary constitutionalism). But see William E. Nelson, *The Fourteenth Amendment: From Political Principle to Judicial Doctrine* (Cambridge, MA: Harvard University Press, 1988), 7 and after (ambiguities of the amendment prevented its fuller explication), and Harold Hyman, *A More Perfect Union* (New York: Knopf, 1973), 438–440 (Republicans did not intend the amendment to restructure federalism fundamentally).

13. Judiciary Act of 1869, 16 Stat. 44. The politics of the act, as opposed to its efficacy, are the subject of some debate among historians. Compare Kermit Hall, "Judiciary Act of 1869," in Kermit L. Hall et al., eds., *The*

*Oxford Companion to the Supreme Court* (New York: Oxford University Press, 1992), 548 (efficiency the primary motive for the enactment), with Justin Crowe, *Building the Judiciary: Law, Courts, and the Politics of Institutional Development* (Princeton, NJ: Princeton University Press, 2012), 159 (politics the primary consideration).

14. Conformity Act of 1872, 17 Stat. 196, 197. But see E. W. Hinton, "Court Rules for the Regulation of Procedure in the Federal Courts," *ABA Journal* 13 (1927), 8, arguing for a uniform federal system of rules in civil and criminal cases.

15. Osborn v. Bank of the United States, 22 US 738, 819 (1824) (Marshall, C. J.); Jurisdiction and Removal Act of 1875, 18 Stat. 470. Civil Rights Act of 1875, 18 Stat. 335–337. The act prefigured the Civil Rights Act of 1964. J. Morgan Kousser, "What Light Does the Civil Rights Act of 1875 Throw on the Civil Rights Act of 1964?" in Bernard Grofman, ed., *Legacies of the Civil Rights Act of 1964* (Charlottesville: University Press of Virginia, 2000), 33–42.

16. On post–Civil War lawyers and business, see Lawrence Friedman and Grant M. Hayden, *American Law, An Introduction*, 3rd ed. (New York: Oxford University Press, 2017), 240; Figures for federal courts from Federal Judicial Center, History of the Federal Judiciary, http://www.fjc.gov/history/caseload.nsf/page/caseloads_private_civil; and http://www.fjc.gov/history/caseload.nsf/page/caseloads_civil_US. Greg H. Williams, *Civil War Suits in the US Court of Claims* (Jefferson, NC: McFarland, 2006), 11, 181. The old court of claims was ended in 1982, http://www.fjc.gov/history/home.nsf/page/courts_special_coc.html. Some of its business and all of its bench was transferred to the US Court of Appeals for the Federal Circuit. A new US Court of Federal Claims has a bench of sixteen judges nominated by the president and confirmed by the Senate who sit for fifteen-year terms and hear cases of money claims against the United States based on the Constitution, http://www.fjc.gov/history/home.nsf/page/courts_special_cfc.html.

17. Minute Books, DC N.D. Ga, 1849–1862, 1867–1871, NARA Atlanta.

18. Elizabeth Lee Thompson, *The Reconstruction of Southern Debt: Bankruptcy after the Civil War* (Athens: University of Georgia Press, 2004), 95, 143; William M. Wiecek, "The Reconstruction of Federal Judicial Power, 1863–1875," *American Journal of Legal History* 13 (1969), 334; bankruptcy petitions, D. C. N. D. Ga, 1867–1868, NARA Atlanta; Bankruptcy Dockets, DC E.D. Mo., June 1867–June 1868; Kansas City NARA.

19. Docket Books, Circuit Court, District of Massachusetts, 1857–1870, NARA Boston; Thompson, *Reconstruction of Southern Debt*, 143.

20. *California Reports*, 16 (July/October terms, 1860), 50 (July/October terms 1875); *Illinois Reports*, 40 (1863–1866), 59 (1871); *Indiana Reports*, 14–15 (1860), 33–34 (1870–1871); *Kansas Reports*, 3 (1866), 9–10 (1872), 16 (1876); *Alabama Reports*, 35–36 (Book 27) (June 1859/January 1860 sessions),

55–56 (Book 37) (December 1876 session); *Mississippi Reports*, 36–37 (Book 18) (1858–1859), 52–53 (Book 26) (1876); *North Carolina Reports*, 52 (1859–1860), 74–75 (1876). These are representative of the other states' Supreme Court reporters.

## Conclusion

1. Herman Melville, "Conflict of Convictions," 17; "Inscription at Pea Ridge," 166; and "Dupont's Round Fight," 30, all in *Battle-Pieces and Aspects of the War* (New York: Harper, 1866); Daniel Farber, *Lincoln's Constitution* (Chicago: University of Chicago Press, 2003), 199; Stephen C. Neff, *Justice in Blue and Gray: A Legal History of the Civil War* (Cambridge, MA: Harvard University Press, 2010), 223–234.

2. John Nicolay, diary entry August 23, 1864, quoted in William E. Gienapp, *Abraham Lincoln and Civil War America: A Biography* (New York: Oxford University Press, 2002), 170; James F. Simon, *Lincoln and Chief Justice Taney: Slavery, Secession and the President's War Powers* (New York: Simon and Schuster, 2007), 263; Gideon Welles, Diary Entry, September 16, 1862, in Howard K. Beale, ed., *Diary of Edward Bates, 1859–1866* (Washington DC: American Historical Association, 1930), 1:137.

3. Oliver Wendell Holmes Jr., "Review of Holdsworth's England Law" (1909), in Richard Posner, ed., *The Essential Holmes* (Chicago: University of Chicago Press, 1992), 207; G. Edward White, *Justice Oliver Wendell Holmes: Law and the Inner Self* (New York: Oxford University Press, 1995), 72; Oliver Wendell Holmes Jr., *The Common Law*, ed. Mark DeWolfe Howe ([1881]; Boston: Little, Brown, 1963), 5.

4. Herman Belz, "The Constitution and Reconstruction," in Eric Anderson and Alfred A. Moss Jr., eds., *The Facts of Reconstruction: Essays in Honor of John Hope Franklin* (Baton Rouge: Louisiana State University Press, 1992), 216; Michael Les Benedict, "Preserving the Constitution: The Conservative Basis of Radical Reconstruction," *Journal of American History* 61 (1974), 67; Kenneth Stampp, *The Era of Reconstruction, 1865–1877* (New York: Knopf, 1966), 14; Edward A. Purcell Jr., *Originalism, Federalism and the American Constitutional Enterprise, a Historical Inquiry* (New Haven, CT: Yale University Press, 2007), 89–90, 189–206. The ironies of the peace thus abound—a war for free labor freeing giant corporations to oppress laborers; a war to protect slavery ending slavery. Alan Trachtenberg, *Reading American Photographs: Images as History, Matthew Brady to Walker Evans* (New York: Hill and Wang, 1989), 115.

5. On the failed promise of full legal equality, see, e.g., Charles Lane, *The Day Freedom Died: The Colfax Massacre, the Supreme Court, and the Betrayal of Reconstruction* (New York: Henry Holt, 2008), 251–258; Edward L. Ayers, *The Promise of the New South, Life after Reconstruction* (New York: Oxford University Press, 2007), 7–8; Cynthia Nicoletti, "Strategic Litigation and the Death of Reconstruction," in Sally

E. Hadden and Patricia Hagler Minter, eds., *Signposts: New Directions in Southern Legal History* (Athens: University of Georgia Press, 2013), 265. But see Melissa Milewski, *Litigating across the Color Line: Civil Cases between Black and White Southerners from the End of Slavery to Civil Rights* (new York: Oxford University Press, 2018), 34, 175.

6.  Mark Twain, "A Tramp Abroad," in *Writings of Mark Twain* (New York: Harper and Brothers, 1907), 203; Gregory C. Sisk, *Litigation with the Federal Government*, 4th ed. (Philadelphia: ALI-ABA, 2006), 21–22; Richard L. Abel, *American Lawyers* (New York: Oxford University Press, 1989), 167–168.

7.  See, e.g., Jack Goldsmith, *The Terror Presidency: Law and Judgement inside the Bush Administration* (New York: Norton, 2009), 151–161; Eric Lichtblau, *Bush's Law: The Remaking of American Justice* (New York: Random House, 2009), 156–158.

8.  See, e.g., Allan A. Ryan, *The 9/11 Terror Cases: Constitutional Challenges in the War against Al Qaeda* (Lawrence: University Press of Kansas, 2015), 191; but see Farber, *Lincoln's Constitution*, 196–197, raising questions about the limits of presidential powers in crisis times. The old Constitution of "Calhounism"—nullification and extreme states' rights—may be dead, but embers of it still burn in concepts like "new federalism." See, e.g., Christopher P. Banks and John C. Blakeman, *The US Supreme Court and New Federalism, from the Rehnquist to the Roberts Courts* (Lanham, MD: Rowman and Littlefield, 2012): "issues litigating the proper boundaries between federal and state governments" remain "closely watched and controversial" (2).